LIES
TRICKERY
OBFUSCATION

How Dysfunctional Societal Institutions and Prepossessed Intellectuals Deceive the General Public

John Ross Brown

Self-Fulfilling Prophecy: A concept introduced into sociology by Robert Merton (see his Social Theory and Social Structure, 1957), and allied to William Isaac Thomas's earlier and famous theorem that"when people define situations as real, they are real in their consequences. Merton suggests the self-fulfilling prophecy is an important and basic process in society, arguing that 'in the beginning, a false definition of the situation evokes a new behaviour which makes the originally false conception come true. [It] perpetuates a reign of error."

—Oxford Reference

Defense mechanisms refer to innate involuntary regulatory processes that allow individuals to reduce cognitive dissonance and to minimize sudden changes in internal and external environments by altering how these events are perceived. Defense mechanisms can alter our perception of any or all of the following: subject (self), object (other), idea or feeling.

—George E. Vaillant

The preservation of the vision of the anointed has led many among the intelligentsia to vigorous and even desperate expedients, including the filtering out of facts, the redefinition of words and—for some intellectuals—challenging the very idea of truth itself....

—Thomas Sowell

Facts are stubborn things; and whatever may be our wishes, our inclinations, or the dictates of our passions, they cannot alter the state of facts and evidence...

—John Adams

...the only possibility for coexistence is to opt for a broader perspective, a domain of existence in which both parties fit in the bringing forth of a common world....A conflict can go away only if we move to another domain where coexistence takes place. The knowledge of this knowledge constitutes the social imperative for a human-centered ethics.

—Humberto Maturana and Francisco Varela

Contents

Acknowledgments

Warm appreciation is extended to my wife Nora who supported this work through providing loving encouragement as well as enduring long hours of research and writing.

Sincere gratitude is expressed to professor, philosopher and author Dr. Stephen R. C. Hicks for his critical review and thoughtful suggestions in the development of this entire work. His breadth of knowledge within the academic realms of philosophy, pertinent epistemological matters and Western history offered both astute guidance and challenging critique.

Immense tribute is offered to the Gregory Bateson Society of Chicago which developed from a course focused on "Theology and the Work of Gregory Bateson" at the Chicago Theological Seminary led by Clinical Psychologist and Theologian Dr. George Cairns. Along with Dr. Cairns, this author joined with University of Chicago Professor Emeritus of Molecular Biology Dr. Martin Matthews as well as Clinical Social Worker Gary Ronjak in initiating an ongoing series of every second month gatherings that continued for more than a decade. The group rapidly expanded to include a diverse assortment of educators, physicists, graduate students, psychotherapists, engineers, physicians and psychologists. While the topics of conversation were much focused on the theoretical conceptions and wide ranging work of Bateson, the ideas of many other social philosophers, theologians, psychological theorists and social scientists became part of the compelling and always valuable discussions.

Professional recognition is afforded to the Gestalt Integrated Family Therapy Institute of Chicago, founded by Dr. Jennifer Andrews and Dr. David Clark. As faculty and a member of the board of directors this author joined a group of innovative psychotherapists in an ongoing effort to both advance an integrated approach to understanding certain human problems and create a derived therapy model to provide effective remediation of troubling issues. Over the period that the Institute was active, teaching and training experiences with the following world renowned theorists and psychotherapists were also important features: Laura Perls, John Weakland, Paul Watzlawick, Salvador Minuchin, Jay Haley, Carl Whitaker, Steve de Shazer, Insoo Kim Berg, Michal White, Cloe Madanes, Harold Goolishian, Joseph Zinker, Tom Anderson, Gianfranco Cecchin and Luigi Boscolo ("The Milan Team") as well as many other theorists.

Notable Observations of Human Life

He who controls the medium controls the message. He who controls the message controls the masses.
—Master Propagandist of the German Nazi Regime
Joseph Goebbels

Some things are believed because they are demonstrably true. But many other things are believed simply because they have been asserted repeatedly.
—Economist Thomas Sowell

His (commonly unconscious) beliefs about what sort of world it is will determine how he sees it and acts within it, and his ways of perceiving and acting will determine his beliefs about its nature.
—Anthropologist Gregory Bateson

Everyone is entitled to their own opinions, but they are not entitled to their own facts.
—U.S. Senator and Sociologist Daniel Patrick Moynihan

How many legs does a dog have if you call its tail a leg? Four. Calling a tail a leg doesn't make it a leg.
—A variation of a quote by United States President
Abraham Lincoln

Far more crucial than what we know or do not know is what we do not want to know.
—Social Philosopher Eric Hoffer

It ain't what you don't know that gets you into trouble. It's what you know for sure that just ain't so.
—Variously attributed to: Mark Twain, Will Rogers, Josh Billings, Artemus Ward, and Kin Hubbard

Truth is powerful and it prevails.
—Abolitionist and Women's Rights Advocate Sojourner Truth

The aim of argument, or of discussion, should not be victory but progress.
—Philosopher of Science Karl Popper

CHAPTER 1

A Brief Introduction to Domains of Experience

What is truth?

—Pontius Pilate

Sometimes, truth really is as plain as the nose on one's face. After a practical joking uncle "snatches" the nose off the face of his young niece, he "proves" that he has indeed taken her nose by showing the "visible evidence" of her nose that now exists between his index finger and middle finger. To provide persuasive confirmation of this social construction of reality, his co-conspiring sons immediately express shock and voice concern. The child at once touches her nose and is somewhat reassured, but a quick trip to look at her face in a mirror reveals the definite truth of the matter; everything is alright, her nose is still attached to her face. As she returns to her uncle, he laughingly shows that the "nose" between his fingers was just his thumb protruding between them. The child has most certainly learned that she can be tricked by others, but she has also discovered two very effective testing procedures by which to determine the validly or falsehood of certain proclamations of truth, i.e., tactile and visual/observational examination of pertinent elements of external reality. Additionally, the girl's double-checking of fact is seemingly an example of establishing validity by repeating a testing procedure, which is a technique somewhat analogous to replication practices as used in modern scientific research projects. Both of these testing methods are empirical, in that the discovery of truth is revealed through observation and experiment. These tests of truth fittingly apply to phenomena in the external day-to-day domain of her life experience.

Not all efforts to establish fact or the accuracy of a hypothesis are so straightforward and readily available. For example, when physicists investigate factors peculiar to the domain of quantum mechanics, where the element of observation is extremely small, one can never know both the exact position and momentum of a subatomic particle at a given specific time. Ongoing research by physicists reveals "…that one cannot assign exact simultaneous values to the position and momentum of a physical system. Rather, these quantities can only be determined with some characteristic 'uncertainties' that cannot become arbitrarily small simultaneously." ("A Quantum experiment supports Heisenberg's Uncertainty Principle," sciencefury.com.) In further outlining the peculiar nature of subatomic entities, a detailed article titled "What is Uncertainty principle? Werner Heisenberg's Theory" offers the following information:

> Ordinary experience does not offer any hint as to this theory. It is easy to calculate both the position and speed of, say, an automobile since the uncertainties for ordinary objects suggested by this theory are too negligible to be observed.…The result of the uncertainties only becomes important for the extremely small masses of atoms and subatomic particles.…Additionally, the uncertainty principle is defined in terms of the momentum and position of a particle. (thewhatis.org, April 8, 2020)

While the issue of uncertainty experienced in the study of subatomic particles was for many years believed to be related to certain effects linked to particular methods of observation, more recent research has determined that

> The uncertainty is rooted in the quantum nature of the particle. Quantum particles cannot be described like a point-like object with a well-defined velocity. Instead, quantum particles behave as a wave—and for a wave, position and momentum cannot be defined accurately at the same time. One could say that the particle itself does not even "know" where exactly it is and how fast it travels—regardless of the particle being measured or not." ("Quantum uncertainty: are you certain, Mr. Heisenberg?" sciencedaily.com, January 18, 2012)

Fortunately for the young niece, her nose does not manifest in the peculiar external "subdomain" of uncertain quantum mechanics, but rather has a certain and exact position in the "see-touch" dimension of external human experience. Thus, the uncertainty inherent to subatomic particles has no relevance to matters that are available for objective study and analysis in the day-to-day world of human beings. In realms where entities are beyond simple observation, the procedures employed to reach knowledge and realize veracity claims must be tailored to fit the nature of the entities encountered. Standard empirical methods of truth testing are simply not suited to phenomena found in the domain of things that are extremely small.

It is likely that for several minutes the girl with the "stolen nose" experienced some manner of cognitive doubt and bewilderment as well as anxiety and generalized emotional instability. Her very real experience of these internal processes and states are neither measurable or observable, i.e., they cannot be touched or directly seen. Yet, she can certainly explain what was occurring if asked about her internal experience between the occurrence of her nose being "stolen" and later receiving the objective results of both tactile and observational truth testing. Most importantly, because these internal events cannot be directly observed when queried about her inner experience she could certainly lie about what she experienced, as defense mechanisms may be employed as a way to avoid appearing foolish to others as well as a way to diminish or entirely avoid an internal sense of embarrassment. Thus, she could both lie to others and lie to herself. Matters related to individual internal human truth obviously require a different method of reaching validity conclusions from those of either the empirical techniques used in the everyday "see-touch" world or those investigative methodologies that are unique to the dimension of subatomic entities.

A matter of pertinent interest for this present work is the socially constructed worldview crafted by the uncle and his co-conspiring off-spring team of tricksters. By means of the uncle's persuasive rhetoric, a sleight-of-hand act of trickery, and the social validation provided by a group of corroborating cousins, the young niece was inducted into a world where the impossible became possible—if only for a brief time. Through the use of lies and trickery, a belief system was socially constructed where truth became subject to obfuscation. However, an appeal to that which can be objectively verified allowed the girl to escape the grasp of a social worldview based on falsehood, plainly demonstrating that a worldview can indeed be socially composed based on a lie. Thus, in the inter-subjective inner human domain of socially constructed realities regarding what is possible in the objective external world, specific procedures aimed at both discerning the nature of such conceptualizations and assessing claims of truth must be developed and employed. Furthermore, since the dawn of civilization, humans have endeavored to realize an advantageous inner visualization of an external social world, leading to producing a wide assortment of directly derived social systems. In order to allow for a determination of the functional validity of these objective social structures, particular investigative methodologies tailored to the observables in the external domain of human social experience must also be generated and impartially utilized.

The scenario outlined above referenced four domains of human experience: 1) an inner personal dimension, i.e., the inner psychological and emotional experience of the young niece, 2) an interior inter-subjective worldview regarding what is possible in the external social world, i.e., the communal perspective socially constructed by the trickster uncle and his offspring collaborators where "nose-snatching" is a genuine human behavioral practice, 3) an observable social world purported to be inhabited by actual "nose-snatching" human actors and 4) the domain of one's individual external life experience where observable, tangible and measurable objects manifest, e.g., the niece's nose.

Significant in this illustrative sketch is the incongruence which arose between the social construction crafted by the lying relatives concerning what is possible in the external social world and the falsehood of this assertion as revealed by the niece as she employed particular methods through which truth was established. Through utilizing two specific empirical testing procedures, she was able to free herself from a state of inner psychological confusion, mitigate emotional distress and, through correcting a false social worldview, she was also released from a manipulated subservient social position.

The balance of this present work will be focused on discussing specific methods of realizing truth in different domains of human experience and explaining the cognitive and behavioral restraining effects of social/psychological self defense mechanisms, as well as analyzing notable contemporary socially constructed realities. The various methods of psychological manipulation and corresponding techniques of social power herein discussed have been utilized both wittingly and unwittingly in an enterprise of human operations which have resulted in constructing social realities that are based on falsehoods rather than truth. This discourse will thus expose certain lies, reveal several rhetorical methods of social trickery and bring into view a number of social strategies that foment obfuscation.

Chapter 2

Post-Postmodernism

There's nothing so absurd that if you repeat it often enough, people will believe it.
                                                           —William James

A lie cannot live.
                    —Reverend Dr. Martin Luther King, Jr.

A generally acceptable definition for a lie is "…an untrue or inaccurate statement that may or may not be believed true by the speaker or writer…." Trickery may be interpreted as "…the practice of crafty underhanded ingenuity to deceive or cheat…." Obfuscation is typically understood as communication that is intended "…to make obscure or unclear…darken…." (Note: All the above definitions are sourced from *Merriam-Webster*, online.)

An observation that is readily available in society is the institutionalization or attempted institutionalization of both beliefs and social practices that are based on falsehoods. Institutionalization may be defined as the social processes by which a practice or belief becomes a formal norm or sanctioned convention in society. The occurrence of this social phenomenon is an essential focus of this present work.

Originally, the lead title of this discourse was *Social/Psychological Self-Defense Mechanisms in Culture and Society*. The concept of social/psychological self-defense mechanisms refers to the social circumstance where a sufficient number of people who share a fallacious belief, desire sanction for a particular favored social behavior or seek validation for an erroneous cultural schema—coalesce with like-minded others employing what is typically seen as individual psychological strategies. In order to cope with anxiety, insecurity, shame, stress, guilt or the cognitive dissonance that may arise when confronted with social objection, self-defense mechanisms become a distributed and readily observable social phenomenon among unified group members.

George E. Vaillant, M.D., was a research psychiatrist and psychoanalyst as well as a professor at Harvard University. Dr. Vaillant also directed Harvard's Study of Adult Development for thirty-five years. In reference to defense mechanisms, Dr. Vaillant offers the following explanation:

> Defense mechanisms refer to innate involuntary regulatory processes that allow individuals to reduce cognitive dissonance and to minimize sudden changes in internal and external environments by altering how these events are perceived. Defense mechanisms can alter our perception of any or all of the following: subject (self), object (other), idea, or feeling. (Vaillant, George E. "Ego Mechanisms of Defense and Personality Psychopathology." *Journal of Abnormal Psychology*, 1994, Vol. 103. No. 1. 44–50, online)

In efforts to challenge normative judgments and societal restrictions, social/psychological self-defense mechanisms foster and allow for group cohesiveness leading to aligned associations and perhaps the formation of a political initiative directed towards the enactment of societal legal codes intended to force public accommodation of desired cultural views and social conduct. Examples of defense mechanisms include denial (refusing to accept actual facts), projection (attributing one's conflictual inner experience, troubling thoughts or unacceptable feelings to other people), rationalization (justifying problematic conceptualizations or confused feelings with a seemingly logical reasoning structure), acting out (performing extreme behaviors rather than rationally processing dubious conceptualizations, effectively expressing difficult feelings or engaging in reasoned debate of personal beliefs or opinions), dissociation (a disconnected view of self in the world, i.e., one's self-image may not be continuous, extreme cases may involve time distortion as well as an expression of multiple selves, e.g., "multiple personality disorder"), regression (escaping to behaviors associated with an earlier stage of development to evade social challenge, ignore unacceptable thoughts or avert distressful feelings) and avoidance (refusing to encounter situations or matters that will bring cognitive challenge or conflict).

However, in some instances, the attempt to insert a fallacious belief within culture or achieve normative status for a fancied behavioral pattern is not accompanied by emotional tension, stress or psychological disturbance among participants in movements aimed at social change; rather, individuals, along with unified groups, can bluntly reject factual data, deliberately advance disinformation, become pugnaciously assertive or engage in violent behavior in order to achieve coveted goals. In order to include these instances of social activity aimed at realizing informal or formal sanction of erroneous beliefs, desired cultural perspectives or coveted social conduct, the lead title was changed to: *Lies-Trickery-Obfuscation*.

A guiding principle of this inquiry can be traced to Emile Durkheim, one of the founders of modern Sociology, who advised: "The first, and most fundamental, rule is: Consider social facts as things." Durkheim further elaborates: "A social fact is any way of acting…capable of exerting over the individual an external constraint; or again, every way of acting which is general throughout a given society.…A social fact is identifiable through the power of external coercion which it exerts, or is capable of exerting, upon individuals." In order to clarify the operating characteristics of social constraints, Durkheim states: "…the public conscience exercising a check on every act which offends it by means of the surveillance it exercises over the conduct of its citizens, and the appropriate penalties at its disposal" (Berger, Peter L., and Thomas Luckmann. *The Social Construction of Reality: A Treatise in the Sociology of Knowledge*. Anchor Books, 1967).

A primary concern of this present manuscript is centered on examining the characteristics and constitutive structure of several social facts in society so that the applied power of societal social constraints, which can be extremely damaging to the individual, can be assessed as warranted based on the veracity, or lack thereof, of these contemporary social assertions and institutionalized practices.

Accompanying the concepts of Durkheim in the guidance of this text is the influential work in the academic area of the sociology of knowledge: *The Social Construction of Reality: A Treatise in the Sociology of Knowledge* by postmodern sociologists Peter L. Berger and Thomas Luckmann (previously referenced). The essence of their thesis as outlined within this social science monograph is that the "social reality" which a citizen encounters in society, and frankly takes for granted each and every day, is a socially constructed reality. Berger and Luckmann assert that "…social order is a human product, or, more precisely, an ongoing human production.…Society is a human product…" The authors further contend that "…all social phenomena are constructions produced historically through human activity." At the conclusion of their treatise, Berger and Luckmann summarize that "The sociology of knowledge understands human reality as socially constructed reality."

However, contrary to what many postmodern sociologists and cultural theorists maintain, a particular socially constructed reality is not axiomatically equated with human truths that can be ascertained through accredited methodologies of confirmation. A social reality can be based on authentic presumptions, valid expositions and legitimate assertions—or fallacious information, oppressive dictums, deceitful rhetoric and inaccurate data. An earnest investigation of social phenomena is not an exercise in creative writing or fanciful linguistic sculpting; rather, it is characterized by a domain specific and rigorous analysis of social matters, i.e., facts. In addition to the sociologists noted above, the scientific findings of Isaac Newton, James Clerk Maxwell, Max Planck, James Watson, and Francis Crick as well as the insightful and cogent work of the scientific and social philosophers Ken Wilber, Lawrence LeShan, Henry Margenau, Stephen Hicks, Karl Popper, Gregory Bateson, Eric Hoffer, Thomas Sowell, Patrick Lee, Robert P. George, Thomas Kuhn and Jürgen Habermas will be importantly referenced in this commentary.

History is replete with false propositions that served as the foundation for socially constructed realities. Unequivocal examples will be utilized to help clarify the distinction between socially constructed realities and human truths. The German National Socialist Party believed that the "Aryan race" was a biologically superior human group and therefore represented a "master race." On the other hand, the Jewish people were believed to be not simply a religious group, but rather a "dangerous race" that lived off of other groups and weakened them. A frequently occurring social credence up until the nineteenth century was related to the subordinate position of women in society. In the words of Sir William Blackstone: "…

the very being or legal existence of the woman is suspended during the marriage…" (Lewis, Jone Johnson. "The Blackstone Commentaries and Women's Rights." thoughtco.com, February 6, 2019).

The socially held belief regarding the subservient nature of slaves has a long history, reaching as far back as the ancient civilizations of the Sumerians, Babylonians and Egyptians as well as numerous archaic societies existing in Asia, the Middle East, Africa, Europe, Central America and South America. Aristotle commentated on the institution of slavery, arguing that some persons are naturally slaves and others are naturally made to rule other persons. In further justifying his position Aristotle states: "And indeed, the use made of slaves and of tame animals is not very different; for both with their bodies minister to the needs of life" ("Philosophers justifying slavery." bbc.co.uk, online).

The caste system in India began as a social structure related to one's occupation, but eventually became completely based on heredity. Everyone's social status and much of one's individual identity became linked in a mostly unchangeable manner to the inherited/genetic circumstances of one's birth. Four distinct groups comprised the social caste system: 1) Brahmin (priests), 2) Kshatriya (nobility and warriors), 3) Vaisya (artisans, traders and farmers) and 4) Shudra (servants and tenant farmers). To take into account those humans born outside of the four castes, another group was designated and identified as "untouchables." These people did not comprise a fifth caste; rather, they were condemned to be completely outside of the caste structure itself. These humans were considered to be so impure that any physical contact with them led to the need to immediately bathe and wash any clothing that came in contact with the "untouchable." This socially condemned group of humans was not allowed to eat in the same room with a member of one of the four castes, and when they died, they could not be cremated.

In each of the cultural/societal examples given above, a granting of "truth" to these beliefs and practices was bestowed by society at large. Entire nations comprising millions of people cultivated and preserved these beliefs, coordinating their day-to-day conduct, so as to comply with associated norms and mores. Additionally, in each of these societies can be found culturally refined political figures, esteemed university professors, honored religious representatives and other learned community leaders who advocated for and personally adhered to these "socially constructed realities."

At this point, the reader is invited to make their own critical judgment regarding the veracity of the several socially constructed realities outlined above. Also proposed is a moment of sober and lucid reflection upon the voguish postmodern philosophical credo asserting that one culture possesses no justified position allowing for a critical assessment of another culture's beliefs and practices based on a cardinal rule of appraisal which demands that all cultures be seen as equally valid social constructions, i.e., "cultural relativism." As a contemporary challenge to this philosophically anchored restraint, consider the abundant documentation of the brutal human oppression intrinsic to the socialist society of North Korea as juxtaposed with the individual and social freedoms enjoyed by citizens within the free-market, capitalist democracy of South Korea.

Unfortunately, contemporary society has not escaped the crowning of social sanction on shared beliefs and human conduct based on lies and spurious rhetoric. In the following pages, societal examples will be identified where lies, trickery and obfuscation have been used to advance socially constructed realities founded on falsehoods.

Every society's way of knowing reality, i.e., Epistemology, is guided by a general formula with peculiar and inherently circumscribed investigative methodologies for generating truths related to important matters of analysis. Thomas Kuhn, in his book *The Structure of Scientific Revolutions* (University of Chicago Press, 1962), used the term "paradigm" for the widely accepted social practices related to techniques of inquiry, which then lead to statements of knowledge. Ken Wilber, in his extensive work on devising a post-postmodern Integral Philosophy, has identified several stages of cultural development with corresponding methodologies for both discerning and bringing forth an understanding of the world. Generally, these broad-reaching cultural worldviews are identified as pre-modern, modern, postmodern and post-postmodern worldviews. Elemental in these worldviews are prescribed investigative procedures in relation to discerning both the nature of phenomena and the related enterprise of comprehending the essence of human experience.

From his historical studies, Kuhn observed that a new paradigm begins to emerge when a crisis is experienced due to the accumulation of unresolved aberrations sufficient to cause practitioners themselves to begin questioning the paradigm itself. The demise of the predominant late medieval premodern epistemology most certainly approached this catastrophic stage with the occurrences of a series of societal calamities including the Great Famine (1315–1317) and the Black Death (1347–1351), where toxic microorganisms (completely unknown to exist at that point in time) led to the decimation of 30 to 60 percent of the European population and 75 to 200 million deaths in all of Eurasia. This prevailing premodern paradigm, which existed for an extended period prior to The Enlightenment, was greatly influenced and guided by a theological worldview.

During this period early scientific ideas such as those developed by Roger Bacon (1219–1292) were not developed to a point of practical efficacy and therefore remained much in the form of intellectual conceptualization.

> Roger Bacon is a name that belongs alongside Aristotle, Avicenna, Galileo, and Newton as one of the great minds behind the formation of the scientific method. He took the work of Grosseteste, Aristotle, and the Islamic alchemists, and used it to propose the idea of induction as the cornerstone of empiricism. He described the method of observation, prediction (hypothesis), and experimentation, also adding that results should be independently verified, documenting his results in fine detail so that others might repeat the experiment. (explorable.com/middle-ages-science)

However, Bacon was a Catholic Franciscan Friar and his worldview was also much guided by theological concerns, as he believed that his work would lead to greater confirmation of the Christian faith. The dominant perspective of this period sought veritable knowledge of human experience by means of mysticism, faith, prescribed religious performances, teachings from authoritative religious figures and guidance from adept practitioners of well-established spiritual practices. While this cosmology greatly contributed to the world's spiritual practices, the internally focused and highly specialized perspective characteristic of this worldview rendered it completely ill-equipped to understand and deal effectively with the horrifying biological plague of 1347–1351. (Note: The philosophical contributions of a variety of premodern western perspectives prior to the late medieval period are not herein considered. Also, Eastern and African cosmologies, while offering profound insights regarding the human experience and containing well-developed theoretical systems of thought, will not be included in this commentary.)

The elements comprising the development of the subsequent dominant worldview called modern philosophy became manifested in the ascension of empiricism, i.e., knowing through sensory experience and employing the cognitive processes of logic and reason. The rigorous work of the "Natural Philosophers," including Copernicus, Tycho, Kepler, Sir Francis Bacon and Galileo was characterized by great precision in observation, exact mathematical measurement and uncanny prediction in regard to the behavior of material objects in the external world. The emphasis on these processes of discernment coupled with disciplined analytical methodologies for bringing forth knowledge of the external world contributed to the formulation of the scientific method. However, it was Sir Isaac Newton who was able to create a new physics that was fully capable of providing a complete system of regulation in regard to the physical cosmos (Newton, Sir Isaac. *The Mathematical Principles of Natural Philosophy*. London, 1686).

With his development of calculus (simultaneously created by Gottfried Leibniz) Newton was able to apply this math to the forces he inferred and bring clarity and unity to the work of several of his predecessors. With his three laws of motion and his principle of universal gravitation a new physics of astounding theoretical elegance, precise analysis and profound predictive power was established. As the scientific method further developed, through systematic observation and testing procedures (i.e., utilization of standardized experimental procedures and rigorous analysis of derived data) microorganisms, such as the bacterium *Yersinia pestis* which is widely believed to have caused The Black Death, could be effectively observed and systematically classified eventually leading to the development of life-saving antibacterial medications. The Enlightenment, also known as The Age of Reason, with its use of empiricism, reason and the scientific method led to a truly profound grasp of knowledge related to the external world and remarkable accomplishments in biology, chemistry, astronomy, physics, agriculture, geology, zoology, botany, etc. Additional social benefits included the emergence of classic liberal political thought and related expressions in society such as individual liberty, social toleration, constitutional government, abolition of slavery, the encyclopedia and dictionary, wider availability of public schools, free practice of religious beliefs in the absence of a government established religion, the inalienable right of the individual to armed defense, advanced university institutions, women's suffrage, private property rights, freedom of political speech and due to the development of open market economies, the realization of substantial financial benefits for the general populace.

Following Kuhn's model, certain limitations of modern philosophy were also realized, albeit in a much less dramatic fashion than the decline of premodernism. The capstone methodologies of empiricism and reason became the vulnerable concepts of this philosophical project. Philosopher Immanuel Kant was occupied with concerns that important aspects of the internal realm of human experience would become thoroughly diminished and marginalized by the Enlightenment's emphasis on empiricism and reason. In the preface of his book *Critique of Pure Reason* (1781), Kant states that his objective in putting forth this exposition was to establish the "limits to knowledge" so as to "make room for faith." He then discussed a rather specific form of faith realized through a practice identified as "free assent." In his critique, Kant argued that the human inquisitor's mind is not a see-through structure with a mere reflective function. But rather, the human process of knowing the external world is through the senses and these senses themselves have impactful structures and causal processes. Thus, reason can only be presented with an internal representation of external reality.

In Kant's view direct experience of the material world is impossible due to the subjective effect of the knower's essentially sequential and influential operations of: 1) sensation, 2) perception and 3) conception. In offering his critique of modern science Kant advanced the proposition that sense organs, neurological pathways and cognitive processes have formative characteristics presenting a "barrier" to awareness of external reality, rather than functioning as the principle "means" of awareness. While vigorous debate on this particular argument endures, Kant assuredly paved the way for an extensive investigation of the variable and creative nature of internal self-experience, eventually leading to certain important advancements in the social sciences.

Although Kant put forth a significant examination and judicious criticism of certain basic tenets of modern philosophy (primarily objectivity), it wasn't until 1979 that the term postmodernism began to be used with the publication of *The Postmodern Condition: A Report on Knowledge* by Jean-Francois Lyotard (Les Editions de Minuit). No doubt Lyotard was influenced by the following quote of Austrian-British philosopher Ludwig Wittgenstein: "But all propositions of logic say the same thing. That is, nothing." (*Tractatus Logico-Philosophicus.* Harcourt, Brace & Company Inc., 1922.) Wittgenstein developed an approach to description and social envisioning called "language games," which refers to actual social activities involving specific and local forms of language resulting in a focus on "the stream of life" in local communities as the means to derive philosophical reflection. This assault on logic and an emphasis on local language provided intellectual guidance for Lyotard's subsequent rejection of "metanarratives" and a concentration on what he called "little narratives" of common day-to-day life and on groups considered marginalized. In rejecting universal reason and truth, Lyotard concluded that human "discourses" have no common basis and therefore conflict and dissension is inevitable, leading to segregation of human communities due to heterogeneity and "dissensus."

Helen Pluckrose and James Lindsay in their book *Cynical Theories* (Pitchstone Publishing, 2020) offer the following comments regarding the central tenets of postmodern philosophy: "At its core, postmodernism rejected what it calls metanarratives—broad, cohesive explanations of the world and society....It also rejected science, reason, and the pillars of post-Enlightenment Western Democracy." Other twentieth century postmodernists such as Michel Foucault and Jacques Derrida will cite the following German philosophers as significant sources of theoretical influence: Immanuel Kant, G. W. F. Hegel, Friederich Nietzsche and Martin Heidegger. (Note: Heidegger was an early proponent of the German National Socialist Party and although he withdrew from open public advocacy he remained a Nazi supporter until the party was disbanded after the Second World War.) In demonstrating the general agreement among postmodernists in their understanding that objectivity is a myth and reason must also be rejected, Professor Stephen R. C. Hicks provides this Foucauldian quote: "It is meaningless to speak in the name of—or against—Reason, Truth, or Knowledge." (*Explaining Postmodernism: Skepticism and Socialism from Rousseau to Foucault.* Ockham's Razor Publishing, 2011).

Professor Hicks usefully provides a summary in his book of several key elements of postmodernism:

> Postmodernism rejects the reason and the individualism that the Enlightenment world depends upon. And so it ends up attacking all of the consequences of the Enlightenment philosophy, from capitalism and liberal forms of government to science and technology....Postmodernism's essentials are the opposite of modernism's. Instead of natural reality—anti-realism. Instead of experience and reason—linguistic social subjectivism. Instead of individual identity and autonomy—various race, sex, and class groupisims. Instead of human interests as fundamentally harmonious and tending toward mutually-beneficial interaction—conflict and oppression. Instead of valuing individualism in values, markets, and politics—calls for communism, solidarity, and egalitarian restraints. Instead of prizing the achievements of science and technology—suspicion tending toward outright hostility.

In further discussing views intrinsic to postmodernism, Hicks notes:

> Postmodern literary criticism rejects the notion that literary texts have objective meanings and true interpretations. All such claims to objectivity and truth can be deconstructed...literary criticism becomes a form of subjective play in which the reader pours subjective associations into the text. In another version, objectivity is replaced by the view that an author's race, sex, or other group membership most deeply shapes the author's views and feelings. The task of the literary critic, accordingly, is to deconstruct the text to reveal the author's race, sex, or class interests.

Professor Hicks adds the following regarding the present difficulties inherent to contemporary postmodern theory:

> In postmodern discourse, truth is rejected explicitly and consistency can be a rare phenomenon. Consider the following pairs of claims. On the one hand, all truth is relative; on the other hand, postmodernism tells it like it really is. On the one hand, all cultures are equally deserving of respect; on the other hand Western culture is uniquely destructive and bad. Values are subjective—but sexism and racism are really evil. Technology is bad and

destructive—and it is unfair that some people have more technology than others. Tolerance is good and dominance is bad—but when postmodernists come to power, political correctness follows. There is a common pattern here: Subjectivism and relativism in one breath, dogmatic absolutism in the next.

Hicks discerningly notes that the present disintegration of postmodern philosophy is readily apparent by pinpointing the far-reaching yet contradictory assertion by its adherents to posit postmodernism as "THE" valid way of knowing, while at the same time boldly claiming that there is "NO" valid way of establishing knowledge. In other words, postmodernism purports that its perspective on all matters is universally true in a world where there are no universal truths, i.e., the postmodern theorist is doing what they claim cannot be done. The renowned 21st century philosopher Jurgen Habermas coined the term "the performative contradiction" for this particular paradox which is intrinsic to the contemporary exercise of postmodern philosophy. Professor Hicks also notes in his book that some postmodern academics have frankly acknowledged that the contemporary practice of their philosophy is no longer an endeavor having to do with reaching an understanding of complex features of human existence or a pursuit of "truth," but rather has been reduced to a political movement aimed at advancing a favored socioeconomic world view. Most importantly, in referring to the postmodern derived literary and cultural analytic method called "deconstruction," Professor Stanley Fish said that deconstruction "relieves me of the obligation to be right...and demands only that I be interesting." Conspicuous in the practice of deconstruction is the necessity to precisely comply with guidelines associated with that of a strict scholarly investigation or risk becoming an endeavor where the very process of analysis turns into something akin to a revealing psychological "projective device." In this way, repressed psychological themes and biased cultural/societal prejudices maintained by the social analyst pervade and corrupt the research project.

A leading figure in 20th century postmodern philosophy, Jacques Derrida, frankly acknowledged that this foremost postmodern analytical methodology was simply not a compelling investigative device: "... deconstruction never had meaning or interest, at least in my eyes, than as a radicalization, that is to say, also with the tradition of certain Marxism, in a certain spirit of Marxism." Duke Professor Frank Lentricchia states that postmodernism "…seeks not to find the foundation and condition of truth but to exercise power for the purpose of social change." Lentricchia further reveals the debilitation of the postmodern school by sharing his position that professors who subscribe to postmodern theory need not emphasize philosophical instruction and related discourse but rather openly and enthusiastically help their students to "…spot, confront, and work against the political horrors of one's time…" (*Explaining Postmodernism: Skepticism and Socialism from Rousseau to Foucault*, previously referenced).

In part due to the leading roles which radical relativism, theoretical paradox and intellectual absolutism have come to hold within the postmodern school, the notable benefits to society as compared to the achievements of modern philosophy, and its offspring called science, are distinctly modest. Ostensibly, the most significant contributions to humankind from postmodernism can be found in the areas of functional psychology (non-neurological psychological endeavors), cultural anthropology, non-quantitative sociological studies, particular models of psychotherapy, creative fiction writing, poetry, performing arts and certain academic schools within the humanities. With the dispirited abandonment of focused and exacting philosophical work, the overt switch to a primary emphasis on social and political action by many of its adherents and the intractable nature of the paradoxes inherent within postmodernism—this philosophical school has also reached the crisis level noted by Kuhn.

The adequacy of the postmodern philosophical project was first fundamentally based on Kant's critical assessment of human observational operations, conceptual processes and the persuasiveness of his accompanying rhetorical arguments. Yet, the modern perspective, much characterized by empirical/reason-based science, proceeded "full steam ahead" alongside these criticisms, as if the challenge to its essential structures had never arisen—and once again raised the question of whether the senses are "barriers" to awareness or the "means" of awareness. Certainly in the domain of Newtonian mechanics, the critique leveled by both Kant and subsequent postmodern philosophers is demonstrably irrelevant and clearly without effective consequence. In the "see-touch" domain of mechanics, which explains how material things are now, based on precise observation and accurate measurement, determines exactly how they will be at a later time.

As physicist and philosopher of science Henry Margenau delineates, if one gains specific and precise data concerning pertinent observables in the dimension of Newtonian physics, exact prediction of future events can be made. Modern Newtonian mechanics very much represents an investigative process by which one is operating as if looking through an unobstructed open window into the external world. To reiterate, advancements in knowledge of the external world and the subsequent realization of practical human benefits in the fields of physics, medicine, engineering, biology, mathematics, technology and many other vital endeavors, guided by modern philosophy's practice of science, have by far eclipsed any able and conspicuous societal contributions derived from either the postmodern perspective or various premodern worldviews.

However, it wasn't until the work on electromagnetic fields by Scottish physicist James Clerk Maxwell (1831–1879) that scientists themselves fully realized that not all phenomena could be understood by Newtonian mechanical models. Regarding this scientific development, psychologist Lawrence LeShan and physicist Henry Margenau precisely state the following in their book *Einstein's Space and Van Gogh's Sky: Physical Reality and Beyond* (Macmillan Publishing Company, 1982): "It first became clear to scientists that the assumption that all phenomena could be visualized and explained by mechanical models was not completely valid through the work of James Clerk Maxwell and the general development of the concept of fields in physics." While this finding helped confirm specific limitations related to modern scientific practice, curiously, this very same disclosure generated a seemingly unrecognized serendipitous discovery in relation to the postmodern project. To wit: not all domains within which humans have experience function according to the same rules of organization and the guiding methods of investigation which are used to derive domain-specific principles will not "fit" elements intrinsic to other distinctive spheres of experience, i.e., different domains operate differently in fact.

Up until this time, philosophers and scientists had generally endeavored to explain human experience according to a singular far-reaching perspective. With Maxwell's discovery, not only were certain limitations of the modern perspective confirmed, but also, by extension and inference, that of premodern and postmodern schools. In just over a century (1860s to 1970s), the conviction that a comprehensive worldview could be developed to explicate the expansive range of human experience came into doubt, while the post-postmodern viewpoints of Domain Theory and the "transcend and include" capabilities of Integral Philosophy began to gain refinement and recognition (discussed in detail below).

In his book *Objective Knowledge: An Evolutionary Approach* (Oxford University Press, 1972), the renowned 20th century philosopher of science Karl Popper also offered a similar integral perspective where he outlines "three worlds" of human experience: 1) a material universe comprised of physical objects, inorganic chemical entities and biological phenomena, each with peculiar laws of organization, 2) a realm of psychological/mental states and 3) a domain comprised of abstract cultural products of thought, e.g., stories, myths, and social conceptions/theories regarding human institutions.

A recurrent and unspoken factor inherent in many social, scientific and philosophical perspectives and commentaries must be noted, which is that, namely, we inquiring humans are animals. To be more specific, humans are mammals. This recognition is of key importance when developing both a historical assessment of philosophical argument and accepting both the abilities and limitations of various schools of inquiry. Cultural anthropologist Gregory Bateson noted in his book *Steps to an Ecology of Mind* (Jason Aronson Inc., 1972) that mammals are keenly interested in relationships. In his study, focused on the behavior of the category of mammals known as dolphins, Bateson states: "...like ourselves and other mammals, they are preoccupied with the patterns of their relationships."

Position and territory are unquestionably two aspects of human mammalian relationships that are foremost in reference to competing philosophical worldviews. The history of both philosophical and scientific debate has clearly been characterized by competition for "top dog position" in laying claim to the authoritative method of inquiry regarding the entire "territory" of human experience. Noteworthy in efforts to achieve this domination, premodern philosophers, modern logicians and postmodern theorists have at certain times each employed their own unique variation of reductionism. In discussing the practice of reductionism, LeShan and

Margenau offer the following interpretation of the Latin root of the word reduction: "…'reducere'—to save." In reference to this particular meaning of reductionism, the authors state: "If one idea seemed strange or unacceptable, its meaning could be saved by reducing it to a more familiar or a more acceptable one." In noting three human characteristics as illustrative of this practice, the authors describe how this type of reductionism leads to such conclusions as "…honor is 'nothing but' a reflex we are conditioned to by our cultural upbringing (an example of postmodern reductionism), that love is 'nothing but' the biological urge to reproduction (a modern form of reductionism), and that consciousness is 'nothing but' changing brain states (another example of modern reductionism)."

The authors further clarify this particular intellectual practice of reductionism by noting that "As long as the universe is seen as continuous, this 'error of origins' can be perceived as a reasonable deduction. But as we have also seen, the idea of a consistently continuous universe with no leaps was destroyed by Max Planck in 1900, and it is no longer a basis of modern science." (Note: Planck is credited as the originator of quantum mechanics.)

> Once we insist that the data in each domain must be taken on their own terms and not squeezed into the Procrustean bed of the sensory realm, it becomes clear that is both valid and scientifically necessary to view honor as qualitatively different from cultural conditioning, love as more than itching in the groin, and consciousness more than brain structure and physiology.… They belong to different domains and each of them must be dealt with on its own terms.… The brain no more secretes consciousness than consciousness secretes the brain. Different domains have different observables. (*Einstein's Space and Van Gogh's Sky: Physical Reality and Beyond*, previously referenced)

With Maxwell's and Planck's findings, the ensuing work by quantum field theory scientists, and the advent of post-postmodern philosophy, the claim to a singular explanatory worldview representing the entire realm of human experience was certainly called into question.

With Popper's "three worlds" referenced as a correlated theoretical model, this present manuscript is offered as a way of realizing veritable knowledge most fundamentally informed by the post-postmodern methodologies and capacities of Integral Philosophy/Theory as developed by Ken Wilber. While Integral Theory is amply complex, containing a number of wide ranging theoretical considerations, the development of this present work will principally employ the felicitous and well established "quadrant" conception. Additional guidance is gleaned from a related conceptual model developed by physicist Henry Margenau and psychologist Lawrence LeShan. Preceding Wilber's quadrant model by more than a decade, in their co-authored book (noted above), these two theorists outline an investigative metamodel termed "Domain Theory." In an effort to elucidate and comprehend the varied ways that humans have endeavored to understand their individual and communal lives, LeShan and Margenau posit that humans have experience in five domains of reality:

1. The "see-touch" domain—the sensory realm (including all human senses) up to the limits of available instrumentation in relation to the investigation of non-living entities.

2. Observable units of behavior of things that are alive—both individual and systemic phenomena. Note: This domain is also accessed via "see-touch" sensory processes and investigative procedures.

3. Things too small to be seen or touched—the non-living microcosm.

4. Things too big to be seen or touched—the non-living macrocosm.

5. A person's inner experience.

During the second half of the twentieth century, foundational aspects of a post-postmodern philosophy were coming to fruition. While this philosophical perspective obviously acknowledges an appreciation that, over time, human understanding continues to unfold and develop (as do all genuine academic approaches to knowledge), most important for this present work is the ability of contemporary post-postmodern theory to transcend earlier worldviews while also retaining many significant and capable conceptualizations from these prior philosophical perspectives.

This intellectual feat is in part possible because Integral Philosophy and Domain Theory have discerned that humans have experience in several distinct dimensions. In refining this post-postmodern perspective, Integral Philosophy offers an assessment of human experience as occurring in the following four quadrants (wisdompage.com):

I	**IT**
Interior-Individual	Exterior-Individual
Intentional	Behavioral
Subjective	Objective
Upper Left	**Upper Right**
WE	**ITS**
Interior-Collective	Exterior-Collective
Cultural	Social
Intersubjective	Interobjective
Lower Left	**Lower Right**

1. The upper left quadrant is the interior individual experience of the person—"I"—(inner self/personal psychological phenomena/ spiritual experiences).

2. The lower left quadrant is the interior social/collective view maintained by the individual—"WE"—(intersubjective perspectives/ culture/social worldviews).

3. The upper right quadrant is the objective individual exterior of the person—"IT"—(individual behavior/chemistry/physics/ neurology/biology).

4. The lower right quadrant represents conspicuous exterior systemic phenomena—"ITS"— (the observable social world/society/institutional structures/external systems).

Note: The quadrants also contain what may be termed as sub-domains. An example of a sub-domain is the microcosm. While this realm includes phenomena that fall within the upper right external quadrant of human experience, the entities under study are disparate from those observed in the Newtonian sphere of mechanics and the laws governing order and change in this peculiar sub-domain are also different. Additionally, in the upper left quadrant of internal self-experience, the constitutive components of self-structure, studied via applicable psychological research procedures, vary radically from appreciable factors intrinsic to transcendent schools of spiritual inquiry. However, so as to avoid added complexity, the crucial point of focus is that the four quadrants reflect actual human experience and are distinct from one another according to the following general framework: 1) interior individual phenomena, 2) interior social conceptions/worldviews, 3) discernable exterior individual phenomena and 4) observable exterior systemic occurrences. In his book *A Brief History of Everything* (Shambhala Publications, Inc., 1996), Ken Wilbur offers a detailed explanation of the quadrant conception.

The underlying compatibility of Domain Theory and Integral Philosophy is readily apparent when one compares LeShan and Margenau's domains of the "see-touch" realm, the sphere of "observable units of behavior of things that are alive" (i.e., the observable individual and social/systemic realms), the "microcosm" and the "macrocosm" with the "external quadrants" of Wilber's model. Within LeShan's and Margenau's model, the area of "a person's inner experience" clearly lies within Wilber's "internal quadrants" (i.e., self-apprehension/individual interior experiences and inner conceptualizations of the social world). The philosophical breakthrough offered by Integral Philosophy is assuredly based on the discernment that humans do indeed have experience in four dimensions. Each of the four domains are equally real and consideration of their unique characteristics and composition is of vital importance in reaching an integral and comprehensive understanding of human experience. Common human experience and understanding as well as directly derived academic disciplines actually do concern themselves with these four dimensions.

As an example, the field of human psychology engages in research and related practices in the following four disciplines: 1) behaviorism, biomedical psychiatry and neuro-psychology (upper right quadrant),

2) family therapy and human systems theory (lower right quadrant), 3) Neo-Freudian models of Self Psychology and Object Relations Theory, plus several cognitively related therapies (upper left quadrant) and 4) Life Script Transactional Analysis, Choice Theory/Reality Therapy and Social Role Theory (lower left quadrant). The matters of concern in each domain differ and processes having to do with operating formulations and organizational change are peculiar not just to the differing domains of focus in the field of psychology, but indeed within the varied realms which comprise human life experience. Additionally, the nature of truth, as well as the methodologies employed to produce domain intrinsic validity claims, vary in relation to the domain of inquiry. Hence, one cannot fully appreciate and accurately understand phenomena in a given quadrant through the operating lens of another quadrant.

LeShan and Margenau assert that two different operations are to be utilized when gathering data related to developing validity tests for the differing domains within which humans have experience. One method is to matter-of-factly observe the data of relevance. This methodology will allow for social confirmation through the sharing of evidence acquired through controlled data gathering procedures. This is the investigative process which fits the domains of the "see-touch" realm, the observable exterior dimension of human experience which includes the "behavior of things that are alive," the microcosm and the macrocosm. It is also the procedure which is to be utilized in studying the external quadrants in Wilber's model. This methodology is essentially that of modern science.

The other procedure employed in efforts to realize legitimacy pronouncements is commonly based on an investigator presenting questions and then, in turn, advancing well-considered interpretations as the subject cooperatively expounds on related aspects of their inner experience. This methodology fits the inside dimensions of human experience and thus corresponds to the LeShan/Margenau domain of a person's interior experience and correlates with the inner realm of individual phenomena, as well as the inner social worldviews maintained by the person as outlined by Wilber. This investigative-interpretive procedure is associated with contemporary hermeneutical practices, varied psychological analyses and narrative related approaches to human study. (Note: LeShan and Margenau mention a third method, but it is that of the "participant observer" and, as such, substitutes the phenomenological experience of the investigator for that of any other person. Thus, this so-called third method actually represents another narrative of inner experience.) Wilber completely agrees with these two methodologies, noting that observation is, in fact, the strategy for gathering data coupled to reaching truth claims in the two right-exterior quadrants; as well, interpretation of expressed inner experience is the key strategy for the realization of validity related information for the two internal self-quadrants. In presenting his theory of "three worlds" Popper also makes a comparable distinction between two types of knowledge: 1) subjective knowledge and 2) objective knowledge. Margenau died in 1997, and with LeShan, offered no notable expansion of their original presentation of Domain Theory. However, Wilber subsequently developed his similar and wholly compatible theoretical model to a refined level of analytical potency and practical efficacy.

After data is gathered via one of the two methods outlined above, Wilber posits that there is a "type" of truth that fits each of the four quadrants and "being in touch" with that truth essentially means being attuned to genuine domain intrinsic validity claims. While the focus of this work is located primarily in the two external quadrants, certain characteristics of truth unique to each of the four quadrants will be outlined below. (Note: As an accomplished philosopher and writer, Ken Wilber has published over 25 books and his work has been translated into 30 languages. He is best known for the development of his systemic philosophy—"Integral Theory"— which seeks a bold synthesis of human knowledge and experience. Much of the subsequent commentary is based on information derived from Wilber's previously referenced book: *A Brief History of Everything*. For greater detail regarding quadrant specific truths and certain tests appropriate for validity-related claims, the extensive published work of Ken Wilber is recommended for study.)

Upper right quadrant ("IT"): Propositional truth has to do with a process of basic mapping or developing a theoretical correspondence in relation to objective external phenomena through which a hypothesis can be confirmed or disconfirmed. Entities in the "see-touch" realm of the exterior upper right quadrant have simple location (position) and can be measured and quantified. The scientific practice of developing a hypothesis related to the matter of concern, conducting controlled experiments, analyzing the resultant data and checking the findings against the original hypothesis is fundamentally the methodology by which truth is determined. Replication of research projects adds sound assurance to validity conclusions.

A simple example from the "see-touch" domain of human experience will provide a useful illustration of the predictable and reliable nature of mechanics. Over 400 years ago, Italian scientist Galileo Galilei hypothesized that the rate at which a body falls is independent from its weight or form, refuting Aristotle's contention that heavier weight objects fall faster than lighter weight items and that the shape of an object also influences its rate of descent. Thus, if a one-hundred-pound metal ball and a one-pound wicker basket are placed in a vacuum chamber (so as to create an environment absent of certain atmospheric concerns) and both are dropped at precisely the same time from a height of twenty feet, the two objects will reach the surface at exactly the same moment. Objective scientific research has conclusively determined that no matter how many times this experiment is repeated with objects of varying weight and shape, they will without variance meet the surface at exactly the same time. In a fantastic replication of this experimental test (and one which Galilei probably could not envision), astronaut David Scott, while standing on the surface of the Moon in the midst of a lunar atmosphere offering negligible interference in the year 1971, dropped a feather and a hammer at the same moment and they predictably landed on the surface of the Moon at the same time. (A video of this actual experiment is available at: https://moon.nasa.gov/resources/331/the-apollo-15-hammer-feather-drop/) Of course, Col. Scott was only able to reach the Moon due to the revolutionary findings of Galileo Galilei, as well as the precise scientific research of Sir Isaac Newton as revealed in his astonishing physics.

The work of Galilei and Newton, as well as many other physicists, established certain truths regarding the nature of observable entities, as well as the behavior and relationship between physical elements and forces in the "see-touch" domain of human experience. Assuredly, after the scientific discovery of the objective truth that the Sun is the center of the solar system, a return to advocating for the false geocentric model of the solar system is simply not possible for persons capable of comprehending rigorous and replicated findings from basic scientific investigations. It is noteworthy that no "cultural relativism" can be said to have bearing in this objective domain, as elements intrinsic to an intangible abstract culture occur only within the domain of inter-subjective human conceptualization. Obviously, humans themselves appeared billions of years after the manifestation of non-living material entities, as well as the precisely run systems and predictable processes of change peculiar to the "see-touch" domain of mechanics. Undeniably, there are objective "Universal Truths" or "Grand Narratives" within this domain/realm of human experience which humans can know—even on the moon—and those who say otherwise are either completely ignorant in matters related to this realm of human life or are being dishonest. This is the investigative quadrant that is best explicated through the practice of modern science and is characterized by the astounding achievement of specific predictability, where the future state of material events can be foretold from knowing pertinent present conditions.

However, when interests are turned towards studying the sub-domain of the microcosm where entities cannot be observed in the same manner as those in the "see-touch" domain, specific predictability is typically replaced by statistical probability estimates. Truths realized in this external domain of human experience have, without question, produced astonishing benefits to humankind. However, an investigative restriction frequently characterized by a reductionist viewpoint, e.g., "if you can't measure it, it is unimportant," has often produced a rather limited and quite impoverished perspective of human experience. Theoretical physicist Erwin Schrodinger, who won a Nobel Prize as well as the Max Planck Medal, offers the following discerning comment on the limits of scientific explanation:

> I am very astonished that the scientific picture of the real world around me is deficient. It gives a lot of factual information, puts all our experience in a magnificently consistent order, but is ghastly silent about all and sundry that is really near to our heart, that really matters to us. It cannot tell us a word about red and blue, bitter and sweet, physical pain and physical delight; it knows nothing of beautiful and ugly, good or bad, God and eternity. Science sometimes pretends to answer questions in these *domains* [emphasis added], but the answers are very often so silly that we are not inclined to

take them seriously. (Schrodinger, Erwin. *Nature and the Greeks*. Cambridge University Press, 1954)

Because, in this quadrant, truth-related findings are typically exact and consistently replicable, the expression of social/psychological defense mechanisms by groups who are troubled by such precise scientific data can be quite strident and vehemently dismissive.

Upper left quadrant ("I"): This is the dimension where the internal experience of the individual self occurs, and matters concerning truth/veracity are related to a self-constitution distinguished by authenticity, trustworthiness, compositional harmony, inter-quadrant congruence, truthfulness and internal honor/integrity. Notably, in regard to one's internal experience of honor, the book *Chapters of the Fathers* (Translation by Hirsch, Samson Raphael. Philipp Feldheim Publisher, 1979) explains: "He who chases after honor, honor runs away from him; He who runs away from honor, honor chases after him." In other words, the honor achieved by constructing and maintaining internal self-integrity is both more assured and of greater worth than external accolades which may or may not be received when seeking the recognition of others. It is important to emphasize that a person's internal self-truthfulness must also be congruent with pertinent inter-quadrant truths, i.e., while one can sincerely form and promote a favored self-characteristic, the belief or characteristic itself can be based on a falsehood. Thus, people can lie to themselves as well as lie to others. If an individually-constructed belief (upper left quadrant) entails personal characteristics, skills or abilities that are linked to pertinent and primary factors intrinsic to other quadrants, then those characteristics must be congruent with the demonstrable facts joined to that domain of experience in order to achieve inter-quadrant congruence, which then allows for internal truthfulness.

Interior elements of individual self-experience are intangible (as they have no simple location) and are often characterized by a great deal of imagination in relation to the construction of personal characteristics and identity structures. The recognition and detection of individual self-defense mechanisms in this domain of human experience occurred primarily through the psychoanalytic research of Sigmund Freud. Freud discovered that humans use several self-deceptive cognitive strategies, e.g., denial, dissociation, rationalization, displacement, projection and repression to protect their self-structure from anxiety, guilt, shame, unacceptable thoughts or the cognitive conflict that can occur when confronted with challenges to certain aspects of self-composition. In relation to internal deceptive practices, longshoreman and social philosopher Eric Hoffer states in his book *The Passionate State of Mind: And Other Aphorisms* (Hopewell Publications, 1955): "We lie the loudest when we lie to ourselves."

Truth in this quadrant is realized through achieving a self-constitution which harmonizes with discoverable internal certitudes, as well as with relevant and limiting aspects of other pertinent quadrants. This is a human dimension where premodern contemplative practices, contemporary spiritual guidance methodologies, substantiated modern psychological assessment techniques, efficacious postmodern psychotherapies, as well as advantageous post-postmodern self-development endeavors, can all be employed to help humans realize a self-structure marked by a truth tied to internal harmony, inter-quadrant congruence and compositional truthfulness. Distortions in this domain are often marked by functional psychological disturbances such as chronic insecurity, which is typically characterized by a dismal self-appraisal of overall inadequacy. Insufficiently structured emotional management capacities can lead to self-harm, acting out on others or dramatic personal "melt downs." A commanding narcissistic self-composition can foment malicious manipulation of others, as well as criminal exploitation.

Yet, it is also from within this domain that the Holocaust survivor and psychiatrist Viktor Frankl could give an account of the following inner self-experience:

> A thought transfixed me: for the first time in my life, I saw the truth as it is set into a song by so many poets, proclaimed as the final wisdom by so many thinkers. The truth—that love is the ultimate and final goal to which man can aspire. Then I grasped the meaning of the greatest secret that human poetry and human thought and belief have to impart. That salvation of man is through love and in love. I understood how a man who has nothing left in this world still may know bliss, be it only for a brief moment. In the

contemplation of his beloved. (Frankl, Viktor. *Man's Search for Meaning.* Beacon Press, 1959)

A similar insight was expressed by the mystic St. Teresa of Ávila: "It is love alone that gives worth to all things." This domain of human experience is notably distinguished by a constitution of self which falls along a continuum from "scoundrel to saint," e.g., Pol Pot to Mother Theresa, Dr. Joseph Mengele to Dr. Albert Schweitzer or Adolf Hitler to Father Maximilian Kolbe (a Catholic priest who willingly substituted his life so a Jewish husband and father could escape execution in Auschwitz).

In order to become a person who is universally regarded by others as fully genuine, compassionate and magnanimous, one's self-structure must be characterized by authenticity, internal honor/integrity, trustworthiness and a truthfulness which is positively marked by inner compositional harmony as well as inter-quadrant congruence. Noteworthy in this quadrant/domain is the work of psychologist Abraham Maslow, who created a seminal psychological model outlining a developmental path towards what could be called, at least at the pinnacle, "the truth of a well-constructed self" identified as "self-actualization."

Lower left quadrant ("WE"): In this domain, matters of concern are related to internal cultural conceptions realized within "intersubjective space." Significant contributions have been realized from postmodern-influenced theoretical developments and considerations in relation to proffering an understanding that "subjective space" is itself intimately and importantly related to language-constituted "intersubjective space." In regard to the function of language in this matter, a review of the work of Chilean biologist and social philosopher Humberto Maturana by Alan Stewart suggests that "individuals who become members of a social system do so by some form of coordination of their activities. Maturana proposes that the means by which coordination is coordinated is by language..." (Stewart, Alan. "Constructivism and Collaborative Enterprises." https://www.univie.ac.at/constructivism/pub/seized/construc.html). It is in this domain of human experience that the work of sociologists Peter Berger and Thomas Luckmann finds its fitting expression and application. Thus, truth in this domain has to do with intersubjective accord and amicable social admission—not the individual-based authenticity and truthfulness characteristic of the upper left quadrant of subjective inner self-experience.

Because culture offers the common context where much of a person's social perceptions will have a type of meaning, criteria by which truth is judged are related to reciprocal understanding, inter-quadrant congruence and the extent of both individual and communal justness intrinsic to a proffered social world view. In demanding and reaching this saving measure of enduring value for differing social ideas, the collective benefit of "an ethics of us" can be achieved. In their book *The Tree of Knowledge: The Biological Roots of Human Understanding* (Shambhala Publications, Inc., 1987), Chilean biologists and social philosophers Humberto Maturana and Francisco Varela state that "the only possibility for coexistence is to opt for a broader perspective, a domain of existence in which both parties fit in the bringing forth of a common world....A conflict can go away only if we move to another domain where coexistence takes place. The knowledge of this knowledge constitutes the social imperative for a human-centered ethics."

From this quadrant, the sociocultural models that produce the observable societies that humans share together in physical space arise (lower right quadrant). This dimension is characterized by an extensive range of social imagery. The concepts of social toleration, equality of all humans, fair economic opportunity and individual liberty tangibly demonstrated most frequently in democratized nations with open market economies are indications of reaching a superior level of truth in this quadrant. In contrast, the ethnically focused and divided (i.e. tribal) genocidal cultural perspective of Germany's National Socialist Party led to inequality and social intolerance resulting in agents of the government killing 12 to 15 million civilians. Likewise, the democide/politicide intrinsic to Karl Marx's divisive economic class conflict worldview called socialism/communism concretely manifested in the 20th century societies of the USSR, China, Cambodia, North Korea, Yugoslavia, Cuba, Ethiopia, Rwanda and Indonesia resulted in representatives of government actualizing forceful social intolerance through the killing of 70 to 100 million citizens—NOT international war combatants. These ghastly socially constructed realities demonstrate that a human society can mutually ascribe to a cultural worldview which values a time bound or conspicuously abstract collective identity over the innate worth of the tangible individual. And, when coupled with associated ethics and norms, they constitute a culture/society that is much more than simply "untrue."

Germany's National Socialism and Marx's socialism/communism are early prototypical forms of the postmodern related regressive and dangerous "Cultural/Intersectional Marxist" practice of ascribing societal value and innate worth to each human being based on an arbitrary categorization of persons into sex, race, ethnic and other divisive "groupisms." The transformation of Marx's socioeconomic class conflict model to a conflict/power theory based on other divisive social groupings was primarily derived from the writings of both the Italian Cultural Marxist theorist Antonio Gramsci and the "Critical Theory" conceptions related to Germany's Frankfurt School. In writing about the Marxist theorists associated with the Frankfurt School, Nicki Lisa Cole, Ph.D., states:

> In the aftermath of Marx's failed prediction of revolution, these individuals were dismayed by the rise of Orthodox Party Marxism and a dictatorial form of communism. They turned their attention to the problem of rule through ideology, or rule carried out in the realm of culture. They believed that technological advancements in communications and the reproduction of ideas enabled this form of rule....Their ideas overlapped with Italian scholar Antonio Gramsci's theory of cultural hegemony. ("The Frankfurt School of Critical Theory." thoughtco.com, October 15, 2019)

So as to emphasize the unifying relational genetic constitution of all humanity, note that before there was a focused social conceptualization of Mongoloid, Australoid, Negroid, Capoid or Caucasoid there was The Human Being. Modern scientific research has demonstrated that all humans share 99.9% of the same genetic makeup (Highfield, Roger. "DNA survey finds all humans are 99.9pc the same." *The Telegraph*, December 20, 2002, online). Prior to the development of complex social systems and related advanced civilizations such as Mesopotamia, Egypt, Ancient Greece, The Roman Empire, Spain, Great Britain, Nazi Germany, Communist China or the Union of Soviet Socialist Republics, there was The Human Being. Before the expression and practice of cosmologies derived from the Vedas, Zoroaster, Moses, Confucius, Buddha, Jesus, Muhammad or atheism, there was The Human Being. And, preceding the socioeconomic systems of early trading, feudalism, mercantilism, capitalism and socialism/communism, there was The Human Being. Conspicuously, grave markings have always been specifically characterized by the name of an individual person, never the name of a particular category of superficial features or a time bound and period unique "class" or "group."

An image search on the internet will provide a photo of the grave site of Karl Marx. This grave site boldly features both a bust and the name of a human being, i.e., Karl Marx, not the name of an ethnic, racial, sex-gender, cultural or era-linked socioeconomic group. The social philosophy of Eric Hoffer is sagacious regarding this enduring truth: "It is the individual only who is timeless. Societies, cultures, and civilizations—past and present— are often incomprehensible to outsiders, but the individual's hungers, anxieties, dreams, and preoccupations have remained unchanged through the millennia" (Hoffer, Eric. "Thoughts of Eric Hoffer, Including:" *New York Times*, April 25, 1971, online). In emphasizing the wonder, as well as the equivalent moral value, of each individual human being Dr. Laura Perls, psychologist and co-developer of Gestalt Psychotherapy, was fond of saying that "No matter how you cut the pie, it comes up apple" (Personal communication, October 11, 1986).

For truth to be realized in the lower left quadrant, it must encompass and embrace inter-quadrant congruence and harmony in order to avoid troublesome and perilous social strife due to quadrant discord. Allowance for the equitable expression of divergent social designs, while at the same time, enshrining the concept of moral justness for each individual human citizen must be at the forefront of proffered social worldviews. While there are certainly various ways to envision a social world, there is clearly not an equal number of viable and truthful ways of constructing a human society. Social/psychological defense mechanisms in this domain of human experience are commonly observed in politically prejudiced propaganda, the characterization of disfavored speech with a variety of pejoratives, the manifestation of the postmodern form of the ancient Greek social practice of ostracizing now known as "canceling," verbal abuse of persons seen as opposed to revered social perspectives, and minimizing or fully censoring disapproved social media platforms or internet programing, as well as refusing to broadcast both information and social occurrences that jeopardize the social narrative of preferred political coalitions and related groups.

Lower right quadrant ("ITS"): Within this domain exists the observable phenomena intrinsic to external human interactional systems. While the upper right external quadrant is focused on individual external experience and typically has to do with single fact propositional truth, validity concerns in the lower right quadrant are related to the functionality of systems. Social systems being phenomena located in the external realm of human experience manifest simple location. Sociologist Emile Durkheim was an adherent to the tenets and practices of modern science, thus his admonition to "Consider social facts as things" mirrors the objective characteristics of external factors in the lower right quadrant of human experience.

> Chief among his claims is that society is a sui generis reality, or a reality unique to itself and irreducible to its composing parts. It is created when individual consciences interact and fuse together to create a synthetic reality that is completely new and greater than the sum of its parts. This reality can only be understood in sociological terms, and cannot be reduced to biological or psychological explanations. The fact that social life has this quality would form the foundation of another of Durkheim's claims, that human societies could be studied scientifically. For this purpose he developed a new methodology, which focuses on what Durkheim calls "social facts" or "elements of collective life that exist independently of and are able to exert an influence on the individual." (Emile Durkheim [1858–1917]. *Internet Encyclopedia of Philosophy*, online)

The empirical investigative methodologies related to the analysis of objective data derived from modern science are the essential procedures utilized to produce valid findings in this domain. Social systems that are based on erroneous internally constructed social realities, such as the lie that the Jews were a dangerous race, not simply an ethnic and religious human group or the socially constructed caste system in India that maintained the untruth that the genetic factors of one's birth determined one's value and social status as a human being, obviously did not allow for well-functioning social systems.

Clearly, inter-quadrant congruence and harmony are essential so that intractable quadrant confusion and dysfunctional quadrant discord can be avoided. Truth in this dimension typically has to do with the following questions and concerns: "does the organization actually work in the way is it is alleged to perform," "is the arrangement a generally functional social enterprise or is it marked by conspicuous aspects of dysfunction," "does objective data correspond with what proponents say regarding specific aspects of the system/social phenomena" and "does the social structure provide for genuinely broad human benefit?" In regard to the horrific failure of socially constructed political systems to realize broad social benefit, political science professor Rudolph Rummel coined the term "democide" for government-directed killing of citizens for motivations related to politicide and genocide. He concluded from his academic research that the socially constructed ideas related to democracy, manifested in tangible governmental institutions, are the least likely to result in the murder of its citizens. Professor Rummel was also a key researcher in "democratic peace theory" and reported that between 1816 and 2005 there were 205 wars between non-democracies, 166 military conflicts between non-democracies and democracies, and no wars between democracies (Rummel, Rudolph. "Democratic Peace." hawaii.edu).

Truth assessment is replicable in this domain by engaging new research personnel utilizing additional sample sets, employing identical analytical procedures and then presenting objective findings. Factors of economic activity, assessment of the social consequences of political policies, as well as other specific aspects of human social systems can be analyzed through modern scientific methodologies. However, the complexity inherent in certain systems can present significant challenges to existing theoretical models, data collection and investigative procedures. Cherished world-views can compromise the very structure of the research project with an aim towards producing desired outcomes. The discounting of unfavorable research findings due to prejudiced political preferences, risks to the public reputation of established governmental officials or endangerment to the viability of politically associated bureaucratic structures is a familiar occurrence in public media discourse. Also, the complete censoring of negative outcome studies considered jeopardizing of favored social policy by social media internet sites, as well as among biased members of the press, is commonplace. Nevertheless, given the implementation of an objectively designed scientific research project (including replication projects), study conclusions in this domain of human experience can be very reliable. The social effect of legitimate examination results can be highly influential, therefore social/psychological defense mechanisms employed among offended or disgruntled groups are often manifested in vigorous and contentious modes of behavior.

The capability of post-postmodern Integral Theory can be explicitly demonstrated in assessing the veracity of a self-constructed individual identity (upper left quadrant) where a hypothetical woman believes that she has extraordinary superpowers featuring the ability of unaided bodily flight, great physical strength and possesses an impenetrable force field which will protect her from physical injury of any kind. Accompanying her construction and satisfied ownership of these highly-valued aspects of self is a firm restriction that these superpowers cannot be revealed to others, personally manifested or publicly displayed until a special communication is received from a yet to be known authoritative messenger. It is conceivable that this woman could continue her life with this superpower self-identity held intact and totally private because she never received an authoritative communication allowing her to apply or speak about her extraordinary abilities to others. In this way, the quadrant/domain of internal experience holding the subjectively self-constructed characteristics of a person possessing superpowers can be seen as being maintained without variance, external social challenge or practical test.

Expanding this hypothetical scenario to the lower left quadrant (the internally composed perspective of a social world) and the lower right quadrant (objective elements within society) the woman continued to see slightly veiled messages on a social media site suggesting that there may be other people in possession of unusual superpowers. Because of the repetitive nature of these messages and her interpretation that the communications seemed specially directed to her, she eventually replied. After a lengthy series of investigative questions, she was given access to a well-shielded website located on the "dark web." The high level of security helped convince her that this was surely a genuine authoritative message of permission to communicate about her powers to this select group. On this website she indeed found a group of people who maintained her conviction about enjoying superpowers essentially identical to hers. She continued to engage in extremely secure communication with this group. The woman, with a self-constructed belief in superpowers, was encouraged and further assured of the truth of her extraordinary capabilities, as well as those of the other group members, by the confidentiality exquisitely maintained by all members. Soon, the group began to periodically meet in jointly negotiated public spaces that were deemed safe from eaves-dropping and free of electronic monitoring devices. The internal belief in the actuality of her colossal powers, as well as a social world inhabited by other people with superpowers, became invigorated by means of the social validation realized through the sharing of various details about each person's exceptional characteristics.

This hypothetical woman, with yet to be exercised superpowers, has just read the first of a series of highly dramatized and heart-wrenching arti-cles in the local newspaper boldly proclaiming that due to the horrendous number of murders in her city and the devastating ineptitude of the mayor to effectively address this issue, a "TRUE Superhero" must be found in order to protect innocent lives. After several weeks of impactful articles describing how a "TRUE Superhero" could save numerous human lives in the face of the grievous and continual failure of the mayor, she determines that this is assuredly another authoritative communication regarding her exceptional powers. She securely mails a note concerning her reception of a genuine authoritative message granting "Permission to Employ Super-powers" to a favored group member. Preparing for battle, she is determined to utilize a full expression of her extraordinary powers in the service of protecting innocent humans from the lethal conduct of violent criminals.

On a hot summer night, on the 61st floor of her apartment build-ing, she leaps to flight. However, fundamental elements inherent to the exterior upper right quadrant said "NO" to the unaided flight of a human body. The subjective "truth" of her claim to have "superpowers of flight," as well as a "protective impenetrable force field," was shown to be false via objective and quantifiable factors in the upper right quadrant. The primacy of this domain of human experience, in relation to the Newtonian based mechanics of flight, conclusively invalidated her personally constructed and socially corroborated "truth" of a human having autonomous aerial ability. Additionally, outside of myth or fiction, the absence of documentation in public libraries or pertinent research facilities (the lower right quadrant) where a human was able to fly without the use of an aeronautical apparatus or other relevant mechanical aid was maintained.

The hypothetical woman with a self-constructed and socially authenticated belief in superpowers has been bluntly confronted with the realities of exercised quadrant confusion, i.e., quadrant discord. The surviving members of the group of those with self-constructed and socially confirmed superpowers are now left with the task of integrating this grim data into their personal self-identities. Some group members immediately conclude that they have gravely "misconstructed" their self-composition in regard to the possession of certain exceptional abilities, detransition from their self-formed superpower identity and leave the group. Others enlist a variety of social/psychological defense mechanisms and are convinced that the author of the newspaper articles was obviously not an authentic courier; as a result, they will wait patiently and cautiously for communication from a yet to be revealed authentic messenger.

While the above hypothetical example may at first glance seem extreme or far removed from actual human self/social construction and associated behavioral practice, certain details of the mass suicide of 39 adult members of the Heaven's Gate cult in March of 1997 may cause pause of a cursory judgment. The recognized leader of this social group, Marshall Applewhite, composed a self-structure (upper left quadrant) which featured exceptional spiritual abilities and an identity where he viewed himself as a special leader with a vital message for the human race. (Note: There are several online videos of Mr. Applewhite revealing his identity claims.) In the lower left quadrant, an understanding of the social world featured an apocalyptic prognostication of imminent human decimation to be followed by a monumental proceeding comparable to a total reprocessing of the Earth.

Assessing the lower right quadrant of Mr. Applewhite's social world reveals an associated micro-society (at one point, the group was estimated to total close to 200 like-minded associates) coalescing around the socially constructed reality that the only way to escape destruction and achieve what was called the "Next Level" was to leave their bodies so as to reach this safe supernatural realm. Interestingly, despite securing a large section in the *USA Today* newspaper publicizing his vital message and special leader designation, Mr. Applewhite was unable to garner the support of politicians, key members of the media, influential religious leaders or notable university academics. Also, he was unable to persuade a significant portion of the general population to accept his special identity and adopt his cataclysmic worldview. Thus, the socially constructed reality proffered by this group remained a marginalized perspective within society.

Undaunted by the lack of broad societal support or endorsement from elite members of society, Mr. Applewhite identified the coming appearance of the comet Hale-Bopp as "The Message" that the time had arrived to leave Earth. Believing that a spacecraft was closely linked with this comet to take the members of this specially selected group to the "Next Level," it was strangely deemed necessary to commit suicide in order to reach the spacecraft. On March 26, 1997, after willfully consuming a lethal cocktail of alcohol and phenobarbital, a total of 39 group members were found dead with a purple cloth draped over their bodies, wearing black shirts, black sweatpants, black running shoes and each member had a five dollar bill along with three quarters in their pockets. An additional curious detail is that Applewhite and a number of the other males had willfully been castrated in Mexico City prior to the expected rendezvous with the spacecraft.

A brief analysis of this dreadful event will immediately disclose a pronounced occurrence of both quadrant confusion and quadrant discord. Clearly, both a spacecraft and a comet are observables in the "see-touch" domain of the upper right quadrant of human experience, whereas the mystically apprehended qualities of an incorporeal soul/spirit are distinctive elements inherent to inner spiritual self-experience (upper left quadrant). Recognizing that an immaterial soul/spirit would not require a material space vehicle for transit to an immaterial supernatural realm is assuredly evident.

Marshall Applewhite could have simply chosen to maintain the exceptional details of his self-composition and social perspective within the two internal quadrants and perhaps only share them with those who ascribed to his extraordinary narrative. In this way, he would have continued to live for a longer period of time while demonstrating and appreciating the creative, as well as fanciful, ways in which humans can construct a self-identity and social worldview. However, the guaranteed ramifications of actualized quadrant confusion (i.e., quadrant discord, revealed through brash behavioral expression) decisively established the falsehood of the self-constructed and socially validated exceptional spiritual leader identity of Mr. Applewhite.

In order to further explicate the concept of quadrant confusion, note that in the sketch of the woman with superpowers objective scientific factors and requirements related to physical flight (upper right quadrant) were arbitrarily reduced to mere human desire and wish as well as to the imaginative capacity of subjective psychological self-construction (upper left quadrant). Likewise, Mr. Applewhite demonstrated a remarkable display of quadrant confusion by conflating certain obvious and invariable characteristics of the external natural world (upper right quadrant) with those of an inner experienced supernatural realm (upper left quadrant). As a result, he failed to recognize that an immaterial entity, i.e., soul/spirit cannot make use of a material structure, e.g., a spaceship. Hence, both the woman with superpowers and Mr. Applewhite, when behaviorally expressing their individually constructed and socially affirmed deluded identities—experienced palpable and indeed inevitable discordant occurrences (lower right quadrant).

Consequently, while individual humans can clearly produce novel self-compositions and groups can rally to a variety of inventive social constructions along with directly derived societal configurations, not all self or social constructions are necessarily true. The reader is invited to utilize Integral Theory to further reflect on the details of this tragic human event and contemplate possibilities for more expansive post-postmodern investigations of certain contemporary self-composed identities and notions, as well as socially constructed realities. Just as the hypothetical women with superpowers left behind like-minded associates, two members of the Heaven's Gate religious cult remain alive. These two persons were commissioned to maintain the teachings of the group, and as a matter of fact, continually monitor a web site (heavensgate.com) in efforts to accomplish their assigned goal. It is probable that suitable social/psychological defense mechanisms are employed by this couple to enable continued allegiance to the socially constructed reality promoted by the group.

In retrospect, the effort to comprehend and resolve the microorganism-caused Black Death through faith and mysticism (well-practiced methods of deriving spiritual knowledge within the individual inner domain of human experience) by certain premodern inquisitors was a profoundly misguided undertaking. The endeavor by some early psychologists to explain particular features of inner self-experience via the machine-like model of modern science (which certainly well describes the "behavior" of observables in the "see-touch" domain of Newtonian mechanics) was a deeply mistaken enterprise. In the same way, the contemporary attempt by various advocates and practitioners of postmodern theory/philosophy to employ subjective self/social constructivist theory (which fits particular phenomena inherent to the inner quadrants of human experience) as an explanatory model of the objective nature of genetically-determined human mammalian binary sex-gender is thoroughly misplaced.

All three examples outlined above are glaring illustrations of quadrant confusion and represent peculiar forms of reductionism. Additionally, these examples align well with the following variant of an often-told story: A police officer while on night patrol observes a man in a parking lot on hands and knees seemingly searching for something. The officer drives to the man's location and asks him about his unusual conduct. The man states that he is looking for his lost keys. After helping the man search for several minutes, the officer asks him more precisely where he believes the keys were lost. The man replies, "In the northeast quadrant of the parking lot." The officer asks him why he is then searching in the southwest quadrant of the parking lot. The man responds, "Because I see much more clearly in the light found within the southwest quadrant." As Gregory Bateson commented, it is quite often the case that, "From the manner of the search, we can read what sort of discovery the searcher may thereby reach; and knowing this, we may suspect that such a discovery is what the searcher secretly and unconsciously desires" (Bateson, Gregory. *Mind and Nature: A Necessary Unity*. E. P. Dutton, 1979).

Since the interest of this work has to do with lies and errors within human society, a final observation from Bateson is propitious:

> Pathology is itself a possibility only of Creatura, (i.e., the domain of living things) for at the level of Pleroma (i.e., the domain of non-living entities), direct physical causation makes error impossible. It is never the physical universe that makes mistakes. The physical universe provides randomness and entropy, but error is a biological phenomenon—if, by the term error, we

wish to suggest the existence or value of a possible something which would be "right" or "correct," the error being a difference of what is and what might have been. (Bateson, Gregory, and Mary Catherine Bateson. *Angels Fear: Towards an Epistemology of the Sacred*. Macmillan Publishing, 1987)

This balance of this work will be focused on observables in the external domains of human experience (upper right and lower right quadrants). Therefore, the approach employed to evaluate the legitimacy of the "socially constructed realities" or "social facts" included in this commentary will entail: 1) explicit identification of the socially constructed realities or social facts of concern, 2) citing pertinent findings established through modern scientific investigations, 3) referencing objective examination results derived from social science research, 4) employing logical reasoning where fitting, 5) establishing which of the four quadrants are related to the matter of concern and 6) identification of quadrant confusion, quadrant discord and peculiar forms of reductionism.

In the late 1700s, Edward Gibbon, the acclaimed author of *The History of the Decline and Fall of the Roman Empire* (London, 1776), stated that "All that is human must retrograde if it does not advance." As a full twenty percent of the twenty-first century is now realized, Gibbon's observation is clearly both up-to-date and felicitous. The theoretical system of Domain Theory and the quadrant conception derived from Integral Philosophy are best understood as post-postmodern metatheories offering identification of specific investigative methodologies which correspond to observables and related truths intrinsic to each of the four quadrants of human experience. Through the utilization of examining techniques proper to each quadrant, as well as inviting an integration of tried and efficacious findings gleaned from premodern, modern and postmodern investigations, earnest appreciation is granted to the wondrous and complex lives we live as human beings.

The intent of this section was to provide an adequate theoretical guide that would convey a consequential understanding of both the methodology and conclusions contained within this discourse. For those social facts herein identified and scrutinized through the processes detailed above, this text may be seen as a post-postmodern investigation and commentary having to do with truth concerns related to certain contemporary socially constructed realities and proposed "individual truths." This document was written for all persons who possess a fervent desire for greater human harmony actualized by means of an enhanced level of intellectual honesty within society.

CHAPTER 3

Trans-Sex-Gender

Teiresias was roaming through either the rocky crags of Mount Cithaeron (in Thebes) or through the mountain valleys of Cyllene (in Arcadia). Either way, at one point, he happened upon two snakes copulating. Disgusted by the scene, he struck them and wounded at least one of them. Hera didn't like this one bit, so she turned Teiresias into a woman. He spent the next seven years of his life living as a priestess of Hera. It was during this time that he gave birth to his most famous child, Manto, a famous prophetess herself. At the end of the seventh year, he came across the same two snakes mating again. Having learned his lesson, this time Teiresias made sure not to touch them and, as a result, he was freed from his sentence and regained his masculinity. (greekmythology.com. 2020)

Sex-Gender Is a Genetically-Determined Immutable Human Characteristic

Life forms on planet Earth are now understood by researchers to have first appeared from 3.5 to 3.8 billion years ago. Writer Vivien Cumming, in an online article titled "The Real Reasons We Have Sex" (bbcearth. com. July 4, 2016), indicates that the first occurrence of sexual reproduction among living creatures occurred approximately 1.2 billion years ago among a group of red algae. In studying fossil records, scientists have determined that these life forms were the first to manifest reproductive spores/cells in male and female structures and relied on water currents to transport the dichotomous reproductive spores to other red algae. Based on examining 385 million year-old fossils located in rocks, investigators have also concluded that the first occurrence of sexual reproduction involving internal fertilization, as in mammalian reproductive processes, appeared in a primitive fish called *Microbrachius dicki*. Significant in this finding is that these particular living creatures demonstrate the first physiological arrangement of what biologists call "dimorphism," i.e., females and males actually look different from one another. Also, of pertinent interest for this present work is the important discovery that the tiny shrew-size creatures called morganucodontids were the earliest of mammals and date to about 210 million years ago.

While sexual reproduction has been the process whereby mammals have reproduced lineage over a period of 210 million years, it is only human mammals that can actually speak about their differing binary reproductive sex organs and reflect upon various aspects and particulars concerning the process of sexual coupling, e.g., sexually focused flirting in language, anticipatory mental envisioning of sexual activity, coordination of physical positioning during sexual engagement via language, linguistically recall prior sexual engagements, offer descriptions in literature, create depictions in film, craft displays in visual art and concoct unique names for the differing binary sexual reproductive organs. While other mammals have peculiar systems of analogic communication, only by means of language are humans able to specifically, abstractly and creatively communicate about concepts, issues or things in the past, present and future. Assuredly, neither camels, cougars nor caribous are psychologically concerned with their differing binary genitals, experience cognitive confusion regarding individual sex-gender identity, engage in reflective deliberation with respect to socially shared conceptions regarding possible sex-gender roles or debate about the conspicuous exercise of sex-gender roles in their species-defined and binary sex-gender delimited society. Language further enables humans to "talk about" ideas, social artifacts or material things from a storehouse of accumulated societal knowledge, individual memory and, amazingly, from elaborate speculation or pure imagination. Only humans enjoy the phenomenon of language, which is wonderfully characterized by a complex and highly abstract meaning-endowed system of visual symbols and verbal productions. Language is arguably one of the most extraordinary and impactful abilities which humans possess.

In the book *Tao Te Ching*, the Chinese mystic and philosopher Lao Tzu stated that "Naming is the origin of all particular things." In regard to the matter of human sexual reproduction, the names sex and gender most certainly refer to "particular things." Because humans communicate through both analogic methods (as do all other animals) and a peculiar abstract language system, it is vital that a shared meaning of names and words be realized so as to enable the individual to effectively relate and functionally coordinate their day-to-day movements within the observable social world. For this present work, the words sex and gender will be notably linked with the distinctive process of sexual reproduction, i.e., the union of the dichotomous small and mobile male sperm and the large female oocyte producing a novel human zygote with a distinct genotype and directly linked phenotype sex-gender differences between males and females. Most notably, the human domain of inquiry regarding the observable elements which have to do with these corporal matters is the external individual upper right quadrant of human experience where the methodology of modern science is fittingly employed to reach valid findings.

The equivalency of the two terms "sex" and "gender," as used in this present work, is based on historical and extensive research in the biological sciences as well as the etymology of the word "gender." The word "gender" is a compound word with the root "gen" carrying the meanings of "give birth," "a producer of something" or "beget." Specific Latin origins are interpreted as "race, kind, family or species." The suffix "der" is understood by etymologists to mean a thing or person who accomplishes something and is typically used to create what is called an agent noun, i.e., a noun which specifies an agent who does something. In the case of "gen-der" the "accomplisher" or "doer" ("der") references the two (and only two) distinct biological entities who sexually take part in reproductive joining/coupling and giving birth ("gen") to "kind" or species. Additionally, of linguistic and semantic importance is the identification of the root "gen" in the following words that have to do with production, origin, identification, kind or family: genitals, gene, generate, genesis, generic, genealogy, generable, genetics, genre, genus, progeny and indigenous. In further revealing the origin and historical meaning of the word "gender," the following reference is most important: "The 'male-or-female sex' sense is attested in English from early 15c. As 'sex' (n .) took on erotic qualities in 20c., 'gender' came to be the usual English word for 'sex of a human being'" (etymonline.com).

Notwithstanding the observation that, since the mid-to-late twentieth century, the word "gender" has undergone a cultural/societal change in usage, deviating from certain etymological origins and historical usage in scientific investigations engendering semantic obfuscation, this present work will employ the well-grounded etymological meaning and quintessential biological interpretation and application of the word "gender," i.e., that gender references specific features of a living entity which renders it capable, due to possessing one of two possible sets of complementary reproductive systems including binary gametes (eggs or sperm), of "generating" species identical and sex-gender binary offspring via sexual reproduction. In studying mammals, scientists have consistently defined sex based on the biologically consistent and ubiquitous observation that males produce structurally unique small and mobile gametes, while females produce large and structurally different non-mobile gametes. This observable fact, of course, applies to all mammals who invariably reproduce offspring via compositionally differentiated gametes. Thus, gender and sex are synonyms that refer to dissimilar living entities precisely marked by producing structurally unique gametes and possessing dichotomous reproductive systems which are distinctly involved in complementary joining/coupling in an organic sexual process that realizes the reproduction of binary male and female offspring, along with the essential foundational biological characteristics that identify their specific species.

Dr. Ryan T. Anderson, in his book *When Harry Became Sally: Responding to the Transgender Moment* (Encounter Books, 2019), states that

> I wanted to cite the standard texts on when the life of a human being begins, and I found that the scientific community is rather clear on the matter when political debates aren't involved: the life of a new human organism—a human being—begins at conception, when sperm and egg fuse to form a single-cell embryo, a zygote.

Dr. Anderson, in quoting *Langman's Medical Embryology*, also notes that the biological scientific community also agrees, and is unambiguous on, stating when sex is determined: "An X-carrying sperm produces a female (XX) embryo, and a Y-carrying sperm produces a male (XY) embryo. Hence, the chromosomal sex of the embryo is determined at fertilization." In further scientific identification of the precise process of sex determination, Anderson adds the following quote from *Human Embryology* by William J. Larson: "The male sex is determined by presence of a Y sex chromosome (XY), and female sex is determined by absence of a Y chromosome (XX)." In fact, binary sex-gender has been the foundational structural arrangement for the reproduction of all mammals for over two hundred million years.

In this "see-touch" domain of biology (upper right quadrant) in which the methodology of modern science is the approach by which truth is realized, there exists no suitable application of individual or social constructionist theory as informed by postmodern philosophy regarding these objective and consistent findings of scientific research. In the same way, an attempt to utilize the modern scientific concept of the kilogram to quantify the "weight" of one's depressive experience, or express through horsepower or electric voltage terminology the "energy potential" related to a person's demonstrated industriousness, would also reveal a profound ignorance of distinct domains of human experience, i.e., quadrant confusion.

The wide array of biological and chemical differences between men and women is discussed in an informative article by writer Cecile Borkhataria, which states that "...researchers analyzed 20,000 genes and found 6,500 of them are expressed differently in men and women..." The author further notes that "Gene expression for muscle building was higher in men and that for fat storage higher in women." In regard to a specific medical concern, the article reports: "A gene that was active in women's brains may protect the neurons from Parkinson's disease— which has a higher prevalence and earlier onset in men" ("The REAL Difference Between Men and Women." dailymail.com, May 2017). In other words, in about one out of every three genes studied, the genes were expressed differently between women and men. These findings have profound implications on the development of male vs. female body characteristics, as well as the manifestations of various diseases. Sex-gender-specific scientific research, as well as the medical interventions employed to treat differing disease occurrences between men and women, are also clearly of vital importance.

In a discourse by David P. Schmidt, Ph.D., titled "The Truth About Sex Differences" (pychologytoday.com, November 7, 2017), the author explains that,

> Ironically, just as the evidence is mounting that psychological sex differences are real, denial of differences has become rampant. Attempts at respectful and productive conversations about biological sex differences often end with name-calling (genetic determinist!) or outright cancelation of events, not to mention the very public firing of a Google software engineer for writing a memo on the topic.

Schmidt suggests that one of the reasons that conversations about sex differences end in difficulties "is the widespread lack of foundational knowledge about sex and gender." (Note: Schmidt's use of the term gender is seemingly equivalent to the concepts of "sex-gender identity," "internally envisioned/constructed sex-gender roles" and "sex-gender roles," as detailed below and used consistently in this present work.) The author adds that "… denying men's and women's different psychologies is not merely a denial of reality; it has serious health consequences for significant segments of the population."

In referencing the way in which the Y chromosome of the human male fetus sets off an amplification of binary genetic sex differences, Schmidt notes that males are routinely prenatally exposed to elevated levels of androgen. Indeed, the elevated quantities of this biochemical androgenic hormone is directly associated with, and contributes to, the accentuation of specific phenotype characteristics of the human male (as well as contributing to a unique sex-gender identity expression); essentially, it is amplifying characteristics that are determined by the initial and foundational binary XY chromosomal structure. The author resolutely proclaims that "…some psychological sex differences result from direct effects of genes.…" In further support of this conclusion, Schmidt notes the research of psychologist Janet Hyde, saying that "Hyde and her colleagues have found that a serotonin-transporter gene, 5-HTTLPR, which exists in short and long versions, the short version being associated with higher negative emotionality, is more closely linked to the emergence of neuroticism-related traits in women than in men." The author references other gene variants affecting other neurotransmitters that are disproportionally expressed in females and highlights the probability that these genetic differences may indeed account for one of the most evident psychological sex differences, i.e., "... the higher prevalence of depression among women than men."

Schmidt discusses several other psychological and behavioral sex differences, and also includes a useful chart outlining additional discernible male vs. female disparities. The author concludes with a statement that openly asserts his position as an objective scientist:

> There are sex differences whose development society needs to actively redress, such as the greater risk of severe autism in males and depression in females. There is only one way to develop the tools necessary for subduing such undesirable developments—understand their biological provenance. And that starts with recognizing their existence.

Ross Pomeroy, in writing for *Real Clear Science,* reveals that "...cells can be male or female....Cells in women's bodies have two X chromosomes (XX), while cells in men's bodies have one X and one Y (XY). Thus we get our male and female cells." Pomeroy then clearly notes: "...male and female cells are fundamentally dissimilar on a genetic level." The importance of understanding this fact is precisely stated by the author: "Like people, cells are also male and female, and they are plainly not the same. Their unique characteristics must be accounted for in scientific research" ("Male or Female? Why a Cell's Sex Matters." realclearscience. com, November 18, 2013).

On August 30, 2016, Carissa R. Violante published an article on the Yale School of Medicine's website titled "Every Cell Has a Sex: X and Y and the Future of Health Care" (medicine.yale.edu). The author, in referencing Yale's Dr. David C. Page, emphasizes that "...researchers and health care practitioners need to fundamentally change how they approach the study and treatments of disease to reflect differences between males and females that exist with every cell of their bodies." Also from the work of Dr. Page, Violante stresses the following conclusion in her report: "...there are intrinsic biochemical differences between XX and XY cells that affect tissues and organs across the entire body and have a significant impact independent of sex hormones. And medical practitioners must understand these differences to properly treat their patients." (Note: "Although most body cells have two matched sets of chromosomes, there are two cell types that are exceptions: reproductive cells and mature red blood cells. Reproductive cells—that is, sperm or eggs—have only a single chromosome set. In this way, when a sperm and egg meet and fuse, the result is a new cell with the two paired sets. Mature red blood cells have no nucleus, so they have no autosomal or sex chromosomes—only the chromosome present in their mitochondria" ("Chromosomes." askingalot.com).

The *NCI Bookshelf*, a service of the National Library of Medicine, National Institutes of Health, presents an online research report titled "Exploring the Biological Contributions to Human Health: Does Sex Matter?—Every Cell Has a Sex" (Wizemann, T. M. and M. L. Pardue. ncbi.nlm. nih.gov. 2001). The report notes that "Surprisingly, recent studies show that the Y chromosome carries genes that are involved in basic cellular functions and that are expressed in many tissues (Lahn and Page, 1997)." In discussing cellular peculiarities in relation to the Y chromosome, two distinct classes of what are called "functional clustering" are highlighted with the article explaining that "Some of these genes are involved in basic cellular functions, thus providing a basis for functional differences between male and female cells." In detailing the unique effect of the X chromosome on cellular operations, the following information is provided: "...females have twice the dose of X-chromosome-linked (sic) genes that males have....Although many are responsible for general cellular functions and are expressed widely in different tissues, others are specific to particular tissues or particular time points during development, and several are known to be responsible for steps in gonadal differentiation" (Pinsky et al 1999). Most importantly, the article states that "The discovery that some genes are expressed only for the maternal allele and that others are expressed only from the paternal allele, a phenomenon called genomic imprinting, reinforces the concept that there are multiple biochemical differences between the gametogenic cells of males and females...." The report concludes that

> These findings argue that there are multiple, ubiquitous differences in the
> basic cellular biochemistry of males and females that can affect an individual's

health. Many of these differences do not necessarily arise as a result of differences in the hormonal environment of the male and female but are a direct result of the genetic differences between the two sexes.

On February 13, 2020, biologists Dr. Colin Wright and Dr. Emma Hilton published an article in *The Wall Street Journal* with the headline "The Dangerous Denial of Sex." The website fairplayforwomen.com offered an overview of the article and presented important and relevant information from this work (February 14, 2020). In regard to the postmodern belief that sex-gender is not a binary and genetically determined reproductive physical reality of human mammalian life, but rather a non-physical, abstract and arbitrary phenomenon of social/psychological construction, Wright and Hilton provide the following rebuttal:

> The argument is that because some people are intersex—they have developmental conditions resulting in ambiguous sex characteristics—the categories male and female exist on a "spectrum," and are therefore no more than "social constructs." If male and female are merely arbitrary groupings, it follows that everyone, regardless of genetics or anatomy should be free to choose to identify as male or female, or to reject sex entirely in favor of a new bespoke "gender identity."

These two biologists then add this succinct critical assessment of this postmodern construct: "To characterise this line of reasoning as having no basis in reality would be an egregious understatement. It is false at every conceivable scale of resolution."

Further scientific details are then offered to firmly anchor the position argued by Wright and Hilton:

> In humans, as in most animals or plants, an organism's biological sex corresponds to one of two distinct types of reproductive anatomy that develop for the production of small or large sex cells—sperm and eggs, respectively—and associated biological functions in sexual reproduction. In humans, reproductive anatomy is unambiguously male or female at birth more than 99.98% of the time. The evolutionary function of these two anatomies is to aid in reproduction via the fusion of sperm and ova. No third type of sex

cell exists in humans, and therefore there is no sex "spectrum" or additional sexes beyond male and female.

Wright and Hilton then plainly state their key conclusions and concerns:

> Sex is binary....Denying the reality of biological sex and supplanting it with subjective "gender identity" is not merely an eccentric academic theory. It raises serious human-rights concerns for vulnerable groups including women, homosexuals and children....The time for politeness on this issue has passed. Biologists and medical professionals need to stand up for the empirical reality of biological sex. When authoritative scientific institutions ignore or deny empirical fact in the name of social accommodation, it is an egregious betrayal to the scientific community they represent. It undermines public trust in science, and it is dangerously harmful to those most vulnerable.

It is most relevant to note that both forensic scientists and archeologists can determine the sex-gender of a mere skeleton even if thousands of years old, simply by a detailed examination of certain aspects of pelvic structure and sex-gender unique physical features of the human skull. Obviously, this determination is accomplished with absolutely no reference to psychological, cultural or sociological factors in relation to the skeletal remains of a human being.

Kara Dansky, who earned a law degree from the University of Pennsylvania and is currently a member of the steering committee for the Woman's Human Rights Campaign (WHRC), is in full agreement with Wright and Hilton's scientific statement that sex is binary—male and female—and that lying about or obscuring this truth is harmful to society. Dansky offers this admonishment: "Every single person is either female or male, there's nothing wrong with saying that....The obliteration of the material reality of biological sex should scare everyone" (Sahakian, Teny. "Lifelong Democrat, feminist warns party to stop trying to abolish biological sex or lose votes." foxnews.com, 11/19/21). Dansky clearly possesses an accurate understanding that one's sex-gender is genetically determined and that the terms sex and gender are synonyms. In her new book *The Abolition of Sex: How the "Transgender" Agenda Harms Women and Girls*

(Bombardier Books, November 8, 2021), she resolutely presents the following assessment of the trans-sex-gender phenomenon: "The truth is there is no such thing as 'transgender'…the entire agenda is grounded in and fueled by an industry whose aim is to abolish the material reality of sex." (Note: Dansky seemingly uses the phrase transgender as synonymous with the term trans-sex-gender as specified in this writing.) The author continues, saying that

> This assault on women's sex-based rights is not occurring in a vacuum or by accident. It is being perpetrated by a vicious and brutal industry that operates openly and yet manages to sneak under the radar. Its aim is to abolish sex in the law and throughout society. We are all victims of this assault, but those most harmed are women and girls, i.e., female human beings.

Sexologist and Neuroscientist Dr. Debra Soh provides the following unequivocal proclamations regarding sex and gender: "There are only two genders.…Not three, not seventy-one, and certainly not an infinite number. Gender is not a spectrum, a continuum, a kaleidoscope, a prism, or another majestic-sounded metaphor that gender activism has dreamed up." Adding emphasis regarding the total number of genders, Dr. Soh assertively states that "There are only two: female and male. There is zero scientific evidence to suggest that other genders exist." In an effort to bring the irrefutable findings from biological science into the contemporary discussion of sex and gender, Soh adds that

> …humans are a sexually dimorphic species, with two types of gametes: eggs and sperm. Intermediate gametes don't exist. Since biological sex and gender are both defined by these parameters, gender is, by definition, like sex—either male or female; binary not a spectrum…Gender is not a continuum or a rainbow or a diverse spectrum. It exists as two discrete categories, female and male, not as two polarities along a shared continuum along which human beings appear with equal likelihood. (Soh, Debra. *The End of Gender.* Threshold Editions, 2020)

Biologists Heather Heying and Bret Weinstein further substantiate the binary nature of sex-gender, saying that "…among plants and animals, there are only ever two types of gametes (reproductive cells)." The two biologists also emphasize the biological determination of dimorphic sex-gender in human mammals, saying that "In mammals…sex is determined chromosomally." And, in regard to the matter of trans-sex-gender, Heying and Weinstein offer an observation that is scientifically invariable: "…no mammals…have ever been known to change sex" (Heying, Heather and Bret Weinstein. *A Hunter-Gatherer's Guide To The 21st Century: Evolution and the Challenges of Modern Life.* Portfolio/Penguin, 2021).

Assuredly, persons capable of utilizing discerning and dispassionate faculties will concede that the dichotomous genetic/biological differences between males/men and females/women have been thoroughly explicated by modern biological science. Succinctly stated, in regard to the reproductive and general physiological nature of the human species: males are not females and females are not males.

Based on the above facts, consistently revealed through the practice of modern science and the etymological origin of the word gender, the hyphenated term sex-gender will be consistently used in this work. The phrase sex-gender quite suitably refers to the binary physical genitals, dichotomous gametes and sex-gender specific biochemical reproductive characteristics of human beings. Additionally, employing the words female and male, girl and boy, woman and man, as well as she and he, will provide a scientifically informed return to the fully established biological fact of the binary (not three, four, five, etc.) sex-gender composition of humans, founded on the unalterable truth of the dichotomous structure of sex gametes.

The commonly used phrase "transgender" is a compound word. (Note: The accurate term "trans-sex-gender" will be consistently used in this work.) The etymological origin of the prefix "trans" conveys the meaning of across, beyond or through, and is related to the term "tere" which signifies crossover, pass through or overcome (etymonline.com). Additionally, the word "identity" is defined as: "…the condition of being the same with something described or asserted…sameness in all that constitutes the objective reality of a thing…" (*Merriam-Webster*, online). Regarding the word "identity" the *Online Etymology Dictionary* offers the following information: "…sameness, oneness, state of being the same, from French…from Medieval Latin… sameness.…" Thus, a "trans-sex-gender identity" would be the term used to designate a male human—whose claimed trans-sex-gender identity—entails the self-determined, and distinctly supernatural, capability to demonstrably bodily "crossover" from being a generator of mobile sperm to becoming an egg provider (and fetus nurturer) in an actual process of sexual reproduction; and, of course, vice versa with related physiological, chromosomal and biochemical sex-gender characteristics, as well as other pertinent biological markers in the case of a woman who claims to be trans-sex-gender. Outside of mythology, e.g., the Greek prophet "Teiresias" or the creation of fictional characters, there is no documentation of a human being who has ever displayed this corporeal transformative ability.

Noteworthy, in regard to the subject of trans-sex-gender, is the ability of some fish to truly change their sex-gender. In a July 10, 2019, article titled "How Can Some Animals Change Sex? The Answer Is Rooted in Stress," published in the online journal *Inverse,* writer Sarah Sloat states that "For the majority of organisms, sex is not something that can change. This is not true, however, for a fish called the bluehead wrasse. These fish can go from female to male, complete with sperm making testes, within a matter of ten days." Referencing researcher Erica Todd, Ph.D., of the University of Otago, Sloat further reports that "We found that sex change requires a complete genetic rewiring of the gonad. Genes needed to maintain the ovary are turned off, and the new genetic pathway is steadily turned on to promote testes formation" (inverse.com. [a publication of the Bustle Digital Group]). Also of interest is the observation that an estimated number of 500 different fish can change sex-gender in adulthood through a process known as sequential hermaphroditism. In the online journal *Inside Science*, writer Rodrigo Perez Ortego comments, in reference to the same University of Otago study, that the bluehead wrasse is able to make this sex-gender switch due to possessing "duplicate genes." This information is additionally based on related research linked to Laura Casas, a molecular biologist at the Institute of Marine Research in Spain, who indicates that "the ancestors of most fishes had their entire genetic repertoire doubled three hundred million years ago—a phenomena known as whole-genome duplication." Casas adds that "While this is not the first example of a pair of genes doing very different things, it is the first time anyone has laid out how genes that serve one function in a female's body can be 'repurposed' for sex change in a hermaphrodite fish…" ("Duplicate Genes Let These Fish Switch Sex." insidescience.org, July 10, 2019).

Obviously, humans do not possess "duplicate genes," as does the bluehead wrasse, and therefore cannot switch sex-gender via the processes identified in this study. There is absolutely no known human biological process that can scientifically describe how a metamorphosis or transformation from a person's genetically determined sex-gender physical and biochemical arrangement to that of the sex-gender structure of the opposite sex-gender could occur. (Note: While the bluehead wrasse is only able to switch from a female to male sex-gender reproductive biological arrangement, the broad-barred goby fish demonstrates the rare capability to switch from both female to male as well as to a functionally genuine male to female reproductive physiology.)

Galileo Galilei discovered when observing the behavior of two falling bodies (upper right quadrant of human experience) that these entities will fall at the same rate of velocity regardless of weight (if placed in a vacuum per earlier noted experiment). The only way for the result of such an experiment to deviate from this absolute truth would be if another object was somehow introduced to disrupt the descent of one of the falling objects. Analogously, as an XX or XY chromosomal organized zygote develops, the "descent" of the infant at birth will respectively be a female or male baby. (Note: Recall Ken Wilber's definition of "propositional truth" within the upper right quadrant.) The developmental errors called "Disorders of Sexual Development" (DSDs) are sometimes presented by postmodern trans-sex-gender activists as foundational "disrupters" in relation to mammalian sex-gender reality. However, Dr. Anderson comments in his book *When Harry Became Sally* (previously referenced) that in all cases where humans manifest DSDs "…they are either male or female but with a disorder in their development.…Disorders of sexual development (DSDs) occur in roughly one out of every 5,000 births" (i.e., .02%) (Lee, Peter A. et al. "Global Disorders of Sex Development since 2006: Perceptions, Approach and Care." *Hormone Research in Paediatrics* 85 [2016]: 159).

In further discussing DSDs, Dr. Anderson offers the following quote:

> As the pediatric endocrinologist Quentin L. Van Meter writes, "The 2006 consensus statement of the Intersex Society of North America and the 2015 revision of the statement does not endorse DSD as a third sex." After all, biological sex is grounded in the organism's organization for reproduction.

There is no third gonad. With DSDs what can develop are dysfunctional ovaries and testes.

The term "third sex" is plainly oxymoronic as the word sex refers to two (binary) differing biological organizations arranged in a structurally complementary system for species reproduction, never three or more. In fact, the etymological origin of the term sex is the Latin word "sexus," which indicates a state of being either female or male (etymonline.com). The .02% occurrence of DSDs represents only one category of numerous developmental disorders which occur throughout the mammalian biological world. In fact, one's pet dog can also manifest a DSD. It is important to note that most people who identify as trans-sex-gender do not suffer from a DSD and the majority of persons with a DSD do not identify as trans-sex-gender.

However, the focus of this work is not on the wide variety of biological errors related to human development (Note: Recall Gregory Bateson's definition of error in living systems: " …the existence or value of a possible something which would be 'right' or 'correct', the error being a difference of what is and what might have been"); rather, it is on advancing an integral assessment of the contemporary matter commonly referred to as transgender, i.e., trans-sex-gender, as well as offering vitally needed clarification regarding this individual and social issue. Domain Theory and, in particular, the well-established theoretical approach of Integral Theory offer a most welcome methodology by which to understand and explicate the confusions in this matter and contribute to an intellectually sound and pragmatic resolution regarding related controversies.

To reiterate, the exterior "see-touch" domain of the individual (upper right quadrant), where modern science offers the most applicable and effective process of reaching valid conclusions, offers no record of research findings detailing the discovery and study of an actual trans-sex-gender human who has transitioned from female to male and impregnated a female or a male who changed to a human female biological organization and became impregnated by a human male. Biological science simply does not offer a detailed explanation of a transformative process that would allow for a male human to become an egg/oocyte-producing female (derived from ovaries) capable of conceiving, nourishing a fetus by means of a womb-located placenta, birthing and nursing a newborn baby with functional mammary glands. Scientific research also does not outline a process by which a female human can become a male capable of impregnating a female through producing semen containing sperm resulting from the possession of testes, a prostate, seminal vesicles, bulbourethral glands as well as a penile sperm delivery organ—which is clearly intrinsic to human sexual coupling, i.e., a trans-sex-gender human mammal.

LeShan and Margenau have provided useful insight and commentary on the human tendency to turn to reductionism when confronted by contradictory evidence in efforts to support a favored theoretical position or perspective, saying that "...if one idea seemed...unacceptable, its meaning could be saved by reducing it to a more familiar or a more acceptable one" (*Einstein's Space and Van Gogh's Sky: Physical Reality and Beyond*, previously referenced). The practice of reductionism can, in some cases, be reasonably classified within the category of human social/psychological self-defense mechanisms, e.g., intellectualization and rationalization. Thus, when the definition of trans-sex-gender deviates from, and avoids connection to, an actual structural biological change from a male to a female who notably carries eggs in ovaries, conceives, internally carries a developing embryo in a womb for approximately nine months, gives birth and feeds the birthed infant with functioning mammary glands (and, of course, mirror opposite transmuting changes of the human female to male), the opportunity for the occurrence of reductionist thinking and the expression of social/psychological defense mechanisms becomes much more probable.

In regard to the concept of trans-sex-gender, the four quadrants of human experience as detailed in Integral Theory provide the following clarification and guidance: 1) in the upper right quadrant (individual external experience, the "see-touch domain") the term "sex-gender" is the suitable term for the genetically/biologically constructed binary genital formations, dichotomous gamete structure and peculiar biochemical characteristics of male and female human beings, 2) in the upper left quadrant (inner individual experience) the phrase "sex-gender identity" will be employed to refer to the nature of a person's psychological recognition of, and relation to, their genetically/biologically constructed binary genital formations, dichotomous gamete structure and peculiar biochemical characteristics, 3)

in the lower left quadrant (inner conceptions and intersubjective constructions of the social world) the expression "internally envisioned/constructed
social sex-gender roles" will be used to describe one's sense of how their
bio-genetically determined sex-gender and sex-gender identity may relate
to—and influence—individual expression and social transactions in a
conceptualized social world and 4) in the lower right quadrant (the visible
world of concrete human social action) the term "sex-gender roles" will
indicate the observable performance of internally envisioned/constructed
sex-gender roles in the social realm of human life.

To assist in further understanding the concepts "sex-gender,"
"sex-gender identity," a human's inner experience of "internally envisioned/
constructed social sex-gender roles," as well as the domain of observable
human actions where the observable performance of "internally envi-
sioned/constructed sex-gender roles" manifest, i.e., "sex-gender roles,"
the following comments by biologists Heather Heying and Bret Weinstein
are useful: "…sex role…is the behavioral expression of…sex. In humans
we call this…gender expression." (Note: Heying and Weinstein seemingly
use the term "gender" as equivalent to "sex-gender identity," "internally
envisioned/constructed sex-gender roles" and "sex-gender roles" as used
in this manuscript.) After succinctly defining "sex-role" as the behavioral
expression of sex, these two scientists then turn their attention to the social
phenomenon of trans-sex-gender, saying that "…sex-role reversal—what
we might call gender switching in humans—is not the same as changing
sex. In mammals and birds, with our genetic sex determination, there is
no sex change possible—no pigeon or parrot, no horse or human, has ever
changed what sex they actually are. Behavior, though—call it sex role…is
highly labile (open to change)."

The authors continue their astute assessment with noting an occurrence of quadrant confusion in the contemporary trans-sex-gender matter
by commenting that "'acting feminine'…is not the same as 'being feminine' (sex)." Heying and Weinstein then carry this particular occurrence
of quadrant confusion to its logical conclusion, i.e., quadrant discord,
saying that "If you want to, be a woman who gets into bar fights or a man
who wears makeup, but don't imagine that getting into bar fights makes
you a man, or that wearing makeup makes you a woman. Bar fights and
makeup are signals to the outside world, proxies. Proxies are not the thing

itself..." Emphasizing the consequences of quadrant confusion, as well as
the repercussions of quadrant discord in relation to the societal issue of
trans-sex-gender, Heying and Weinstein state:

> ...ask people to believe things that are patently untrue and they will be ever
> less likely to form a coherent worldview, one based in observation and real-
> ity, rather than fantasy. Men will never ovulate, gestate, lactate, menstruate,
> or go through menopause. Women who identify as men might, but that is
> different. (*A Hunter Gatherer's Guide to the 21st Century: Evolution and the
> Challenges to Modern Life,* previously referenced)

Most importantly, it must be precisely stated and emphasized that
a person's sex-gender identity, internally envisioned/constructed social
sex-gender role and enacted sex-gender societal role, are not based on
"no-thing" but rather they are based on "some-thing" and the "some-thing"
all three of these conceptualizations or performances are based on is the
"thingness," i.e., the objective and very tangible reality of binary physical
reproductive sex organs, dichotomous sex gametes, as well as the distinctive
biochemical arrangements of male and female humans. In regard to this
fact, Dr. Debra Soh astutely provides this observation: "I'm not sure how
an entire movement has managed to overlook this, but if a person says
that they are both genders or neither, this still depends on the concept of
gender being binary. Even for those who identify as gender-nonconforming,
it means that they are still less like one gender and more like the other"
(*The End of Gender,* previously referenced).

Additionally, the internally formulated variations of professed
"non-gender" or "agender" self-compositions (upper left quadrant)
are clearly based on a psychologically deceptive non-accepting or
non-identifying circumvention of a human's unavoidable relationship to
a genetically constructed and quite noticeable binary biological reproductive physical organization. Unquestionably, genitals are as integral to
a person's perceptual experience as are their eyes, tongue, hands, nose,
teeth, feet, ears and, of course, the palpable reality of one's entire body, i.e.,
genitals are experienced and used on a daily basis. As a person observes
(upper left quadrant) their bare body in a mirror, they will continually
witness the obvious evidence of their genetically constructed binary

sex-gender human mammalian reproductive morphology (upper right quadrant). The observable and palpable truth of one's biological/physical reproductive organs (upper right quadrant) directly influences a person's individually-composed sex-gender identity (upper left quadrant). Thus, when a person espouses a non-gender identity or something akin to an agender identity, they are clearly not cognitively associated with their genetically constituted mammalian binary sex-gender reality; rather, they are psychologically dissociated from their biologically determined dichotomous genitals, binary gamete reproductive structures and related reproductive biochemical organization.

Plainly, it is one thing to be rather uninterested in biological sex matters, or to be little concerned with one's binary sex-gender reproductive organs, but it is quite another matter for a person to say that they have no genetically constructed sex-gender reality. In an analogous manner, a 5' 6" person can claim they are fat or obese in spite of looking in their bathroom mirror at their 85 pound body. This human phenomenon is described as anorexia nervosa and is associated with a very specific type of psychological misrepresentation and self-deception. In a report titled "Anorexia nervosa" by Jane Morris and Sarah Twaddle (NCIB/BMJ. pubmed.ncbi. nlm.nih.gov, April 28, 2007), the somber nature of this human malady is emphasized: "Anorexia nervosa has the highest mortality of any psychiatric disorder." Morris and Twaddle indicate that "The core psychological feature of anorexia nervosa is the extreme overvaluation of shape and weight." This human ability to psychologically deceive one's self through denying and, indeed, dissociating from visual and tactile senses is quite sobering. The fact that a 5' 6" person suffering from anorexia nervosa can clearly observe and verbally state their weight when standing on a scale, look into a mirror at their 85-pound body, completely detach from otherwise reliable tactile perceptive abilities, and all the while reject the objective findings of biological science in regard to the range of healthy weight standards for their height is sincerely astonishing.

In view of the broadly understood and accepted phenomena of psychological imagination, creative conceptualization, self-choice and personal agency within the inner self (upper left quadrant), the case for a person's ambivalence, denial or avoidance of genetically-constructed sex-gender corporeal reality, as well as one's desire to adopt, emulate and appropriate the

sex-gender identity of the opposite sex-gender, must be assuredly acknowledged. And of course, there are historical cases of persons preferring and
forming a dissociated inner trans-sex-gender identity. Nevertheless, just
as the majority of people coordinate their cognitive conception of their
body weight so as to be congruent with both their visual and tactile perceptions, as well as scientifically established standards for a healthy body
mass index (BMI), most persons recognize, merge and construct their
sex-gender identity coinciding with their genetically determined binary
sex-gender physical reality. While some postmodern theorists make the
claim that sex-gender identity compositions can be constructed in many
different ways, it remains clear that sex-gender identity cannot be truly
fashioned in just any way, as some ways will be completely devoid of any
relationship to plainly detectible human sex-gender biological reproductive structures.

In an article titled "What is Self-Concept Theory? A Psychologist
Explains" (positivepsychology.com. 18-3-20), author Courtney E. Ackerman affirms this assessment, that "Self-concept does not always align
with reality. When it does, our self-concept is 'congruent.' When it doesn't,
our self-concept is 'incongruent.'" In order to bring clarity to the essential
requirement of congruence in relation to fashioning an internal identity
structure, socially presenting the identity once crafted and, importantly,
ensuring that this identity aligns with relevant and ascertainable objective
facts of one's life, i.e., inter-quadrant congruence/harmony, consider the
following readily recognizable clarifying examples.

A person may sincerely state their "identity" as the present "Mayor
of Prague" or an "agent of the FBI" (upper left quadrant). In what way
can an observer of these identity assertions assess either the presence of
congruence or detect evidence of incongruence and, perhaps, delusion
within these two claimed identities? One might well consider that the
person's physical presentation does not match an internet search of several
current photographs of the Mayor of Prague (Czech Republic) and, when
asked to speak Czech, they refuse, stating that it would be disrespectful
to speak in their "native tongue" while visiting America (upper right and
lower right quadrants). An observer of the second statement ought to
doubt the veracity of a person who boldly and publicly announces their
identity as an "agent of the FBI" and, upon request, is unable to present

official credentials of "identification" or the address and phone number of their FBI office to allow for verification of their stated identity (lower right quadrant). Obviously, neither the person "identifying" as the "Mayor of Prague" or the person "identifying" as an "agent of the FBI" possess an internal subjectively constructed self-identity that is truly the same as that which they claim, i.e., matches external objective reality. Thus, a lack of congruency with respect to confirming features, factors and/or elements from other pertinent quadrants has established the delusional nature, i.e., falsehood of these two identity claims. Ackerman cogently adds this consideration: "To have a fully developed self-concept (and one that is based in reality), a person must have at least some level of self-awareness."

Postmodern cultural anthropologist Gayle Rubin makes the following claim: "Gender is a socially imposed division of the sexes. It is a product of the social relations of sexuality." This postmodern theorist further contends that society can invent "an androgynous and genderless (though not sexless) society in which one's sexual anatomy is irrelevant to who one is, what one does, and with whom one makes love." A similar theoretical construct is advanced by Judith Butler, Ph.D., who offers a gender perspective called "performativity theory" which contends that being a man or a woman is not what someone is; rather, it is what someone does. Lawrence S. Mayer, Ph.D., and Paul R. McHugh, M.D., in writing a special report titled "Sexuality and Gender, Findings from the Biological, Psychological, and Social Sciences" in *The New Atlantis* (Fall 2016), while quoting Rubin's conceptualization (noted above), more specifically focuses on the following gender belief professed by Butler, saying that "Gender is neither the casual result of sex nor as seemingly fixed as sex." Mayer and McHugh indicate that Butler posits that gender is radically independent from bodily traits or biology and is simply an individual, as well as socially constructed, phenomenon. In order to bring greater clarification to this distinctly postmodern theoretical conceptualization, the authors present the following quote by Butler, which defines gender as "…a free floating artifice, with the consequence that man and masculine might just as easily signify a females body as a male one, and woman and feminine a male body as easily as a female one." Mayer and McHugh precisely, yet graciously, confront Butler with the following succinct appraisal and inescapable consequences of her theory:

If gender is entirely detached from the binary of biological sex, gender could come to refer to any distinctions in behavior, biological attributes, psychological traits, and each person could have a gender defined by the unique combination of characteristics the person possesses. This "reductio ad absurdum" is offered to present the possibility that defining gender too broadly could lead to a definition that has little meaning.

In their assessment and critique of Butler's viewpoint, Mayer and McHugh seemingly hint at, yet fail to expressly identify, what are probable products of thought processes influenced and clouded by dissociation. Dissociation is defined as: "the fact of being separate from and not related to something else…the action of separating yourself, or considering yourself to be separate, from something…" (*Cambridge English Dictionary*, online). Thus, when an understanding and definition of the concept of gender (i.e., sex-gender identity) is characterized precisely by being "separate from" the "some-thing" of the dimorphic reproductive genitals of males and females, binary gamete structures, sex-gender unique chromosomal arrangements and peculiar biochemical features—incongruence and, indeed, cognitive dissociation is the result; due to the fact that self-constructed identity notions in the upper left quadrant of human experience are clearly disassociated from demonstrable tangible realities in the upper right quadrant.

Assuredly, a person can internally construct a variety of so-called "free-floating" identity structures (upper left quadrant). However, if a professed sex-gender identity composition is not associated with either male or female genitals, along with related human mammalian reproductive physical realities (upper right quadrant), then it is categorically not a sex-gender identity, e.g., "agender" and "non-gender." Additionally, if a person asserts a trans-sex-gender identity, this internal self-composition is obviously not based on an association with their genetically/biologically constructed sex-gender reproductive reality. Rather, the self-declared sex-gender-identity of a trans-sex-gender person is dissociated (i.e., separated) from their genetically-determined sex-gender truth and then aligned with, and constructed upon, the sex-gender biological truth of another human being, i.e., a person of the opposite sex-gender. Of relevant interest in this matter is research discovering that 30% of people who suffer with Gender Dysphoria have a lifetime diagnosis of

Dissociative Disorder (Collizi, Marco, et al. ``Dissociative symptoms in individuals with gender dysphoria: Is the elevated prevalence real?" *Science Direct, Psychiatry Research,* Volume 226. Issue 1, Pages 173–180, 30 March 2015). Additionally, sexologist and neuroscientist Dr. Debra Soh reports the following in her previously referenced book: "A study for the *American Journal of Psychiatry* showed that 61 percent of patients presenting with gender dysphoria have another psychiatric disorder. In 75 percent of the 61 percent of patients, gender dysphoria was a symptom of another mental illness, such as a personality, mood, or psychotic disorder" (Campo, J., et al. "Psychiatric comorbidity of gender identity disorders: A survey among Dutch psychiatrists." *American Journal of Psychiatry,* 160, 1332-1336. [2003]).

The American Psychiatric Association (APA) is a professional organization comprised of members of the medical community whose professed expertise is related to identifying, classifying and diagnosing mental disorders. The organization publishes the *Diagnostic and Statistical Manual of Mental Disorders* (*DSM*), which represents the key professional guidebook for mental health clinicians, educators and researchers. The language and concepts used in this document disseminates a wide variety of contemporary psychiatric constructs which mental health professionals then use to coordinate professional communication and direct much of their clinical conduct. As a prestigious intuition within society, the professional assessments and conclusions put forth by this organization influence society, while at the same time, pertinent leaning notions in contemporary culture exert influence on certain formal positions held by the leaders of this social group (as occurs with all societal institutions). With this observation in mind, in the latest *DSM,* the authoritative decision makers within the APA removed the term and diagnostic category of "Gender Identity Disorder"—i.e., a sex-gender identity that is not identical to one's genetically determined sex-gender reality. At the same time, the decision was made to begin using the phrase and diagnostic category "Gender Dysphoria" to characterize and emphasize the emotional stress, behavioral difficulties and impairments in social functioning that may be experienced by persons who are significantly troubled by an internal incongruence between their preferred, sensed and expressed sex-gender identity and their genetically-determined sex-gender truth. Thus, both professional assessment and clinical concern was shifted away from issues related to specific psychologically dissociated identity issues, having to do with genetically determined dimorphic mammalian sex-gender objective reality—to troubling emotions that may be experienced due to a confounding distress resulting from an incongruent self-relationship (upper left quadrant) with respect to one's biologically determined binary sexual reproductive structures and systems (upper right quadrant).

To further illustrate the influence of trending cultural/societal social constructions on professional institutions and their members, consider the following quote referenced by Dr. Ryan Anderson: "It is counter to medical science to use chromosomes, hormones, internal reproductive organs, external genitalia, or secondary sex characteristics to override gender identity for purposes of classifying someone as male or female." This is a statement by Dr. Deanna Adkins, a professor at Duke University School of Medicine and director of the Duke Center for Child and Adolescent Gender Care. Anderson provides an astute critique of this medical physician's assertion:

> Adkins doesn't say if she would apply this rule to all mammalian species. But why should sex be determined differently in humans than in other mammals? And if medical science holds that gender identity determines sex in humans, what does this mean for the use of medicinal agents that have different effects on males and females? Does the proper dosage of medicine depend on the patient's sex or gender identity? (*When Harry Became Sally: Responding to the Transgender Moment*, previously referenced)

Dr. Adkins, in her statement, plainly demonstrates an intellectual occurrence of quadrant confusion, as well as the ethos of a belief system, that is consonant with a subjective postmodern neo-Gnosticism. In a Senate Judiciary Committee hearing, Senator Josh Hawley expressed the biological fact that because women experience pregnancies—men cannot get pregnant. In responding to this scientific statement Khiara Bridges, a law professor at Berkeley, expressed essentially the same quadrant confused notions as well as subjective postmodern neo-Gnostic belief as Dr. Adkins: "There are trans men who are capable of pregnancy as well as nonbinary people who are capable of pregnancy" (Saunders, Joe. "Watch:

Pretentious Berkeley Professor Can't Handle Question from Sen. Hawley." westernjournal.com, July 12, 2022). In regard to the sort of "mind over matter"—i.e., self vs. biology—metaphysical ideology set forth by Dr. Adkins and Professor Bridges, Robert P. George (Professor of Jurisprudence at Princeton University) succinctly states that "Sex is constituted by our basic biological organization with respect to reproductive functioning; it is an inherent part of what and who we are. Changing sexes is a metaphysical impossibility because it is a biological impossibility" ("Gnostic Liberalism." *First Things*, December, 2016, online).

Researchers have endeavored to discover physiological and hormonal factors (upper right quadrant) that may contribute to the development of a trans-sex-gender inner experience (upper left quadrant). Some trans-sex-gender activists have eagerly looked to researchers for confirmation of their "born in the wrong body" or "I was born this way" assertions. Mayer and McHugh, in their previously referenced report, present a thoughtful and objective review of several relevant research papers, including studies looking at brain structure and functioning, as well as hormonal factors. In noting that some studies offered suggestive findings, none of the research could be considered conclusive, as Mayer and McHugh state that

> In summary, the studies presented above show inconclusive evidence and mixed findings regarding the brains of transgender adults. Brain activation patterns in these studies do not offer sufficient evidence for drawing sound conclusions about possible associations between brain activation and sexual identity or arousal. The results are conflicting and confusing.

The authors then point to particular concerns with studies of the sort reviewed: "It is important to note that, regardless of their findings, studies of this kind cannot support any conclusion that individuals come to identify as a gender that does not correspond to their biological sex because of an innate, biological condition of the brain."

Mayer and McHugh then further detail their concerns with the studies reviewed, saying that "The question is not simply whether there are differences between the brains of transgender individuals and people identifying with the gender corresponding to their biological sex, but

whether gender identity is a fixed, innate, and biological trait, even when
it does not correspond to biological sex, or whether environmental or
psychological causes contribute to the development of a sense of gender
identity in such cases. Neurological differences in transgender adults
might be the consequence of biological factors such as genes or prenatal
hormone exposure, or of psychological and environmental factors such
as childhood abuse, or they could result from some combination of the
two." The authors point to a significant weakness in studies offered thus
far on the trans-sex-gender issue:

> There are no longitudinal, or prospective studies looking at the brains of
> cross-gender identifying children who develop to later identify as transgender
> adults. Lack of this research severely limits our ability to understand causal
> relationships between brain morphology, or functional activity, and later
> development of gender identity different from biological sex.

An important general agreement regarding the limitations of brain
imaging research among psychiatrists and neuroscientists is also noted
by Mayer and McHugh, who say that

> ...there are inherent and ineradicable methodological limitations of any
> neuroimaging study that simply associates a particular trait, such as a cer-
> tain behavior, with a particular brain morphology. (And when the trait
> in question is not a concrete behavior but something as elusive as "gen-
> der identity." The methodological problems are even more serious.) These
> studies cannot provide statistical evidence nor show a plausible biological
> mechanism strong enough to support causal connections between a brain
> and the trait, behavior or symptom in question.

In offering a reasoned assessment regarding the studies reviewed,
the authors note that

> Studies like those discussed above of individuals who already exhibit the
> trait are incapable of distinguishing between causes and consequences of the
> trait. In most cases transgender individuals have been acting and thinking for
> years in ways that, through learned behavior and associated neuroplasticity,

may have produced brain changes that could differentiate them from other members of their biological or natal sex.

Finally, the authors provide these conclusive comments:

> Unlike the differences between the sexes, however, there are no biological features that can reliably identify transgender individuals as different from others. The consensus of scientific evidence overwhelmingly supports the proposition that a physically and developmentally normal boy or girl is indeed what he or she appears to be at birth. The available evidence from brain imaging and genetics does not demonstrate that the development of gender identity as different from biological sex is innate. Because scientists have not established a solid framework for understanding the causes of cross-gender identification, ongoing research should be open to psychological and social causes, as well as biological ones.

Most importantly, regardless of what factors may be related to the formation of an inner trans-sex-gender psychological identity (upper left quadrant), a trans-sex-gender identity is nonetheless dissociated, i.e., disunited in composition precisely due to being decoupled from one's genetically determined dimorphic reproductive biological reality (upper right quadrant).

The post-postmodern capacities of Integral Theory allow an understanding to be realized that recognizes a human's sex-gender (upper right quadrant) is "who one is," i.e., one of two possible human mammalian binary sex-genders (Note: All of earth's 6,300+ species of mammals possess binary gametes, dimorphic reproductive genital structures and distinct dichotomous sex-gender related biochemical arrangements) and their sex-gender identity, internally envisioned/constructed social sex-gender role and actuated sex-gender role are "what one does" (upper left, lower left and lower right quadrants). Thus, in the composing of one's sex-gender identity, the necessity of meeting the truth requirement of inter-quadrant congruence and harmony cannot be over emphasized. For each individual human mammal, the psychological joining with a language-characterized, and meaning-endowed, social world, as well as the development of a self capable of crafting internal identity structures, is experienced well after one's sex-gender is genetically determined and constructed. This recognition is of essential importance for the development of a post-postmodern integral understanding of matters related to sex-gender identity. Thus, the postmodern sex-gender identity conceptualizations of both Rubin and Butler, as presented by Mayer and McHugh, exhibit both elements of cognitive dissociation and theoretical reductionism as a result of quadrant confusion, directly fostering inevitable behavioral repercussions that evidence quadrant discord.

Academic, semantic and social critique derived from Postmodern Philosophy/Theory in relation to the term gender has gone beyond a "deconstruction" of the term among those who ascribe to, or are impacted by, the contemporary state and practice of this philosophical worldview, to a virtual "decomposition" of the word. The following report will demonstrate this assertion: "'I'm otherwordly': Ex-transgender man, 33, who now identifies as an 'agender alien' reveals that they had their (sic) nipples and eyebrows REMOVED to 'look less human'" (*Daily Mail*, March 1, 2019, online). This feature reports that a person named "Jareth Nebula transitioned from female to male and changed their (sic) name at the age of 29." In the article, Jareth Nebula explains that "After coming out as transgender and believing I had finally found myself, I realized I was wrong—I wasn't male or female, or even human…I don't think or feel like humans. I can't explain it to others—I'm simply otherworldly." The account further indicates that Jareth is "agender," avoiding sex-gender identification as a either male or female and prefers to be referred to by the pronoun "they." In the report, Nebula adds certain details regarding personal viewpoints related to the construction of internal self-identity, saying that "I didn't feel comfortable as either gender or even anything in between. I know I'm in a human form and that's how I'm perceived by others—but to me, I'm an alien with no gender…" Nebula summarizes the concept of self-identity formulation in the following manner: "Who is anyone to tell you who you can or can't be? If someone wants to identify as anything, even an animal, let them."

It is probable that most persons would agree that evidence affirming the existence of additional "otherworldly" aliens who possess no reproductive sex-gender physical reality—while at the same time living in "human form"—is presently uncertain. Yet, the actual existence of a group of "otherworldly" beings would allow access to specific and important data that would allow discovery of whether these other amalgamated human-celestial beings would "identify" as: 1) one of two possible human genetically determined sex-gender identities, i.e., male or female, 2) an adopted sex-gender identity of the opposite sex-gender, i.e., a trans-sex-gender identity, 3) a vacillating or ambivalent sex-gender identity having to do with either male or female reproductive biological physical reality or 4) an identity that has no relation whatsoever to human reproductive binary gamete structure, dimorphic physical genitals and unique biochemical sex-gender facts of existence, i.e., "agender" or "non-gender." Whatever the case may be, the probability that virtually every cell in Nebula's human form carries an XX chromosome is essentially 100%. Also, given typical developmental processes at a 99.98% probability level, the distinct genital structure of a baby girl was available for detection at Nebula's birth, as well as the internal reproductive organs and biochemical arrangement of a human female (upper right quadrant).

There decidedly was no initial identifying choice for Nebula regarding these genetically constructed sex-gender structural realities, as they predated the development of a psychological self with the capability to decide and assert preference regarding: 1) the composition of an individual sex-gender identity, 2) the crafting of an internal vision regarding sex-gender identity social enactment and 3) publicly performing according to the social precepts linked to a preferred sex-gender social role identity. Whether Nebula decides to compose a sex-gender identity that is identical to genetically determined dimorphic reproductive genital formations, binary gamete biological structures and related biochemical characteristics (upper right quadrant—"IT"—), or not, is certainly a matter of individual preference (upper left quadrant—"I"—). Suffice it to say that Jareth Nebula's "agender otherworldly alien existing in human form" identity (upper left quadrant) is definitely not an identity formation that is linked in any way to genetically constructed sex-gender observable and quite tangible reproductive physical reality (upper right quadrant). Interestingly, the article did not reference a specific group of other persons who are in support of Nebula's belief that a human being can transition to become an agender otherworldly alien while living in human form. With respect to the foregoing, recall Mayer and McHugh's concern about a "reductio ad absurdum" occurring when "gender is entirely detached from the binary of biological sex."

To once again stress, genetically/biologically determined human sex-gender binary genotype and phenotype expressions, i.e., tangible body-based reproductive physical structures and systems, are in absolutely no way derived from, based on or influenced by one's individually internally crafted sex-gender identity, internally envisioned/constructed social sex-gender roles or socially performed sex-gender roles. The information ("…from Latin term informare: 'to shape, give form to, delineate…'" etymonline.com) contained within genetic/DNA coding instructions sets the rules of formation and absolutely determines the processes guiding the construction of sex-gender genotype configurations leading to related phenotype expressions, i.e., dichotomous genitals and binary gamete forms, as well as the unique biochemical composition of binary human male and female mammals. The abundant biological and genetic research readily available, such as the astonishing and pioneering work of James Watson and Francis Crick, is conclusive in regard to the genetic determination of human binary sex-gender organization.

The tangible truth of human binary sex-gender formations and sexual reproductive processes is aligned with 210 million years of procreative success among a myriad of different species of mammals. The fact that the corporeal and distinctly purposeful reproductive binary gametes and dimorphic genital structures among mammals preceded the appearance of humans, their singular and unprecedented language system, and every possible human sex-gender identity or non-identity conceptualization, is simply an indisputable truth. While all mammals possess binary sex-gender biological arrangements, they do not possess language and therefore cannot abstractly consider or communicate about their binary sex gamete differences, peculiar biochemical configurations and dichotomous genital structures, let alone abstractly construct a related sex-gender psychological identity. Yet, an aligned group of postmodern trans-sex-gender activists muddled by social/psychological defense mechanisms, as evidenced by their avoidance and/or denial of biological science, insist that individual cognitive conceptualization determines one's sex-gender. This espoused notion not only demonstrates an incomprehension of basic biological science, but it also offers an instructive example of conceptual quadrant confusion. Concordia University professor, researcher and author Gad Saad adds this relevant observation:

There are people, fortunately very few, who truly suffer from gender dysphoria. But their existence should not lead us to reject the biological facts that irrevocably shape who we are. To elevate one's "self-identity" above reality is hardly liberating. It is a rejection of truth. It is perhaps not surprising then that postmodernism is so rampant amongst radical feminists, social constructivists, and trans activists. It is the ultimate liberator; it frees us from objective truth by celebrating "my truth." (Saad, Gad. *The Parasitic Mind: How Infectious Ideas Are Killing Common Sense.* Regenery Publishing, 2020)

In this regard, a brilliant insight into a troublesome feature of human cognitive experience as expressed by John Milton in his epic work *Paradise Lost* (London, 1667) is worthy of note: "The mind is its own place, and in it self…Can make a Heav'n of Hell, a Hell of Heav'n."

The reductionist ("error of origins") thinking intrinsic to the predominant postmodern trans-sex-gender perspective is well-described by LeShan and Margenau. In their discussion of reductionism, the authors state that "As long as the universe is seen as continuous, this 'error of origins' can be perceived as a reasonable deduction. But as we have also seen, the idea of a consistently continuous universe with no leaps was destroyed by Max Planck in 1900, and is no longer a basis of modern science." An "error of origins," i.e., reductionism, plainly occurs when advocates of certain trans-sex-gender perspectives employ the social/psychological defense mechanisms of denial, rationalization, intellectualization and avoidance with respect to the findings of biological science and incorporate the scientific truth of sex-gender determination within the upper left quadrant of inner human experience. As a restraint on the tendency to regress to reductionist thinking when meeting "unacceptable" data, the authors suggest taking an investigative approach commonly used by physicists, saying that "In each domain of experience that they study physicists ask certain questions: 'What are the observables in this domain?' 'What kind of measurements can be made here?' 'What are the laws relating the observables in this domain?'" (*Einstein's Space and Van Gogh's Sky: Physical Reality and Beyond*, previously referenced).

In following LeShan and Margenau in the recognition of distinct domains of human experience and the related study of the peculiar observables located in these domains, in regard to the matter of trans-sex-gender, it is nontrivial to emphasize that while tangible penises, vaginas, sperm, oocytes/eggs as well as testosterone and estrogen do objectively exist (upper right quadrant), they do not exist in one's mind (upper left quadrant). It is crucial to understand that the "observables" located within mind are only internal "ideas about" penises, vaginas, sperm, oocytes/eggs, testosterone and estrogen. Thus, reaching congruence in cognitive conceptualization and linguistic expression, with respect to a relationship with tangible realities in the external upper right quadrant, is essential in order to realize veracity within the human sphere of sex-gender identity formations in the upper left quadrant. (Recall this previously cited definition of identity from *Merriam-Webster* [online]: "...the condition of being the same with something described or asserted...sameness in all that constitutes the objective reality of a thing....") In reference to this important matter, Gregory Bateson astutely comments:

> In language, the maps with which we are cut loose from correspondence with "territory"; not only are we constrained...to deal with ideas of coconut palms rather than actual coconut palms, we can sit on a tropical island and imagine oak trees, lie about them, or by simple linguistic transformation take any proposition about an oak tree or a palm and convert it to its opposite. Human language, alas, is...so flexible that it tends to falsify. (Bateson, Gregory, and Mary Catherine Bateson. *Angels Fear: Towards An Epistemology Of The Sacred*. Macmillan Publishing, 1987)

As an illustration of the above discourse, a hypothetical case study of the life of 33-year-old Dr. Cadence Faith Williams will be employed. Williams professes and maintains the following valued identities: 1) sex-gender identity, internally envisioned/constructed social sex-gender role and actuated sex-gender role: female/woman, 2) ancestry identity: Black, 3) cosmology/religion: atheist, 4) vocational identity: founder and CEO of a software development firm, 5) athlete: golfer, 6) relationship/partner identity: single (with no children), 7) identifying preference of sexual practice: lesbian, 8) nationality identity: North American/USA , 9) socioeconomic self-assessment: upper middle class, 10) educational identity: Ph.D. computer science, 11) political identity: Libertarian and 12) valued social group identities: Mensa, national regional officer for a university associated sorority, Vice President of River Creek Country Club, Treasurer for the Association for Women in Science, Midwest Wine Connoisseurs Club, New Atheism Philosophy Club and Recruitment Chairperson Libertarian Party.

By carefully noting the "observables" in each of the four quadrants of Williams's life experience, one is able to guard against quadrant confusion by studying the characteristics, as well as the essential structure, of domain specific entities, and ascertain which features of human life are mutable and which characteristics are biologically/genetically permanent. In the upper right quadrant are found several biologically/genetically determined characteristics of Williams's life experience: binary sex-gender physical composition of a female/woman, hair color and eye color. These features of human mammals are all genetically determined and cannot be altered at a later point in life development in order to substitute genetically derived characteristics which may be personally preferred or coveted. Additionally, Cadence has an ancestry linked to an African origin, a human characteristic that is directly derived from her parents who were both born in Nigeria. Thus, Williams cannot become a person of Cambodian or Lithuanian ancestry, she cannot self-create or develop sperm producing testes, a prostate and a functioning penis to transfer semen/sperm, her hair color can only be temporarily chemically altered and eye color is genetically fixed. Furthermore, the manifestation of a psychological self that has the ability to make conscious choices among malleable identity compositions develops well after the life conception of a human being.

After a detailed and thoughtful consideration of the Koran, Dr. Williams has chosen to reject an atheist cosmology and religiously identify as a Muslim (upper left quadrant). This choice of a new cosmology also contributed to a change of sexual practice identity from lesbian to heterosexual, so as to comply with her now firmly-held and vigorously-espoused spiritual beliefs. Because of these newly developed convictions, she also constructs a belief that she must psychologically and functionally disassociate from the Midwest Wine Connoisseurs Club, New Atheism Philosophy Club, River Creek Country Club and the Libertarian Party (now identifying politically as an Independent). Additionally, she self-composes a new internal relational self-image and realizes a desire to marry a Muslim man and become a mother.

In the lower left quadrant, Williams has now adopted a worldview that is most fundamentally informed by Muslim religious teachings. She now rejects many of her previous social perspectives, including views on sexual practice and consuming alcohol. She has significantly modified her cultural views of a preferred human society to those which more closely align with a traditional Muslim social worldview. In the lower right quadrant, Williams attends her local Mosque with absolute consistency, she no longer associates with prior wine club cohorts, country club members or with her former lesbian friends. She sold her business, eventually married a Muslim physician from Montenegro, moved to the capital city Podgorica, achieved a flexible and quite lucrative European based consulting position, gave up playing country club golf, became pregnant and is very excited to give birth and nurture her first child.

In this hypothetical example, Dr. Cadence Faith Williams has demonstrated the human ability to change several self-constructed identities related to one's life experience. The incontrovertible evidence that many people have changed once cherished self-compositions to other identities is plainly evident. The following accounts represent just a few of numerous examples of persons who have changed self-composed and highly valued self-identities. The renowned English philosopher Antony Flew was at one point considered to be the world's best known atheist, but later in life adopted an identity as a deist. A July 7, 2016, article in *Woman's Day* magazine describes how a 40+ year old heterosexual man, a father as well as a member of the Mormon Church, changed his sexual practice identity from heterosexual to homosexual. Dan Barker was a Christian musician and preacher who eventually chose to become a prominent atheist and author. Dr. Rosaria Butterfield (Ph.D. Ohio State University) was a tenured professor of Woman's Studies and English at Syracuse University specializing in feminist and queer theory. When she chose to adopt a Christian identity, she abandoned her lesbian sexual practice identity, left university teaching, eventually got married to a man and became a mother to several children. She is also an author focused on writing about Christian spiritual matters, lectures on her personal conversion experience and engages in an outreach ministry.

Matthew Crawford earned a Ph.D. at the University of Chicago in Political Philosophy. He then became a university professor, but soon afterwards abandoned his identity as a professor within academia. After next selecting an identity as an intellectual working for a Washington D.C. "think tank," he rejected this identity after just five months. Crawford next became identified as the sole owner of a motorcycle repair shop, yet soon transitioned to become identified as an author, publishing his first book through Penguin Books (2010) titled *Shop Class as Soulcraft: An Inquiry into the Value of Work*. Of wider national recognition is the story of Anne Heche, famously the lesbian partner of Ellen DeGeneres. Heche left her lesbian relationship with DeGeneres, eventually developed a relationship with cameraman Coleman Laffoon with whom she had a child. After a breakup with Laffoon she developed a relationship with actor James Tupper and birthed another child. Brazilian born citizen Eduardo Saverin, a co-founder of Facebook, became psychologically troubled and emotionally dysphoric with his acquired identity as an American citizen, primarily related to certain financial restrictions and associated bureaucratic difficulties. Saverin chose to abandon his identity as a United States citizen and reside in Singapore. Michael Glatze, the co-founder of the group "Young Gay America" and managing editor of *XY Magazine*, changed his sexual practice identity to heterosexual. His story was portrayed in a 2015 Sundance Film Festival movie titled *I Am Michael*, which was adapted from the June 16, 2011, *New York Times Magazine* article "My Ex-Gay Friend." The observation that countless people have chosen to change career identities, citizenship identity, religious identity, sexual practice identity (e.g., many people have chosen to switch between the following sexual practice identities: heterosexual, bisexual, homosexual, polygamous, polyandrous, polyamorous as well as celibacy), marital status, social group affiliations, educationally related identities as well as a host of other self-composed or actively acquired individual and social identities—is blatantly obvious.

The next hypothetical example is added to provide additional details regarding the phenomena of alterable human identities as well as the nature of non-mutable genetic/biological human structures and realities. Chun Kim professes the following valued identities: 1) sex-gender identity, internally envisioned/constructed sex-gender social role and actuated sex-gender role: male/man, 2) ancestry identity: South Korean/Asian, 3) religious/cosmological identity: Buddhist, 4) relationship identity: married with one child, 5) vocational identity: documentary film producer, 6) educational identity: bachelor's degree from U.C.L.A., 7) socioeconomic self-assessment identity: middle class, 8) identifying preference of sexual practice: heterosexual, 9) athlete: avid tennis player and 10) national identity: South Korean with an American work visa.

In the upper right quadrant of Kim's life experience, the following genetically/biologically established characteristics include: genetically constructed binary sex-gender composition of a male/man, hair color and eye color. To repeat some important details from the example of Dr. Cadence Faith Williams, Kim's sex-gender, hair color and eye color are genetically determined and are therefore not malleable. Additionally, Kim's biologically founded identity as a father is unchangeable. Due to the fact that Chun Kim's parents are both Korean with a very long family heritage, ancestry is also firmly fixed.

After much doubt and an overall disenchantment with Buddhist religious doctrine, Kim has recently come to a decision to adopt an atheist cosmological perspective. Also, after a significant waiting period, Chun Kim has gained legal identity as an American citizen. For some time, Kim has experienced a sense of psychological alienation from self-identification as a male/man. He states that he is extremely uncomfortable and often dysphoric (upper left quadrant) with respect to the physical reality of his male biological reproductive features and characteristics (upper right quadrant). He now much prefers dressing in clothing, along with other accessories, that are more aligned with what women typically utilize in their daily garb (lower right quadrant). At the age of 28, Kim decided to begin self-identifying as a woman (upper left quadrant). This announcement was both surprising and troubling to his wife of four years, soon resulting in a marital divorce. Chun Kim began using the name of Hani Kim (achieving a legal name change), consistently dressing in attire most often worn by women, using facial makeup products marketed to females and adopting both grooming practices and hair-styling forms typically employed by women. Hani is also contemplating the use of a medical specialist to utilize specialized hormonal treatments and is further considering surgical modification of certain body features to more closely mirror those of human females.

Kim has demonstrated the human ability to change the following self-identity formulations: religion/cosmology, national citizenship, marital status, legal name—as well as construct a dissociated sex-gender-identity, internally envisioned/constructed sex-gender social role and actuated sex-gender role. Each of these alterations of self-identity configurations and behavioral practices are located in the two left internal quadrants and the lower right external quadrant. To reiterate, Kim cannot alter genetically determined biological sex-gender reality, hair color, eye color or biological fatherhood, which are all observable human biological/genetic factors located in the upper right quadrant of human life experience. And of course, Kim's ancestry predated the development of a self-structure with the capability of even reflecting on this matter.

Perhaps the best known contemporary example of transitioning, so as to adopt a sex-gender identity aligned with that of the opposite sex-gender, is the broadly published case of Caitlyn Jenner (née Bruce Jenner) who now self-identifies as a woman. An earlier example of a person who changed their sex-gender identity is WW2 veteran Christine Jorgenson (formerly known as George Jorgensen), who famously summarizes the decision to self-identify as the opposite sex-gender in the following announcement to family members: "Nature made a mistake, which I have corrected, and I am now your daughter." Dr. Renee Richards, who formerly was known by the name Dr. Richard Raskind, is another early example of a person changing their sex-gender identity to the opposite sex-gender. The daughter of Cher and Sony Bono, Chaz Bono (née Chastity Bono), after first identifying as a female/woman and lesbian, transitioned to identify as a male/man. Another well-known example of this human phenomenon is that of the former U.S. Army analyst Chelsea Elizabeth Manning (née Bradley Edward Manning), who self-transitioned so as to identify as a woman.

Intrinsically coupled with the contemporary issue of trans-sex-gender "transitioning" is the matter of "detransitioning." In the April 30, 2017, online edition of the Australian journal *Independent*, details of the detransitioning of a person named Zahra is discussed (Zatat, Narjas. "'Going back': Why a woman transitioned into a man—and then changed her mind"). In the feature, Zahra offers the following statement: "It's not a thing to say to someone I used to be a boy and now I'm a girl... again." At the age of 14, Zahra states that she despised her body. She began to think that perhaps she was gay, but after doing personal research, along with ongoing self-reflection, she began to have a sense of being "trapped in the wrong body." At the age of 18, she began using the name of Zane and used pronouns commonly associated with males/men. A psychiatrist eventually diagnosed her with Gender Dysphoria, and referred her to an endocrinologist who began treating her with testosterone. She soon grew facial hair and her voice got much deeper. Through this process, she indicates she twice attempted suicide. Eventually, Zane decided to transition back to identifying as a woman and returned to using the name Zahra.

An article in the *Daily Mail* features details of the detransition of Laura Jensen back to Walt Heyer (Collins, Laura. "Let's see how Caitlyn Jenner feels in eight years." November 7, 2019, online). In 1983, two years after using hormone treatment as an integral part of his choice to identify as a woman, Heyer selected gender reassignment surgery. For a period of eight years, Heyer lived as Laura Jensen claiming a self-identity as a woman. In the article, Heyer provides the following assessment of the trans-sex-gender issue: "I finally understood that the surgery never changed me into a woman. And once you've come to that realization that you're not really a woman, then transitioning back really isn't a big deal because you're still a man." So, after eight years identifying as the woman Laura Jensen, Heyer transitioned back to identifying as a man and returned to using the name Walt Heyer. A website regarding the trans-sex-gender issue is maintained by Heyer and he is both a public speaker and the author of four books focusing on this individual and social phenomenon. A report in *The Guardian* describes various aspects of the de-transitioning of Elan Anthony, who once said of his sex-gender identity that "I believed I was female and that could never change." Anthony offers the following comments regarding his transition and detransition experience:

> I started to realise that I could have dealt with my own issues so much better without changing my body because that has brought so many more difficulties. Detransitioning isn't as unusual as you might expect, but it is underground, and the trans community isn't happy discussing this. (McFadden, Joan. "Transition caused more problems than it solved." September 16, 2017, online)

In a March 12, 2022 article titled "Detransitioners Flood Social Media With Testimony, Photos 'The Darkest Time In My Life'" (dailywire.com), writer Mary Margaret Olohan references a number of personal stories focused on persons who have decided to psychologically change back to a sex-gender identity that is identical with their genetically determined sex-gender reality, after psychologically constructing an incongruent/ dissociated trans-sex-gender identity. Olohan also presents the following information from a study conducted by Dr. Lisa Littman, Associate Professor of the Practice at the Brown University School of Public Health:

> …out of 100 detransitioners who participated in the study, 60% detransitioned after they became more comfortable identifying as their biological sex. The peer-reviewed study also found that 49% of that group detransitioned over "concerns about potential medical complications from transitioning," and 38% detransitioned after "coming to the view that their gender dysphoria was caused by something specific such as trauma, abuse, or a mental health condition."

Olohan adds these details from the study: "The majority (55.0%) felt that they did not receive an adequate evaluation from a doctor or mental health professional before starting transition and only 24.0% of respondents informed their clinicians that they had detransitioned." From the abstract of Dr. Littman's study the article offers this quote: "There are many different reasons and experiences leading to detransition.…More research is needed to understand this population, determine the prevalence of detransition as an outcome of transition, meet the medical and psychological needs of this population and better inform the process of evaluation and counseling prior to transition."

In order to expand compassionate recognition of this community, international "Detrans Awareness Day" occurs annually on March 12. Detransitioners, supporters and concerned parents have organized to bring both a much-needed awareness, as well as an improved understanding of the unique health care needs of destransitioners, to empathic members of society. The website detransawareness.org highlights the accounts of numerous people who have chosen to psychologically switch back to a sex-gender identity that is identical, i.e., corresponds with their biological sex-gender reality. The website also includes helpful resources, professional references, personal interviews and provides notices of upcoming events focused on issues related to the destransition community.

Unquestionably, the occurrence of detransitioning is well-documented with numerous examples available for review and, when joined with the practice of transitioning, clearly demonstrates that, in the internal upper left quadrant of human experience, a person can compose a dissociated trans-sex-gender identity—potentially resulting in a fully deluded self-composition—as well as publicly perform an array of opposite sex-gender roles (lower right quadrant). Yet, the person may then choose to psychologically switch back to a self-constructed sex-gender identity that is congruent with and identically mirrors their genetically determined binary sex-gender. Thus, while sex-gender identity is clearly a malleable psychological development, i.e., an immaterial occurrence, one's material dimorphic sex-gender is demonstrably proven to be a non-mutable genetically determined corporeal truth. (Note: The online *Cambridge Dictionary* defines "delusion" as "something a person believes and wants to be true, when it is actually not true.")

Towards An Integral Post-Postmodern Model of Trans-Sex-Gender Indentity

Since the ability of a human to actually transition their sex-gender to the opposite sex-gender is an absolute physical/biological impossibility, i.e., there is no truly existing "Teiresias" and humans do not possess the "duplicate gene" structure of either the bluehead wrasse or broad-barred goby, which allows for actual sex-gender transitioning so as to reproduce species identical offspring, the question of immediate concern for the matter of trans-sex-gender is as follows: is it possible for a person to claim to be trans-sex-gender and remain in accord with the truth requirements of each of the four quadrants which encompass full human experience, i.e., achieve inter-quadrant congruence? The post-postmodern investigative models of Domain Theory and Integral Theory provide a potent antidote to both the subtle and gross reductionism intrinsic to postmodern theory, on which much of the contemporary concept of transgender, i.e., trans-sex-gender, is most fundamentally linked. The validity requirements related to each quadrant will be considered below in employing a post-postmodern critical assessment of the contemporary trans-sex-gender phenomenon.

In the "see-touch" domain of the upper right quadrant, requirements for the establishment of valid conclusions are related to matters of considered proposition, conceptual representation or theoretical correspondence. For example, Wilber states that propositional truth is a statement that is said to be true if it is congruent with an objective fact, e.g., if one states that it is snowing outside, this statement can be said to be true if the statement matches what one observes when opening their front door. Thus, a stated "propositional" or "representational" map is true if it matches the "territory" of reference. In following LeShan and Margenau, just what are the observables in the "see-touch" realm of the biochemical, physiological and biological domain of the human being in regard to sex-gender? When one observes a human and "opens the front door" and detects a penis, testicles, prostate, small mobile sperm and a peculiar biochemical arrangement featuring a prominent level of testosterone, one is confronting a human male/man. And, if that same "front door" was opened and one observes a vagina, ovaries, large non-mobile oocytes, a uterus and a distinctive biochemical composition characterized by a prominent level of estrogen, one is encountering a human female/woman. And yes, the same test of truth applies to camels, cougars and caribous. As a matter of fact, dimorphic biologically/genetically constructed reproductive organs, differentiated binary gametes and peculiar sex-gender biochemical characteristics related to males and females are consistent among all mammals and have persisted over the course of 210 million years. These recurring biological factual findings most certainly represent an example of something approaching a world's record in the realm of replication research results.

In the upper left quadrant, in the sub-domain having to do with the formation and experience of self-identities, the pertinent "observables" are cognitions, ideas, beliefs, theoretical constructs, abstract compositions of self-characteristics, linguistic interpretations of emotional phenomena, as well as an ongoing thoughtful re-assessment regarding any insistent concern in relation to one's sex-gender identity. Once again, these "observables" are, in fact, not observable. The primary pathway available for learning about the interior of another person's self-experience is through dialogue with the "subject," which, of course, then requires interpretation by the "investigator." Perhaps obvious is the fact that the person may lie to the inquirer and may also lie to themselves. In surveying the matter of trans-sex-gender identity, a primary concern is whether the person believes that they can actually transform or transition into an actual human male from a female physical reality with the associated genetically-determined and fully-functional reproductive biological structural features and biochemical characteristics (and vice versa)—or not. Some of the key factors that are related to establishing veracity in this quadrant are truthfulness, trustworthiness and inter-quadrant congruence. The biological scientific fact that a human cannot undergo an actual transformation into the opposite sex-gender most certainly presents an unmovable obstacle in regard to the matter of realizing internal self-truthfulness and inter-quadrant congruence. Not surprisingly, this roadblock of biological fact elicits a variety of self-defense mechanisms including avoidance, intellectualization, rationalization, repression, acting out as well as the utter denial of the practice and findings of modern biological science.

Remarkably, a fascinating predicament will occur if one were to initiate an inquiry regarding pertinent compositional elements within the interior individual domain of a human who claims to have transitioned to the opposite sex-gender, i.e., a trans-sex-gender person. This quandary is directly related to the unavoidable task of interpreting the expressions of a person who has had to previously interpret the expressions emanating from the individual interior of another person(s), as well as engage in an analysis of the exterior actualized social behavior of that other person(s), namely, a person(s) of the opposite sex-gender of whom the transitioning person desires to emulate. In other words, a person who identifies as trans-sex-gender can have no direct experience of "what it is like" to be a person of the opposite sex-gender; rather, it is only an empathically observed, envisaged, conceptualized and interpreted version of the internal sex-gender identity experience of an opposite sex-gender person. On the other hand, the trans-sex-gender person can very directly describe and express details of their psychological difficulties and emotional struggles associated with the cognitive alienation and dysphoria they experience in relation to their genetically determined sex-gender. Indeed, expressions such as "born in the wrong body" point specifically to a psychological dissociation from one's genetically constructed sex-gender reality, whereas an inquiry into the interior self-experience (upper left quadrant) of a male or female who readily identifies with the physical fact of their biologically determined sex-gender presents no such quandary.

In the lower left quadrant (internally envisioned/constructed social sex-gender role), a person who identifies as trans-sex-gender can likely locate other persons who maintain an internal belief that transitioning to the opposite sex-gender is possible and, when such persons are found, engage in discussions concerning varied conceptualizations of possible role expressions in the social world. Additionally, the notion of developing a political coalition designed to persuade or coerce broader society to adapt their social perspective may also be envisioned. However, because relevant observables in the upper right quadrant, as confirmed by modern biological science, present an uncompromising stumbling block to a belief in an actual transformation from a testicle-and-penis-endowed (as well as semen/sperm-producing) male to a female with a specific biochemical composition, owning unique genitals, possessing specific internal organs which produce large gametes (oocytes), e.g., a "Teiresias"-like transformation and vice versa, variations of just what is possible in this matter are found among those who advocate for trans-sex-gender identity conceptualization and social vision. When the self-defense mechanisms of avoidance and denial of modern biological science are psychologically dominant, a person can more readily maintain a belief that a male/man can become a female/woman and a female/woman can actually transition to become a male/man. However, when there exists acknowledgment of the confirmed and settled facts revealed by modern biological science on this topic, the concept of transitioning to the opposite sex-gender becomes a notion that falls into the realms of internal sex-gender identity, internal conceptions of sex-gender social roles, as well as sex-gender social role performance.

In efforts to sway public opinion on this issue and maintain group cohesiveness, the display of social/psychological self-defense mechanisms among biological science deniers often includes intellectualization, rationalization, denial, acting out and avoidance. Additionally, the postmodern associated and encouraged tactic of crudely attacking objective academic challenge, dismissing pertinent scientific research and aggressively opposing speech that is contrary to a preferred social vision is commonly witnessed and typically characterized by the use of rather simple pejoratives, e.g., bigot, hate speech, transphobic, prejudiced or ignorant.

However, when one gets beyond the demonstration of an array of social/psychological defense mechanisms, boorish insults and various postmodern rhetorical tactics of deflection, the matter of establishing truth in the lower left quadrant remains the most pressing issue. Veracity in this domain has to do with amicable social admission, inter-subjective accord and inter-quadrant congruence/harmony. Therefore, the task of realizing truth in this domain is directly related to accommodating and integrating: 1) the perspective of trans-sex-gender advocates who share some similar sense of alterable internally constructed sex-gender self-identity formations, as well as concepts regarding mutable internally envisioned social sex-gender roles, 2) the social perspective held by persons in society who adamantly refuse to disregard the thoroughly established findings of biological science in terms of the binary genetically determined sex-gender of humans, as well as all other mammals and 3) the irrefutable sex-gender facts revealed by modern biological science. Thus, the massive sticking point for the internally envisioned/constructed social sex-gender roles proffered by some trans-sex-gender advocates is, once again, the inalterable fact of the binary genetic/biological reproductive physical characteristics confirmed by scores of scientific researchers combing over plainly observable data presented by 210 million years of mammalian life.

(Note: Regarding the requirement to realize and maintain inter-quadrant congruence/harmony concerning what is actually possible in the external quadrants, recall that the hypothetical woman associated with the group of those with "superpowers" could not achieve autonomous flight of her human body and a material space vehicle was most certainly unavailable [and would be unable] to transport the "soul/spirit" of a deceased Marshall Applewhite, along with those of his co-believing social group, to an immaterial "next level." Consequently, the social realities constructed and advanced by both the hypothetical "group with superpowers" and the actual "Heaven's Gate" association were demonstrated to be falsehoods by virtue of conceptual errors directly related to quadrant confusion; leading to calamitous social role performances characteristic of quadrant discord.)

In the lower right quadrant of human experience, the observable domain of human action and role performance, the position held by many within the realm of trans-sex-gender activism, is that if a person states they are a female/woman having previously identified as a male/man, they then become instantly a female/woman (and vice versa) based solely on a stated inner preference or experience; and furthermore, they must be socially accepted as such. This "biology need not apply" assertion represents a glaring denial of the biological fact of the genetic determination of one's sex-gender reality. This position has resulted in unending controversy and is perhaps the most obvious example of the quadrant confusion and quadrant discord characteristic of the current trans-sex-gender matter. "Men Keep Committing Heinous Crimes, Then Identifying as Women After Being Arrested. The Media Is Playing Along," is the title of an article written by Laurel Duggan on June 6, 2022 (dailycalller.com).

Duggan highlights the following data in her feature: "In the federal prisons alone, there are said to be over 900 biological males in women's prisons, resulting in massive and ongoing civil rights violations and other torts against women inmates daily." These figures are attributed to Harmet K. Dhillon, CEO of the national civil rights organization The Center for American Liberty. Duggan also presents the following shocking report:

> Peter Cerf, who now goes by Michelle Hel-Loki Angelina according to the New Jersey Department of Corrections…was sentenced to 75 years in prison in 2003 for the murder of a 47-year-old woman. He admitted to kicking her to death, crushing her skull and drinking her blood in a 2003 letter to the *New York Daily News*: "Since I have a most unusual taste for blood, I drank and licked and lapped up my fill." Cerf, who previously identified as a man, now identifies as a woman—and is presently housed at the Edna Mahan Correctional Facility in New Jersey, a women's prison.

The postmodern "mind over matter" neo-Gnostic ideology intrinsic to current trans-sex-gender theorizing, directly contributed to the following incongruous as well as entirely predictable social occurrence—offering a vivid example of both quadrant confusion and quadrant discord. Three inmates at a women's prison, all "identifying" as women, became sexually involved resulting in two pregnancies (Creitz, Charles. "Women's rights activist says pregnant inmates at NJ women's prison 'shoots a hole' in 'trans ideology,'" foxnews.com, 19 April 2022). Without question, the biological male inmate who "self-identifies" as a female/woman in this incident, is not "identical" to the two biological female/women inmates (who also "self-identify" as females/women) who were impregnated by this biological male inmate. Furthermore, the denial of biological science has also resulted in self-proclaimed trans-sex-gender persons excelling in important athletic contests, achieving access to private spaces reserved for persons of the opposite sex-gender and competing for valuable women's athletic scholarships. Examples of these occurrences are readily available for contemporary perusal in various societal media sources.

Beyond those persons who are devotees of Postmodern Philosophy, trans-sex-gender activists and/or biological science deniers, there exists another group of people who, perhaps sympathetically or nonchalantly, grant at least tacit support to the idea that sex-gender is solely a social construct. The observation that there is a measure of social acceptance of this claim beyond adamant postmodernists is, seemingly, a contemporary societal example of the brilliant and important "Asch Conformity Experiments" in the field of social psychology. Dr. Solomon Asch arranged for several groups of eight college students to participate in a social psychological visual comparison exercise. All but one student in each group were designated as actors and these performers were told to give the wrong answer at a particular point in the exercise. All of the students viewed a large card located at the front of the class with a vertical line on the left side and three more vertical lines labeled A, B and C on the right side of the card. One of the lines labeled A, B or C was the same length as the line on the left and the other two lines were clearly of differing lengths. The students were to state whether line A, B or C was equal in length to the line on the left side of the card. The experiment consisted of 18 trials. The seven actors would begin by unanimously picking the line that was of equal length to the line on the left of the card and then, at a specific point, as previously instructed, all seven actors would again unanimously pick the same line, but that particular line was noticeably not of equal length. Asch noted that the non-actor, who always answered last, would deny her or his perceptions and conform to the wrong answer as expressed by the group almost 37% of the time.

An article in the *Daily Mail* describes how Oxford graduate and rapper Zuby declared himself a woman just prior to besting a woman's deadlift record. The Oxford grad stated that "It was done in a humorous way, but it made it more real: it showed the fallacies of the arguments on the other side." In referring to the frequently expressed position by trans-sex-gender activists that there is no strength difference between biological men and women, he further noted that he "posted it a bit tongue in cheek, showing what I think is the absurdity of the argument" ("Oxford-educated rapper 'smashes female weightlifting records while identifying as a woman' in row over transgender athletes." March 3, 2019, online). (Note: Zuby is only a recreational weight lifter.)

In a more serious note, New Zealander Laurel Hubbard, a self-stated trans-sex-gender female, recently won an international weight lifting title. Tracy Lambrechs, another competitor, dropped weight so as not to compete against Hubbard and stated that "I'm more than happy that she has become a female, I have no problem with that as everybody needs to do what they need to do to be happy in life…." Lambrechs then added, "Personally I think that they should be able to compete, but they shouldn't be able to take spots from other female athletes" (Payne, Marissa. "Transgender woman wins international weightlifting title amid controversy over fairness." *The Washington Post,* March 22, 2017, online). It is both curious and blatantly inconsistent that, while Lambrechs expressed support of Hubbard in regard to transitioning (so as to identify as a woman), she also switched weight classes so as to not compete against Hubbard and assertively stated that transwomen athletes should not "take spots away from other female athletes." These conflicting statements suggest that Lambrechs would probably fall among 37% of the "Asch Conformity Experiment" subjects who, while accurately perceiving what is "right before their eyes," nonetheless vocally deny their perception and yield to group clout leading to expressing conclusions contrary to self-perceived reality.

Seemingly, UK broadcaster Piers Morgan would comparatively find himself among the 63% of participants in an "Asch Conformity Experiment" who assertively expressed exactly what their perceptions indicated. Regarding this matter, Brittany Chain wrote an online report on February 27, 2020, in the *Daily Mail* titled "Piers Morgan slams gold medal-winning transgender weightlifter for destroying women's right to a fair go as she closes in on a berth at the Tokyo Olympics." In the article, Morgan made the following statement in regard to Hubbard's weight lifting win: "…women's rights to basic fairness and equality are getting destroyed at the altar of political correctness." Morgan further argued that "Trans women with biological male bodies have a massive physical advantage against women born with female bodies in any sport where power & strength are significant factors.…" The article also includes a photo of a very tall and physically massive Hubbard standing next to biological women competitors and, upon viewing the image, determining which "line" is metaphorically the correct answer presents a non-perplexing problem.

In the 2019 Pacific Games in Samoa and Australian International & Australian Open in Melbourne, Hubbard's body weight was recorded at just over 290 pounds ("LAUREL HUBBARD BIO…" *celebsiren.com*, July 30, 2019). Hubbard realized admission to the 2021 Olympics in Japan and thus became the first biological male identifying as a woman, i.e., a trans-sex-gender woman, to compete in the women's weightlifting competition. Due in part to a judged "technical detail" in a lift, the 43-year-old athlete did not advance in the competition ("Transgender weightlifter Laurel Hubbard ELIMINATED from Olympics after failing first three lifting attempts as Team GB's Emily Campbell wins silver." FR24 news, August 2, 2021, online). However, Hubbard did win the prevention of Lambrechs, or another biological woman, from the opportunity to represent New Zealand in the 2021 Olympics.

The veracity test of "functional fit in systems" and related inter-quadrant compatibility requirements in the lower right quadrant, present certain trans-sex-gender advocates with a variety of unassailable tangible realities. Private spaces reserved for males/men are equipped with vertical wall-mounted urinals or crudely constructed "horse trough" urine receptacles typically found in sports venues, saloons and military barracks, as well as the quintessential condom-dispensing machines—whereas personal spaces for females/women are notably absent of vertical urinals, "horse trough" structures for urination and condom machines. In their place are partitioned horizontal toilets and vending machines that dispense sanitary products related to female menstruation. Undeniably, men use condoms in order to catch and contain small mobile sperm as a contraceptive strategy, which obviously requires testicles, while women utilize tampons and feminine pads for hygiene practices due to monthly menstruation, which distinctly requires female ovaries producing large oocytes. Medical facilities are equipped with sex-gender specific instruments and physicians employ examination practices that are specifically designed to assess health matters related to the binary reproductive organ systems peculiar to men and women. Men are subject to an anus-accessed digital prostate exam, a Prostate Specific Antigen test and a tactile assessment of the testicles for the detection of testicular cancer. These are not medical procedures that are experienced by women. Females/women undergo a regularly-occurring cancer screening breast evaluation and a pelvic examination which is designed to assess the health of the vulva, vagina, uterus, cervix and ovaries. For women between the ages of 21 to 65, a Pap smear, designed to aid in the detection of cervical cancer, is highly recommended. Males/men have none of these physical sex-gender related biological structures and, therefore, do not undergo this sort of examination in a physicians' office.

Clothing for males/men and females/women are also uniquely designed, for example a woman's shirt or blouse often has "darts" to better fit around mammary glands and women's slacks are often tailored with a bit more space in the hip area as compared to men's trousers (recall that this is one of two specific areas of peculiar bone structure that allows for forensic or archeological identification of a male or female human purely from skeletal remains). Supportive-wear includes bras for the larger breasts typically found on women, as well as athletic supporters and "sports protective cups" for the testicles found on males. And most obviously, males/men are not capable of being impregnated as are females/women. While additional observable physical characteristics, social practices and societal artifacts could be offered to further delineate and explicate the biologically determined binary sex-gender physical differences between males and females, a return to the matter of sports competition is most warranted.

The movement called "Save Women's Sports" has been established to "…preserve biologically-based eligibility standards for participation in female sports." The founder of this group is amateur powerlifter Beth Stelzer, who maintains a website with the same title. On this website, a position statement assertively declares that "…defending women in athletics ought not to be a partisan nor religious issue. If we allow males to compete in female sports, there will be men's sports, there will be co-ed sports, but there will no longer be women's sports." The website is replete with studies and scientific facts regarding the numerous geneti-cally/biologically-determined factors that result in physical advantages for transwomen athletes as they compete against biological women in a variety of competitive sporting contests. On the website, there can also be seen testimonies of females who have been placed in a physically dis-advantageous competitive position by transwomen, i.e., men who state that they are now women (savewomenssports.com).

A study by researchers at the Karolinska Institutet in Sweden revealed that biological males who claim to be women, i.e., transwomen, maintained significant muscle mass and strength advantages over biological women even after a year of hormone treatments. The results of this study are summarized as follows: "Despite the robust changes in lower-limb muscle mass and strength…the TW [transwoman] still had an absolute advantage at the 12-month follow-up.…Our results indicate that after 12 months of hormonal therapy, a transwoman will still have performance benefits over a cis-woman" ("Muscle strength, size and composition following 12 months of gender-affirming treatment in transgender individuals: retained advantage for the transwomen." Karolinska Institutet. Department of Laboratory Medicine, Division of Clinical Physiology. Huddinge, Sweden, September 2019). Also, *The Journal of Medical Ethics* published research findings related to the rules established by the International Olympic Committee regarding the participation of trans-sex-gender athletes in women's events and noted the following conclusion in the abstract of this research report: "Particularly important is whether the advantage held by transwomen is a tolerable or intolerable unfairness. We conclude that the advantage to transwomen afforded by the IOC guidelines is an intolerable unfairness" (Knox, Taryn, et al. "Transwomen in elite sport: scientific and ethical considerations." jme.bmj.com, 2019). The authors emphasize, critically and importantly, that hormone therapy will not alter the genetic/biological advantages that transwomen will continue to possess in spite of any hormone manipulation. Transwomen athletic performance advantages that are most certainly retained after hormone treatments include a larger heart size, greater stroke volume (i.e., the amount of blood pumped by the left ventricle), superior lung capacity, enhanced bone dimensions with more strength due to greater compositional density, enhanced articulation of joints, retention of specific musculature mass and strength, and because biological males/men have greater amounts of hemoglobin, they are able to realize a higher level of oxygen in their circulatory system (upper right quadrant).

When trans-sex-gender activists focus solely on hormone differences, along with contrived methods of hormonal alteration to reach what they consider sex-gender equivalency, what is being displayed is plainly a rhetorical "red herring"; that is to say, in advancing this position, what is clearly taking place is a strategy of obfuscation, a "sleight of hand" technique of trickery and a deflection tactic that falls within the realm of social/psychological self-defense mechanisms. Fully acknowledging and embracing the numerous biological differences that demarcate male and female is unacceptable among postmodern trans-sex-gender activists, thus a theoretical reductionism is employed so as to "save" their belief system, i.e., the only difference between male and female athletes is one's personal choice of sex-gender identity and hormone levels.

U.K. biologist Emma N. Hilton and Tommy R. Lundberg, a researcher in sports medicine at the Karolinska University Hospital in Stockholm, Sweden, published a professional paper titled "Transgender Women in the Female Category of Sport: Perspectives on Testosterone Suppression and Performance Advantage." In the abstract, the two researchers state that

Males enjoy physical performance advantages over females within competitive sport…the International Olympic Committee (IOC) determined criteria by which a transgender woman may be eligible to compete in the female category, requiring total serum testosterone levels to be suppressed below 10 nmol/L for at least 12 months prior to and during competition. Whether this regulation removes the male performance advantage has not been scrutinized. Here, we review how differences in biological characteristics between males and females affect sporting performance and assess whether evidence exists to support the assumption that testosterone suppression in transgender women removes the male performance advantage and thus delivers fair and safe competition. We report that the performance gap between male and females becomes significant at puberty and often amounts to 10–50% depending on sport. The performance gap is more pronounced in sporting activities relying on muscle mass and explosive strength, particularly in the upper body. Longitudinal studies examining the effects of testosterone suppression on muscle mass and strength in transgender women consistently show very modest changes, where the loss of lean body mass, muscle area and strength typically amounts to approximately 5% after 12 months of treatment. Thus, the muscular advantage enjoyed by transgender women is only minimally reduced when testosterone is suppressed. Sports organizations should consider this evidence when reassessing current policies regarding participation of transgender women in the female category of sport.

Regarding the objective and measurable effects of suppressing testosterone in transwomen athletes (i.e., biological male athletes who claim to have self-transitioned and become human females) with respect to strength and performance factors, the authors conclude

> ...the data show that strength, lean body mass, muscle size and bone density are only trivially affected. The reductions observed in muscle mass, size, and strength are very small compared to the baseline differences between male and females in these variables, and thus, there are major performance and safety implications in sports where these attributes are competitively significant. These data significantly undermine the delivery of fairness and safety presumed by the criteria set out in transgender inclusion policies, particularly given the stated prioritization of fairness as an overriding objective (for the IOC). If these policies are intended to preserve fairness, inclusion and the safety of biological female athletes, sporting organizations may need to reassess their policies regarding inclusion of transgender women. (https://www.ncbi.nim.nih.gov/pmc/articles/PMC7846503/, December 8, 2020)

(Note: This research project was concerned with elements that fall within the upper right quadrant of human experience, where the practices of modern science were employed to reach conclusions related to objective truth. Recall that no factors or considerations related to either individual or social construction have relevance in this quadrant of human experience.)

In 2019, the USA Powerlifting organization stated that it will not allow transgender women to compete in their sanctioned events. The organization based their decision in part on the advantage in sports, based on the overall greater strength, that males possess over women, saying that

...naturally occurring androgens as the level necessary for male development, significant advantages are had, including but not limited to increased body and muscle mass, bone density, bone structure, and connective tissue. These advantages are not eliminated by reduction of serum androgens such as testosterone yielding a potential advantage in strength sports such as powerlifting. The science behind this policy can be read in Dr. Kris Hunt's 2019 Therapeutic Use Exemption (TUE) Report. Dr. Hunt presented this report at the National Governing Body (NGB) Meeting.... (https://www. usapowerlifting.com/transgender-participation-policy/)

In 2020, the State of Idaho banned transgender women from competing in women's, i.e., biological female athletic contests, and in 2021, the States of Florida and Texas enacted similar laws. Additional lawsuits regarding this matter are underway and other legislative bodies have crafted laws to prevent transwomen athletes from competing in biological female athletic events. Without question, the inclusion of transwomen in the realm of women's sports represents an occurrence of quadrant discord that is both blindingly obvious and calls for well-reasoned efforts to resolve this controversy, as well as other conflicting societal concerns surrounding the more general trans-sex-gender issue.

Regarding the question of whether biological males who self-identity as women should be able to compete in sports against biological females who also self-identify as women, sociologist Callie Burt, Ph.D., and associate professor at Georgia State University in the Andrew Young School of Public Policy, states "No" (abc14news.com, April 25, 2020). While it is unknown if Burt has an understanding of Integral Theory, the following comments nonetheless reflect a recognition of distinct domains of human experience:

Sports are separated by sex because of male-female biological differences of which we are all aware. Starting before puberty and accelerating thereafter, males are stronger, faster, and bigger than females, and, it is not close. Furthermore, this sex-difference isn't about socialization or effort; it is about biology. Male physiology (muscle mass, greater hemoglobin, bone strength, hip shape, lower fat composition) is exceptionally advantageous for sport. As others have noted, the fastest female of all time has her world record beaten every year by high school boys....For female athletes to gain benefit from competitive sport, including the possibility of being on teams and winning occasionally, sports must be sex-separated. This is not debatable.

Professor Burt, in employing a keen sense of quadrant/domain distinctions, notes that "People who are transgender experience a 'sex-gender mismatch,' but they still have a sex, and it is on that basis that they are transgender." Burt further clarifies her position in matters related to trans-sex-gender sport competition, stating that "There is no 'human right' to opposite-sex provisions. In other words, maintaining sex-based rights is not discriminatory against people of the opposite sex (including transgender people)." Professor Burt supported the legislation in Idaho that bans born males from competitive female athletics, and thusly summarizes her views on this issue: "In the same way that it is not a violation of civil liberties to check people's eligibility for the Paralympic Games or age-group categories, it is not a violation of civil liberties to maintain the sex-separation of sports and ascertain eligibility. Females' sex-based rights matter, and for sports at least, gender is irrelevant" (Burt, Callie. "Idaho's transgender athlete bill is pro-female, not anti-gender." *idahostatesman.com*, April 21, 2020). (Note: Professor Burt seemingly uses the word "gender" as equivalent to the concept of "sex-gender identity" as used in this present work.)

Author Douglas Murray, in his book *The Madness of Crowds: Gender, Race and Identity* (Bloomsbury Continuum, 2019), recounts the case of Fallon Fox, a transwoman athlete who twice broke the skull of a biological female competitor. Regarding the male biological physical advantages that Fox brings to every MMA fight against biological female competitors, Murray notes that,

> As one board-certified endocrinologist (Dr. Romana Krutzik) explained it, Fox's advantages included the bone density she had accrued from her time as a man, the muscle mass she will have accrued from those years and the testosterone imprint on the brain which does not go away through taking androgens or having surgery. All this could give Fox not just a physical edge but also a potential aggressive edge.

In covering the September 10, 2021, MMA debut of Alana McLaughlin, a transwoman competing against a biological female, the *Times News UK* reported that "A biological male fighter beat the crap out of his female opponent...." The feature adds these details: "38-year old 'Alana' McLaughlin, born a male named Ryan, 'transitioned' 5 years ago after serving in the US Army Special Forces." The article also notes this quote by McLaughlin, "I want to pick up the mantle that Fallon put down....Right now, I'm following in Fallon's footsteps. I'm just another step along the way and it's my great hope that there are more to follow behind me" (September 12, 2021, online). In commenting on this same MMA event, Piers Morgan stated that "I found the bout sickening to watch....It was obvious very quickly that McLaughlin was too strong, and equally obvious that this strength came from the 33 years she spent as a biological man." In commenting more generally on the matter of allowing transgender women to compete against biological women in sporting events, Morgan commented that "This creates a bad enough unfairness in non-contact sports like sprinting and weightlifting, but when it comes to combat sport like MMA it creates a potentially deadly disparity" (Zanotti, Emily. "'Sickening To Watch,' 'Deadly': Piers Morgan Blisters MMA Match Featuring Openly Transgender Fighter." *The Daily Wire*, September 13, 2021, online).

Reporter Valerie Richardson published an article on December 5, 2021, in the *Washington Times* (online) titled "Transgender swimmer Lia Thomas smashes women's records, stokes outrage: Athlete dominated Ivy League freestyle events after transition." In the article, Richardson reported that "The University of Pennsylvania swimmer continued her dominance Saturday at the 2021 Zippy Invitational in Akron, Ohio, with a first-place finish in the 200 yard freestyle, setting a pool, program and meet record with a time 1:41.93....She won the race by nearly seven seconds and her time was the fastest in the country...." The article continues with these additional details: "Her record-breaking victory came a day after she set a pool and meet record in the 500 freestyle preliminaries, then claimed more records in the final with a time of 4:34.06, beating the second-place finisher by 14:39 seconds." In response to this total athletic dominance, Richardson quotes Linda Blade author of *Unsporting: How Trans Activism and Science Denial are Destroying Sport*: "Well of course women's records are being smashed!...Lia competed as male for the first three years in #NCAA. This is not right!" The article notes that Thomas "swam on the men's team from 2017–2020 as Will Thomas, placing second in the Ivy League Championships in freestyle events and making second team All-Ivy in the 2018–19 season. Thomas also won the men's freestyle against Villanova in the 2019–20 season." Richardson then offers this assertive statement by Clay Travis, founder of the sports and politics website Outkick: "It's absurd, it's ridiculous, it shouldn't be allowed to happen.... Women should not be losing to biological men who were good enough to be competing on college swim teams before they decided to identify as women...I can't believe I have to say that, but it makes no sense at all."

Luke Gentile of the *Washington Examiner* published an article on December 24, 2021, titled "USA swimming official resigns in protest of UPenn's transgender swimmer." Gentile notes that an official of USA Swimming resigned her position on December 17, 2021, in protest of the ongoing dominance of Lia Thomas, the University of Pennsylvania's trans-sex-gender swimmer. The article states, "Cynthia Millen resigned while preparing to officiate the U.S. Paralympics Swimming National Championships in Greensboro, North Carolina... 'I can't do this, I can't support this,' she wrote in her resignation letter." The writer further quotes Millen, who said that "I told my fellow officials that I can no longer participate in a sport which allows biological men to compete against women. Everything fair about swimming is being destroyed." In summarizing Millen's professional position regarding the allowance of biological males to competitively swim against biological females, the article offers the following quote: "If Lia came on my deck as a referee, I would pull the coach aside and say, 'Lia can swim, but Lia can swim exhibition or a time trial. Lia cannot compete against those women because that's not fair.'" Millen then assertively recommended a course of action to assure fair competition in women's swimming events, saying that "Now, the 'adults in the room' need to step into the conversation....People are saying, 'Why don't the swimmers just leave?' Well, those are 19-, 20-year-old kids.... It's up to us. We're the ones who are supposed to be providing this fair competition. [The swimming authorities] should be the ones who should be saying, 'Wait a minute.'"

On May 30, 2022, reporter Jennifer Smith published an article in the *Daily Mail* (online) titled "Doctors confirm trans swimmer Lia Thomas

DOES have an unfair advantage even after taking testosterone suppressants." Smith highlights a definitive conclusion asserted by Mayo Clinic's Dr. Michael Joyner and physiologist Dr. Ross Tucker in *The New York Times,* where these two professionals "confirmed Thomas's advantage is inescapable." The feature also reports: "Mayo clinic doctor Michael Joyner said testosterone is the '800lb gorilla' which gives biological men an advantage." Smith also quotes this decisive assessment by Dr. Tucker: "Lia Thomas is the manifestation of the scientific evidence. The reduction in testosterone did not remove her biological advantage."

On June 19, 2022, the *New York Post* featured the following headline: "Lia Thomas banned as FINA votes to restrict transgender women from competitions." FINA is the International Swimming Federation and by a vote of 71.5% of their members, determined that self-declared trans-sex-gender women must be banned from competing against biological women. From all indications, the quadrant discord on display as the biological male Lia Thomas dominated in multiple swimming competitions against biological women and destroyed previously established women's swimming records was simply beyond the pale. Apparently, the social psychological self-defense mechanisms, which FINA members surely employed to initially allow biological males to compete against biological women, were ineffective in this particular case of a biological male totally dominating biological women in collegiate swimming events. However, the presence of certain lies, the persuasive influence of intellectual trickery and the obscuring nature of obfuscating rhetoric among FINA members seemingly remains active, as this new rule exempts persons who have "transitioned" before age 12. Thus, FINA remains focused primarily on hormonal factors, rather than on the established scientific reality of numerous fundamental and non-mutable genetic sex-gender differences between human males and females. Interestingly, the swimming federation is also considering a new "open competition" category that may allow certain persons, who identify as trans-sex-gender, to realize sanction of their swimming achievements. In a paradoxical counteraction, perhaps in defiance of this recent FINA decision as well as an assertion of zealous allegiance to postmodern "mind over matter" neo-Gnostic ideology, the University of Pennsylvania nominated the biological male Lia Thomas for the NCAA's "Woman of the Year Award" (Reilly, Patrick. "UPenn nominates transgender swimmer

Lia Thomas for NCAA's 'Woman of the Year' award." *New York Post*, July 16, 2022, online).

In a similar occurrence, the International Rugby League (IRL) came to a decision that biologically male athletes who claim to be female, will be banned from competing in the biological women's league until a fully developed revised policy is formed (Prestigiacomo, Amanda. "Another International Sport Bans Biologically Male Trans Athletes From Competing Against Women." *The Daily Wire,* June 22, 2022, online).

In a newspaper feature titled "Caitlyn Jenner: Lia Thomas shows NCAA needs to 'protect women's sports,'" the self-proclaimed trans-sex-gender Olympic gold medalist commented that "I've said from the beginning, biological boys should not be playing in women's sports,...We need to protect women's sports." Jenner then continued,

> Obviously this is about Lia Thomas who has brought a lot of attention to this issue....First of all, I respect her decision to live her life authentically. 100 percent. But, that also comes with responsibility and some integrity. I don't know why she's doing this....It's not good for the trans community. We have a lot of issues in the trans community that are very difficult and very challenging. We have a suicide rate that's nine times higher than the general public.

The famed athlete then assertively commented that

> [Lia Thomas] is also not good for women's sports...it's unfortunate that this is happening. I don't know why she's doing it. She knows when she's swimming she is beating the competition by two laps. She was born as a biological male. She was raised as a biological boy. Her cardiovascular system is bigger. Her respiratory system is bigger....Her hands are bigger. She can swim faster. That's a known. All of this is woke world that we're living in right now is (sic) not working. I feel sorry for the other athletes that are out there, especially at Penn or anyone she is competing against, because in the woke world you have to say, "Oh my gosh, this is great." No it's not.

In conclusion, Jenner stated that "We need to protect women's sports, and the NCAA needs to make the right decision tomorrow, and that's to stop this right now....Re-think it. Texas ruled no more transgender athletes in the state—you can only compete in what your original birth certificate says. The IOC is looking into these issues. It's a complicated subject" (Glasspiegel, Ryan. *New York Post*, January 19, 2022).

The conceptual quadrant confusion, as well as the derived social quadrant discord revealed in Jenner's comments, are surely obvious. While Jenner acknowledged support (lower left quadrant) for Thomas to live "authentically" as a male-to-female trans-sex-gender person (upper right quadrant), at the same time, the Olympian also insisted that the trans-sex-gender swimmer is "not good for women's sports" (lower right quadrant). Yet, if Thomas is now an actual woman, i.e., a human female mammal, as Jenner "100 percent" affirmed through supporting (lower left quadrant) the assertion by Thomas regarding his transition/transformation from a human male into a human female (upper right quadrant)—an achievement that researchers in the life sciences universally affirm has never before been realized by any other mammal—the question of authenticity, i.e., truthfulness, becomes undeniably paramount. In other words, if it is possible for a man to "authentically," i.e., truly become a woman, why would the trans-sex-gender advocate Caitlyn Jenner object to a male to female trans-sex-gender person, like Lia Thomas who is now living "authentically" as a woman, from freely participating in all social behaviors and activities traditionally exclusive to women, e.g., unrestricted use of private spaces reserved for females, vie for valuable women's athletic scholarships, insist on receiving gynecological medical services, seek protection from abusive relationships within women's domestic violence shelters, demand placement in women's prisons as well as compete in the wide array of women's sporting events?

The contradictions and quadrant confusion intrinsic to postmodern philosophy and associated neo-Gnostic ideologies, e.g., the "mind over matter" assertion fundamental to the contemporary trans-sex-gender cultural/societal phenomenon, inevitably lead to the sort of social quadrant discord represented by the domination in women's swimming events (lower right quadrant) by the biological male (upper right quadrant) Lia Thomas—who claims to have become an actual female (upper right quadrant) through certain "mind over matter" immaterial psychological operations, as well as internally obscure emotional processes (upper left quadrant).

Thus, the trans-sex-gender advocate Caitlyn Jenner is caught in a paradox often typical of social constructions based on particular subjective postmodern philosophical conceptions, i.e., if Lia Thomas is an actual (true) trans-sex-gender human female (upper right quadrant), then all social activities exclusive to women, along with numerous accordant public recognitions, must be granted to Thomas, including swimming on a female college swim team (lower right quadrant). However, if Lia Thomas is not in truth an actual woman (upper right quadrant), but rather is in truth a male (upper right quadrant) who has psychologically self-constructed a dissociated, i.e., incongruent/inconsonant internal belief (upper left quadrant) that he has somehow autonomously achieved a transformation into the veritable materialization of a human female mammal, then exclusion from women's sporting competitions, prohibiting the utilization of private spaces reserved for human females, as well as disallowing participation in a host of other dichotomous male-vs-female social arrangements, should be enforced through historic and effective mechanisms of social management.

Consequently, the two most crucial questions for Jenner regarding authenticity/truthfulness in this matter are: 1) has Thomas truly, i.e., authentically, autonomously transmuted/transformed into a genuine human female mammal (upper right quadrant) or 2) is Lia Thomas truly, i.e., authentically, a human male mammal (upper right quadrant) who has psychologically self-constructed a dissociated, i.e., incongruent—and perhaps fully delusional—internal belief (upper left quadrant) that, by his own volition, he has achieved an actual transmutation/transformation into the identical/factual configuration of a human female mammal (upper right quadrant)? Based on the published comments of Jenner herein referenced, it appears as though the predicament facing Caitlyn Jenner has to do with psychologically confronting, and then theoretically accommodating, the consequences of honestly acknowledging the scientifically factual nature of the second assessment outlined above.

Recall the previously cited definition of "dissociation" from the online *Cambridge Dictionary*: "the fact of being separate from and not related to something else…the action of separating yourself, or considering yourself to be separate, from something…." Additionally, "incongruent" is defined as: "Made up of parts or qualities that are disparate or otherwise markedly lacking in consistency…discordant, discrepant, dissonant, incompatible, incongruous, inconsistent…." (*The Free Dictionary*, online). "Delusional" is defined as: "believing things that are not true" (*Cambridge Dictionary*, online). Therefore, regarding the question of whether Lia Thomas or any other human can truly change their sex-gender to the opposite sex-gender, the demonstrated inability to achieve inter-quadrant congruence by self-proclaimed trans-sex-gender persons unequivocally reveals the falsehood of all such claims.

A resounding deafening silence is heard from male/men athletes proclaiming that transmen athletes (i.e., women who claim to have transitioned to become men) are creating an unfair competitive advantage in the arena of male sporting events. Several web searches using both the Google and Bing search engines failed to locate a website captioned "Save Men's Sports" or a similar title. It is beyond telling, or just mildly interesting, that male athletes are not exclaiming that transmen athletes possess an unfair genetic/biological advantage over biological male athletes. Plainly, transmen athletes are not winning male athletic scholarships, frequently scoring huge wins, or setting new records in powerlifting, shot put, high jump, boxing, soccer, caber tossing, swimming, running, basketball, football, triathlon, diving, strongest man contests, skiing (water or snow), big wave surfing, polo, tennis, hammer throw, lacrosse, baseball, golf, volleyball, cycling, long jump, javelin, rugby, judo/jujitsu, rowing, lumberjack competitions, pole vault, wrestling, rock climbing, decathlon, hurdles, bodybuilding, discus, karate, skateboarding, mixed martial arts, archery, bowling, fencing, snowboarding, motorcycle racing, hockey or arm wrestling. Only regression to various social/psychological self-defense mechanisms can allow avoidance of the obvious innate physical advantage that transwomen athletes have over biological women, as well as the competitive disadvantage that transmen athletes have when competing against biological males/men. Conspicuously, repeated internet searches have not revealed any current lawsuits or pending government legislation specifically written to halt the participation of transmen in biological men's sporting contests.

As a vivid exercise in emphasizing the obvious physical advantage that men who claim to be women, i.e., transwomen, enjoy over biological females, the athletic achievements of Caitlyn Jenner will be reviewed. In 1976, Jenner was 26 years old, 6' 2" in height and weighed 196 pounds. In 1976, sporting news journals announced that the 26-year-old had won a decathlon gold medal in the Olympics while also setting a new world record with a total of 8,618 points. In the previous two years, the Olympian had also set two additional world records. Other sports accomplishments for Jenner include: first decathlon victory in 1970, achieved 10th place in the 1972 Munich Olympics, grasped a 1974 AAU decathlon championship, gained a Pan-American Games decathlon victory in 1975 and reached victory in the 1976 AAU decathlon. Jenner has also been added into the following hall of fame institutions: Olympic, National Track and Field, City of San Jose, Bay Area Sports and State of Connecticut. Consider what would have been the probable effect on biological women's sporting event outcomes and related records if, in 1974, 1975 or 1976, while in the midst of these amazing athletic triumphs, Jenner had decided that he was no longer a man, but was a woman and began competing against biological women in track and field events.

This next hypothetical example will also dramatically demonstrate the lack of "functional fit" in social systems, which is intrinsic to the matter of transwomen athletes competing against biological women. Ponder what would be the most likely striking effect within the sphere of professional women's boxing if either Deontay Wilder or Tyson Fury were to insist they had transitioned—claiming to have become an actual human female through internal psychological processes related to personal choice, emotional influence and self-determination—and demanded to compete against heavyweight biological women boxers. Juxtapose this scenario with what would be the probable impact on men's professional boxing if a top ranked professional heavyweight female boxer were to express that they have transitioned, claiming now to be a male, and insist on entering the realm of professional men's heavyweight boxing.

Post-Postmodern Integral Theory Congruously Delimits Sex-Gender Identity

Recognizing that the sex-gender of a human biological female can never achieve a transition in the manner with which the bluehead wrasse actually switches to the opposite sex-gender, and the sex-gender of a biological human male cannot, in a "Teiresias"-like transformation, realize the sex-gender of a female and give birth to a daughter (upper right quadrant), just what human characteristics are then mutable in relation to the issue of trans-sex-gender?

Firstly, as previously outlined, following certain domain/quadrant fitting postmodern theories, a person can construct a dissociated self-composition that is aligned with how one interprets pertinent internal self-features of the life experience maintained by a person of the opposite sex-gender. This process will be accomplished through intuiting, as well as concluding, what are believed to be essential psychological elements, pertinent emotional aspects and private interior self-identifying imaging products experienced by an opposite sex-gender person. Data for such an individual internal self-construction will result from viewing the opposite sex-gender through a psychological lens that is formed and honed by affinity, preference, desire, sympathy, aspiration and rapport.

Secondly, in order to compose an internal vision of what might be key conceptions related to the sex-gender roles communally held and promulgated by the opposite sex-gender (lower left quadrant), the verbalized expressions of opposite sex-gender persons will noticeably require keen psychological attention. Additionally, empathically guided observation and study, including details realized through both interpersonal communication and the observation of social performances, will provide the crucial experiences necessary to facilitate the acquisition of a general knowledge related to sex-gender cultural role guidelines. Ongoing scrutiny of public role performances will eventually lead to reaching a more refined appreciation and understanding of probable defining criteria regarding internally shared opposite sex-gender social role regulations. These communally held internal sex-gender social role perspectives powerfully contribute to the network of self-restraints that result in the maintenance of those societal role performances typically displayed by the opposite sex-gender.

Thirdly, so that a person who desires to identify as the opposite sex-gender may demonstrate social role compliance with conduct that is characteristic of their desired sex-gender group (lower right quadrant), typified roles must be surveyed, examined, exercised and repeatedly practiced. Information regarding role acquisition is ubiquitous, namely movies, literature, casual social arrangements, as well as customary structures within societal institutions, unique clothing, distinguishing personal care products, advertising, consumer goods, grooming practices, magazines, social events, family dynamics/structure, music, various internet sites, art and, of course, observation of a variety of every day opposite sex-gender role performances. (Note: The requisite psychological processes outlined above will occur with a level of awareness, depth and complexity commensurate with a person's cognitive acumen as well as age of development.)

Dr. Debbie Hayton, an instructor of physics in the UK, states: "Transgender ideology is indeed transgender nonsense. I believe trans women are male, and women are female; male people are not female people and therefore trans women are not women. I say that as a trans woman" (debbiehayton.com). Hayton has demonstrated no deviation from this assessment as these statements were affirmed in a March 31, 2021, online interview with Konstantin Kisin and Francis Foster titled "Transwomen are men…Including me" (*YouTube*, Triggernometry). In this detailed and candid conversation, Dr. Hayton further affirmed the phenomenon of trans-sex-gender as a troubling psychological issue. Based on Dr. Hayton's succinct analysis of the trans-sex-gender matter, a male/man who claims that he has somehow achieved a complete transformation and has become an actual female/woman, as well as a female/woman who insists that she has changed her sex-gender by means of a self-determined transition/transformation and has, in fact, become a male/man are being untruthful, thus misleading themselves and others.

In an article written by Izzy Lyons and published on December 22, 2019, in *The Telegraph*, the author relates that Hayton "…lives as a transgender woman after changing her gender from male to female in 2012. But unlike many people in the trans-community, she does not believe that her sex can be changed and is vocal about the fact that she will always remain a man." The report also reveals that Hayton has some support for her position among those in the trans-community by printing the following quote from another transwoman, Kristina Jayne Harrison: "The process of having surgery or hormone treatment cannot ultimately transform your sex. Every cell in my body has male chromosomes. I have a prostate. These things cannot be completely deconstructed. It is not possible to be biologically female. But that does not mean I can't live a fulfilling life being treated as a woman." Harrison adds the following reprove for policy makers: "…attempts to 'legally coerce society' into treating males as females in all circumstances is 'inevitably doomed to fail.'"

Lyons also directs attention to the conflicts within the trans-community by quoting Nicola Williams, who is the founder of "Fair Play for Women," a UK advocacy group for women and girls:

> Accusations of transphobia are thrown at women so often for so little that the word has lost all meaning. When even trans people can be called transphobes, I hope people now understand how ludicrous and far-fetched these attacks have always been. The trans movement has been hijacked by gender extremists. ("Transgender woman who wore T-shirt proclaiming that she's still biologically a man is accused of 'hate speech' and faces being thrown off LGBT committee at TUC." *telegraph.co*, online)

Thus, while Hayton may be cast as a "transphobe" by persons either profoundly ignorant of basic biological science and/or suffering from ideological extremism, no doubt Hayton claims a self-developed personal theoretical perspective that may be characterized as "trans-accurate." The very successful "trans" identified American YouTube personality Blaire White (one million subscribers) has consistently affirmed the positions proffered by Hayton and Harrison. Thus, White also assertively stated, in an interview with Konstantin Kisin and Francis Foster, that a person cannot change their sex-gender and noted that gender dysphoria is a genuine human psychological disorder ("Gender Dysphoria is a Mental Disorder." *YouTube*, Triggernometry, July 25, 2021).

In critiquing certain extremist trends among trans-sex gender activists, YouTube creator Arielle Scarcella (more than 700,000 subscribers) on February 21, 2020, posted this headline on her channel: "I'm A Lesbian Woman & I'm Leaving The Insane 'Progressive' Left." Scarcella then offered in her video the following assessment and critique of some specific aspects of contemporary trans-sex-gender conceptualizations, positions and activism:

> I don't think gender is a social construct. I don't think that straight white men are evil. I don't believe that genital preferences are transphobic or

that there are 97 genders. I don't think that male sex offenders belong in women's prisons.

The popular "YouTuber" continued, saying that "Never in my life have I been more cancelled, tortured, tormented and harassed than by members of my own community." Scarcella added that "This community has become so ridiculously intolerant, while preaching love…anyone who goes against the grain and thinks for themselves is immediately outcast. That's not a community that's a…cult." Chances are that Scarcella would join Morgan in the 63% of those in an Asch Conformity Experiment who are not swayed by group pressure, but rather proceed undeterred, insistent on expressing what their unified awareness reveals (Scarcella, Arielle. *YouTube*).

Post-postmodernism, as outlined in Integral Philosophy, is able to transcend the worldview of postmodernism, yet effectively include the particular concepts of both self and social construction derived from this perspective. Integral Theory also transcends the perspective of modernism while including the factual findings from the biological sciences. Due to the insight that humans have experience within four distinct domains, Integral Theory can direct particular perspectives intrinsic to Postmodern Theory to the quadrants where the theory is fitting; as well, it can direct views peculiar to Modern Philosophy, along with the practices of modern science, to the domains where its methodologies of discernment and validity testing are most felicitous—thus contributing to the realization of an "all-quadrant integral worldview."

As mentioned in the beginning of this chapter, assuredly neither camels, cougars nor caribous are consciously occupied with sex-gender identity issues. This is precisely due to the fact that sex-gender identity is not an objective physiological phenomenon (upper right quadrant), but rather, is a subjective human psychological construction/formation (upper left quadrant) that is solely related to genetically determined and unchangeable binary gamete structures, along with other co-occurring reproductive biochemical arrangements and dichotomous physical features (upper right quadrant). Furthermore, dissimilar binary genital organs and gametes as well as associated reproductive systems, are shared by all mammals. While trans-sex-gender activists may say that sex-gender identity is "nuanced" (Note: Nuanced is defined as "A subtle or slight degree of difference…a gradation." *The Free Dictionary*, online), the metatheoretical capacity intrinsic to Integral Theory is able to accurately explicate this particular psychological self-composition as characterized by the following three distinct and delimited psychological identity configurations: 1) a sex-gender identity that is congruent (i.e., identical) with one's genetically constructed sex-gender binary gamete structure, dimorphic genital formations and related biochemical arrangements, 2) a sex-gender identity that is incongruent (i.e., not identical) with, and factually dissociated from, one's genetically constructed sex-gender binary gamete structure, dimorphic genital formations and related biochemical arrangements—and then preferentially self-constructed based upon relevant characteristics adopted/appropriated from the opposite sex-gender or 3) an ambivalent or vacillating male or female sex-gender identity. (Note: Internally constructed psychological self-identities that are completely unrelated to binary biological/genetic sex-gender human mammalian reproductive reality are decidedly not sex-gender identities, e.g., agender, non-gender, etc.)

In the self-aware trans-sex-gender identity expressions of Dr. Debbie Hayton, a complete acknowledgement of the findings of modern biological science is assertively affirmed in regard to the genetic/biological determination of a person's sex-gender (upper right quadrant). With the factual truth of modern biological science established and unabashedly vocalized, Hayton then attests to forming a dissociated, i.e., incongruent (inconsonant) psychological sex-gender identity (upper left quadrant) adopted/ acquired from the sex-gender identity of the opposite sex-gender, as well as readily acknowledging a decision to internally envision and appropriate social role performances that are typified by the opposite sex-gender (lower left and lower right quadrants). In this way, Hayton avoids developing a completely delusional psychology identity structure, by recognizing a fundamental and indeed key requirement essential for the realization of internal truthfulness, i.e., inter-quadrant congruence (harmony)—by fully acknowledging a human mammalian male sex-gender corporeal reality (upper right quadrant).

While it is not possible for a person to truthfully claim to have transitioned (or transformed) into the opposite sex-gender while remaining in accord with the validity requirements of all four quadrants of human experience, Hayton offers a personally sincere position, which is both scientifically valid and thoroughly sensitive regarding the dissociated, i.e., disunified trans-sex-gender psychological/emotional issue. Thus, an outline of a fully adequate and, indeed, probable resolution of this societal concern is shaped by Hayton. To be specific, the prototype solution modeled by Dr. Hayton includes: 1) the complete acceptance of the fact of genetic binary sex-gender determination, as revealed from extensive research findings within the biological sciences (upper right quadrant); in other words, a human being can never truly transform/transition into the physiological/corporeal reality of the opposite sex-gender, 2) an acknowledgement of a person's psychological ability to internally construct a preferred sex-gender identity (upper left quadrant), which is based upon, and organized around, pertinent sex-gender identity characteristics of the opposite sex-gender, while fully recognizing that the sex-gender identity thus formulated is dissociated from, and clearly incongruent/incompatible with, one's genetically determined sex-gender physical reality (upper right quadrant), 3) the recognition of a person's capacity to cognitively formulate, and internally envision, sex-gender social role performances associated with the opposite sex-gender (lower left quadrant), 4) the acknowledgement of a person's capability to assume/appropriate—and then publicly perform a variety of sex-gender social roles, which are typified, as well as routinely displayed, by the opposite sex-gender (lower right quadrant) and 5) a demand that the general public must not be politically compelled to adopt the dissociated/disconnected worldview intrinsic to trans-sex-gender ideology (lower right quadrant).

Certain troubling implications for individual liberty and free political speech, emphasized in Kristina Jayne Harrison's previously quoted admonition and reflected in item five above, is found in a May 25, 2022, article by Genevieve Gluck titled "Norwegian Feminist Facing Up to Three Years In Prison Over Tweets." The online comments under investigation by Norwegian authorities were made by Christina Ellingsen, a representative of the feminist group Women's Declaration International. Ellingsen directed her comments to Chistine Marie Jentoft, a member of a trans activist group called Foreningen FRI. Some of the tweets made by Ellingsen include: "Why does FRI teach young people that males can be lesbian? Isn't that conversion therapy?" Ellingsen later added this question: "Jentoft, who is a male and an advisor in FRI, presents himself as a lesbian—that's how bonkers the organization which supposedly works to protect young lesbians' interests is. How does it help young lesbians when males claim to be lesbian too?" In an ironic twist, Amnesty International Norway joined in the free speech assault on Ellingsen, blaming her for harassing Jentoft through presenting the following statement on national television: "You are a man. You cannot be a mother....To normalize the idea that men can be mothers is a defined form of discrimination against women." Gluck further quotes Ellingsen: "I am under police investigation for campaigning for women's rights, because to certain groups, the fact that women and girls are female and that men cannot be women, girls, mothers or lesbians, is considered hateful....Women are not protected against hate speech in Norway, but men who claim to be both lesbian and a woman, are protected both on the grounds of gender identity and on the grounds of sexual orientation." The paradoxical and contradictory nature of postmodernism as well as the political influence of a Cultural Marxism that has captured Norway, and much of the Western world, is certainly well represented within the body of Gluck's report (reduxx.info).

The socially constructed reality which asserts that a person can change their sex-gender through inner resolve, psychological processes, emotional influence, hormonal manipulation, sex-gender role simulation, social affirmation and particular surgical procedures is entirely untrue. However, through embracing the grace of human dignity and maintaining the decency of mutual respect, empathic concern for those individuals who experience a psychologically dissociated/disunited trans-sex-gender identity, as detailed in this manuscript and affirmed by Dr. Hayton, can assuredly be realized. Unquestionably, as trans-sex-gender activists deviate from the identity conceptualization outlined by Hayton, and insist that a human male can become a female and a female can transition to become an actual human male—and demand that society must accept and validate this fallacious individually/socially constructed reality as true—they will necessarily call upon a variety of social/psychological self-defense mechanisms promoting quadrant confusion and inducing quadrant discord. Clearly, the lies, trickery and obfuscation engineered and proffered by certain trans-sex-gender activists are promulgating cultural/societal falsehoods that are ultimately damaging.

The foremost form of the socially constructed reality commonly called transgender, i.e., trans-sex-gender, is arguably one of the most useful of available cultural/societal artifacts for demonstrating the ongoing and impending demise of postmodern philosophy as currently structured. The inconsistent character of this philosophical worldview as contemporarily espoused, as well as the paradoxical or contradictory composition of many theoretical notions derived from this intellectual perspective, is no doubt much related to the absolutism and radical relativism often maintained by theorists who are guided by this worldview. A recent publication by Dr. Rebecca Tuvel will be referenced as a noteworthy exhibit of the disintegration and, indeed, "Kuhnian crisis" of postmodernism. Tuvel, who is Associate Professor and Chair of Philosophy at Rhodes College, astutely, yet boldly proclaimed—given her quite visible and important teaching position within the ideologically rigid, and intellectually illiberal, milieu commonly found within contemporary university humanities departments—that

> Former NAACP chapter head Rachel Dolezal's attempted transition from the white to the black race occasioned heated controversy. Her story gained notoriety at the same time that Caitlyn Jenner graced the cover of Vanity Fair, signaling a growing acceptance of transgender identity. Yet criticisms of Dolezal for misrepresenting her birth race indicate a widespread social perception that it is neither possible nor acceptable to change one's race in the way it might be to change one's sex. Considerations that support transgenderism seem to apply equally to transracialism. Although Dolezal herself may or may not represent a genuine case of a transracial person, her story and the public reaction to it serve helpful illustrative purposes." (Tuvel, Rebecca. "In Defense of Transracialism." *Hypatia* vol. 32 no. 2, [Spring 2017])

It is not at all surprising that, with the publication of this article, Professor Tuvel sparked more than just a bit of wrangling from an assorted group of postmodernists. Nevertheless, Tuvel (either wittingly or unwittingly) precisely pointed out in her discourse that the "postmodern intellectual emperor has no clothes" through securing a vivid cultural/societal example of postmodern theoretical contradiction, as well as the working of biased political influence on objective academic practice, which are both clearly corrupting and crippling features of contemporary postmodernism. As a thought-provoking exercise in further explicating the inconsistent, and clearly untenable, constitution of the predominant postmodern derived trans-sex-gender perspective, imagine the intellectual dilemma and philosophical conundrum postmodern zealots would have experienced if Diallo (née Dolezal) were to have claimed "I identify as a Black man," not simply "I identify as Black."

In an April 10, 2021, comment posted on a popular social media platform, distinguished biological scientist, ethnologist and author Richard Dawkins (University of Oxford) referenced essentially the same rationally consistent analysis and comparison of the trans-sex-gender vs. transracial matter as Dr. Tuvel: "In 2015 Rachel Dolezal, a white Chapter president of NAACP, was vilified for identifying as Black. Some men choose to identify as women, and some women choose to identify as men. You will be vilified if you deny that they are literally what they identify as." In response to the logically consistent, and scientifically accurate, assessment reflected in his comments, Dr. Dawkins was aggressively criticized by various postmodern trans-sex-gender activists and also experienced the withdrawal of the "Humanist of the Year" award granted by the American Humanist Association to Dawkins in 1996 (Flood, Alison. "Richard Dawkins loses 'humanist of the year' title over trans comments." *The Guardian,* April 20, 2021, online).

The well-documented accounts of both Tuvel and Dawkins highlight the urgent societal need to embrace and utilize the "transcend and include" capacities of post-postmodern Integral Theory in relation to the trans-sex-gender matter. Recall this previously referenced clear-sighted admonition by Maturana and Varela, which states that

> ...the only possibility for coexistence is to opt for a broader perspective, a domain of existence in which both parties fit in the bringing forth of a common world....A conflict can go away only if we move to another domain where coexistence takes place. The knowledge of this knowledge constitutes the social imperative for a human-centered ethics.

The socially constructed reality that proffers the belief that genetically determined mammalian sex-gender reality falls within the purview of human psychological capacities betrays a radical postmodern perspective that is both dissociated in structure and incredibly exaggerated in character. In other words, reducing objective factors from the "see-touch" domain of biology and genetics (upper right quadrant) to the impalpable and subjective upper left quadrant of inner human experience not only represents an obvious occurrence of quadrant confusion, but also discloses an occurrence of postmodern reductionism that is extraordinarily audacious in light of its scientific illiteracy. As postmodern trans-sex-gender advocates employ theoretical perspectives guided by reductionist thinking, the understanding and very definition of sex-gender is "saved" from the domain of objective science (upper right quadrant) through an inexplicable, and patently fanciful, "reducing" of the objective biological phenomenon of sex-gender to the intangible and imaginative compositional capacity of individual psychological processes (upper left quadrant). (Note: Recall LeShan and Margenau's explanation of reductionism from the Latin word "reducere" meaning "to save.")

When informal or formal social sanction is conferred upon a self-constructed identity that is demonstrably unrelated to foundational elements essential to the psychological self-identity socially presented, license is therefore granted for both other persons and aligned groups to profess (and present for societal sanction) other self-composed identity compositions that are also unrelated to fundamental, as well as essential, constitutive factors of the proffered self-identity. With the account of Jareth Nebula noted as a reference (the born female human who self-transitioned to identify as an alien with no gender), consider the following report. Writer Ryan Smith notes the following remarks by the British singer, media personality and model Oli London: "I've really struggled with identity issues, with who I am…it's a very tough one, So I've finally had the courage. I've undergone my racial… transitional surgery. I've transitioned to a non-binary person—they/them, Korean/Jimin and I finally have the Korean look, so I'm actually really happy."

London expressly chose to outline and undergo 18 surgical procedures to alter certain shaping body features and further stated that "I know a lot of people don't understand me, but I do identify as Korean, and I do look Korean now. I do feel Korean. I don't identify as British, so please don't… refer to me as British, because I identify as Korean." The singer assertively continued, "That's just my culture, that's my home country. That's exactly how I look now, and I also identify as Jimin—that's my Korean name…" The online article has a link to a video where London says being "trapped in the wrong body…the last eight years…it's been very tough." The feature also presents the following summary of the media personality's non-binary and "transracial" transitioning:

> I have gone through extreme lifestyle changes to become who I am today and have lived in Korea, I eat Korean food everyday, use Korean skincare, have plastic surgery to look Korean and I speak the Korean language—all of this shapes me as a person and my identify as a non-binary Korean person. ("Oli London Before Surgery Pictures as Instagram Star Identifies as Korean." newsweek.com, June 28, 2021)

Rachel Diallo (née Dolezal) offered the following support for London: "Cultural appropriation is very different from just being authentically yourself. So being true to yourself is a very different journey and experience than stealing somebody's culture in order to profit or gain from it. There's a different thing there, and I think sometimes people are confusing the two." (Smith, Ryan. "Rachel Dolezal defends 'Transracial' Influencer Oli London." newsweek.com, July 2, 2021). In another online article, that further details Diallo's advocacy for London's "transracial" transition, the following proclamation is highlighted: "You know who you are, and don't afford anyone else the right to tell you who you are. Don't let anybody steal your joy.…" Found within this same article, an assertive online comment posted by London advancing a reasoned conclusion similar to that put forth by Dr. Rebecca Tuvel reads:

> If you can be transsexual you can also be TRANSRACIAL. Why are there such double standards & hypocrisy with people criticizing me for being Korean. It's the same as someone who was born in the wrong body and wants to become a man or a woman. I was actually born in the wrong body! (Nightingale, Hannah. "Rachel Dolezal defends 'transracial Korean' influencer Oli London." thepostmillennial.com, July 1, 2021)

In a surprising turn of events—given London's adamant claim regarding his genuine sex-gender and racial transition—a Fox News feature offered an updated report concerning Oli London noting that he "…shocked the world on Friday, announcing that he was in process of detransitioning back to a man after living as transgender-woman for the last six months." In this article London offered the following succinct and quite decisive quote: "I am no longer trans and have gone back to living as man" (Mendelson, Will. "Influencer Oli London explains why he detransitioned back to male, blasts 'hypocritical' haters." foxnews.com, October 17, 2022).

In another article written by Libby Emmons, London also announced he had detransitioned from his transition to a Korean self-identity. Emmons offers these comments about London's sex-gender transitioning experience:

> Oli London is one of a growing number of detransitioners who have gone through gender transition, come out the other side realizing that no amount of medical technology can change their sex, and that perhaps it was ill-advised in the first place, and are speaking out about it.

In this feature London announces: "I found God, I've detransitioned, but I'm also now trying to speak up and spread positive messages to try and help other people in the world that may have identity issues or maybe struggling. I just want to speak out and try to help you know, give people guidance and positivity and spread love," ("Detransitioner Oli London no longer identifies as Korean or trans after finding God." thepostmillennial. com, November 12, 2022). London's new book describing in detail his sex-gender as well as racial transition choice and his twofold decision to destransition is titled: *Gender Madness: One Man's Devastating Struggle with Woke Ideology and His Battle to Protect Children* (Skyhorse, August 15, 2023).

In contemporary society joining Diallo (née Dolezal), Senator Elizabeth Warren and London in insisting that they have transitioned to another "race" through internal processes (upper left quadrant) involving introspection, emotional influence and psychological self-construction includes a German women named Martina Big, who claims to have self-transitioned and become a Black woman (Gibbs, Constance. "White German Woman tells 'Maury' of her transition to becoming a black woman." *Daily News*, September 22, 2017, online). Along with the well-documented account of Oli London, another case that will likely befuddle postmodern philosophy neophytes who are just becoming familiar with current trans-sex-gender ideology, as well as present a philosophical dilemma rife with paradox for more seasoned activists, has to do with a person born as a biological male and given the birth name of Adam Wheeler. Wheeler, while declaring a change of name to Ja Du, also proclaimed the self-constructed personal identities of being both "transracial" and trans-sex-gender, having self-transitioned so as to identify as a woman as well as Filipino (Maningding, Rainer. "Meet the Transgender Woman Who Now Identifies as a Transracial Filipino." *NEXTSHARK*, November 14, 2017, online).

The intriguing and controversial matter of U.S. Senator (and 2020 Presidential Candidate) Elizabeth Warren's claim to a "transracial" Native American self-identity (upper left quadrant) is worthy of detailed analysis (Mill, Adam. "Elizabeth Warren May Be Making U.S. History As The First Trans-Racial Senator." thefederalist.com, October 17, 2018). In order for a self-constructed identity (whether truthful or not) to reach a significant level of societal sanction, the case of Senator Warren highlights the necessity of joining one's self-composed identity with the affirming agreement of a sufficient portion of society. Warren indicated that she was an "American Indian" on her State Bar of Texas registration in April of 1986 (Miller, Hayley. "Elizabeth Warren Listed Herself as 'American Indian' on Texas Bar Registration." *HUFFPOST*, February 6, 2019, online). Additionally, according to a feature written by Josh Hicks, the senator assertively claimed to be a minority. The feature reads: "Warren first listed herself as a minority in the Association of American Law Schools Directory of Faculty in 1986, the year before she joined the faculty of the University of Pennsylvania Law School. She continued to list herself as a minority until 1995, the year she accepted a tenured position at Harvard Law School." The reporter also notes that "Warren contributed recipes to a Native American cookbook called 'Pow Wow Chow,' published in 1984 by the Five Civilized Tribes Museum in Muskogee, Okla. She signed her entries 'Elizabeth Warren—Cherokee'" ("Did Elizabeth Warren check the Native American box when she 'applied' to Harvard and Penn?" *The Washington Post*, September 28, 2012, online).

Only after ongoing public demand, as well as the manifestation of sufficient political pressure to verify her claim to be Native American by means of objective scientific testing (upper right quadrant), did Warren abandon her self-constructed identity (upper left quadrant) and then detransition to a White self-identity. The objective scientific testing utilized in this case revealed the following facts:

> Sen. Elizabeth Warren's newly released DNA results show that the Democrat's Native American ancestry is roughly the same as that of the average white American, and may be less....A 2014 study by Harvard University and 23andMe found that European Americans tested overall for 0.18 percent Native American ancestry, while Ms. Warren's results show she has anywhere from 0.09 percent to 1.5 percent. (Richardson, Valerie. "Elizabeth Warren may be less Native American than the average U.S. white person." *The Washington Times*, October 15, 2018, online)

It is noteworthy that, while Warren was able to scientifically demonstrate a genetic linkage (however small) to a Native American ancestry of between 0.09 and 1.5% (upper right quadrant), her self-constructed identity (upper left quadrant) as a "transracial" Native American was subsequently rejected by authentic Native American leaders, most politicians, cultural elites and a majority of persons within society (lower left and right quadrants).

Achieving inter-quadrant congruence (harmony) in the construction of a self-identity is an essential requirement, if a claimed self-identity is to be assessed as true. This central point can be well-illustrated by reviewing five examples of self-constructed identities previously outlined in this manuscript:

1. The hypothetical woman with "superpowers" composed a self-identity which featured the ability of autonomous flight (upper left quadrant). She was able to gain supportive confirmation of her internally self-constructed exceptional powers through association with a group of other persons who also asserted the self-construction of similar superpowers (lower left and lower right quadrants). However, when attempting to actually exercise her internally constructed belief in the ownership of the superpower of autonomous flight, specific and unyielding objective factors related to the "see-touch" domain of Newtonian physics (upper

right quadrant) discordantly demonstrated the delusional nature of her self-constructed and socially-affirmed superpower self-identity.

2. Marshall Applewhite constructed a self-identity where he viewed himself as having exceptional spiritual abilities, as well as a social standing representing an extraordinary position of leadership for all humanity (upper left quadrant). Applewhite's self-composed identity and novel worldview was supported and informally sanctioned by a microsociety of up to 200 enthusiastic believers (lower left and lower right quadrants). Yet, as Applewhite led a mass suicide in a fantastic attempt to actualize his special spiritual abilities by reaching an envisioned material spaceship, believed to be closely following the Hale-Bopp comet, the quadrant confusion characterized by confounding certain objective factors of the material world (upper right quadrant), with features related to an immaterial spiritual domain (upper left quadrant), resulted in a tragic occurrence of quadrant discord. The evidence of actualized quadrant confusion intrinsic to Applewhite's novel self-composition and imaginative worldview was graphically represented in the discordant and macabre scene of 39 dead human bodies, as well as the conspicuous absence of a spaceship (upper right quadrant). In this dramatic way, the self-constructed identity of Mr. Applewhite was revealed to be a delusional self-composition.

3. Senator Elizabeth Warren constructed a "transracial" self-identity where she experienced herself—and, indeed, publicly presented herself—to be an actual Native American (upper left quadrant). Remarkably, university institutions, influential segments of the legal profession, one specific political party, an assortment of societal elites, as well as an array of political sympathizers, affirmed her self-identity as a Native American (lower left and lower right quadrants). When data related to objective scientific analysis of pertinent genetic factors (upper right quadrant) revealed that Warren possessed about the same amount of Native American DNA as the average American, and maybe less, her self-constructed "transracial" identity was revealed to be a deluded self-identity.

4. Caitlyn Jenner (née Bruce Jenner) proclaimed a self-transition (upper left quadrant) from the sex-gender of a male to the sex-gender of a female (upper right quadrant). Most importantly, Jenner did not claim to be a man who wishes to both adopt/assume an inner sex-gender identity of a woman and socially present as a human female. As clearly indicated by the trans-sex-gender self-identity analysis expounded in this manuscript, and confirmed by Dr. Debbie Hayton et al., Jenner certainly could have acknowledged psychologically constructing an incongruent, i.e., dissociated, inner sex-gender identity (upper left quadrant) aligned with personal interpretations of the internal experience of women (i.e., human female mammals) and engage in performing a variety of social enactments and traditional roles routinely displayed by human females (lower right quadrant). Yet, in spite of this possibility, Jenner remarkably claimed to have somehow employed inner emotional influences, introspective considerations, as well as nonmaterial psychological processes, to facilitate an actual transformation from a male human reality to the configuration of a human female. In response to this proclamation, a wide assortment of entertainers, journalists, media personalities, politicians and trans-sex-gender activists endorsed Jenner's professed self-transformation from a male/man into a female/woman (lower left and lower right quadrants). Additionally, in what is clearly an incongruous and patently untenable societal occurrence of supporting that which is impossible, the State of California formally sanctioned Jenner's claim to have self-initiated a mutation from a male human mammal into a female human mammal (lower right quadrant).

    Without question, these particular occurrences of both informal and formal social sanction are vivid examples of the "Thomas Theorem." Sociologists William Isaac Thomas (1863–1947) and D. S. Thomas (1899–1977) outlined the following observation of a quite consequential social phenomenon: "The theory that if we define something as real, or believe that something is real, it is real in its consequences" (sociologydictionary.org). In further explaining this sociological theorem, the following quote is useful: "The 'Thomas Theorem' states that in a social world, the interpretation of the situation influences the actions of the members of society. This would mean that when a number of people believe that some social issue, phenomenon or event is true, those same people would be driven to act on those issues or phenomena which will then lead to the said issue to occur in reality (Macionis, 2007)" (graduateway.com).

The "Thomas Theorem" is also well-described in the following manner: "Such a 'subjective' definition of the situation by a social actor, group, or subculture is what Merton came to call a self-fulfilling prophecy (as in cases of 'mind over matter')" (oxfordreference.com). Merton's observation is further explained as "A concept introduced into sociology by Robert Merton (see his *Social Theory and Social Structure,* 1957), and allied to William Isaac Thomas's earlier and famous theorem...Merton suggests the self-fulfilling prophecy is an important and basic process in society, arguing that 'in the beginning, a false definition of the situation evokes a new behaviour which makes the originally false conception come true, [it] perpetuates a reign of error'" (oxfordreference.com). The "Thomas Theorem," when joined with Merton's social conception of a "self-fulfilling prophecy," offers a felicitous explanation and cogent understanding of the subjective "mind over matter" (i.e., "Gnostic Liberalism" per Robert P. George) social occurrences in relation to Jenner's claimed sex-gender transformation, as well as the trans-sex-gender phenomenon more generally.

Most importantly, Caitlyn Jenner presented a total of "0%" of scientific findings in relation to validating a claimed sex-gender transformation through producing objective evidence of possessing the following human female biological characteristics and markers: vagina, clitoris, cervix, labia majora, labia minora, Bartholin's glands, ovaries, oocytes/eggs, fallopian tubes, uterus (thus demonstrating the genuine potential to conceive, i.e., to be impregnated), elevated estrogen level, sex-gender peculiar skull and pelvic skeletal structures and the pertinent foundational genetic/biological markers uniquely related to identifying a human female mammal (upper right quadrant). Thus, an objective review of scientific factors specifically related to Jenner's genetic/biological reproductive reality, coupled with scientific research reporting on 210 million years of findings related to unchanging mammalian dimorphic sexual reproductive organ systems and processes (upper right quadrant), reveals an unmistakable occurrence of quadrant confusion in Jenner's case. Due to these objective scientific factors (upper right quadrant), the deluded nature of Jenner's subjective self-constructed claim (upper left quadrant) to have transitioned/transformed from a human male into an objective (actual) human female is categorically established.

5. Bruce Jenner, in the mid-seventies, claimed the sex-gender identity of a male human (upper left quadrant). Jenner powerfully demonstrated and was, indeed, hailed by a large portion of society as being one of the greatest male track and field athletes of all time (lower left and lower right quadrants). Of pertinent significance for this discussion is the fact that, subsequently, Jenner became the biological father of six children. Through objectively demonstrating the ability to generate sperm from a uniquely male reproductive system—including male genitals— he was, in truth, biologically/ scientifically confirmed to be a man, i.e., a male human mammal (upper right quadrant). (Note: The sex-gender identity expressed by Jenner during this period avoids quadrant confusion by maintaining inter-quadrant congruence/harmony.)

In regard to the foregoing, it is important to recall Dr. Debra Soh's reporting on scientific research related to sexually reproducing human mammals, where she states that

> ...humans are a sexually dimorphic species, with two types of gametes: eggs and sperm. Intermediate gametes don't exist. Since biological sex and gender are both defined by these parameters, gender is, by definition, like sex—either male or female; binary not a spectrum....Gender is not a continuum or a rainbow or a diverse spectrum. It exists as two discrete categories, female and male, not as two polarities along a shared continuum along which human beings appear with equal likelihood. (*The End of Gender*, previously referenced)

Furthermore, as biologists Heying and Weinstein have assertively stated, "...no mammals...have ever been known to change sex" (*A*

Hunter-Gatherer's Guide to the 21st Century: Evolution and the Challenges of Modern Life, previously referenced). Since "Teiresias" is only a mythical character of human imagination, and humans do not possess a duplicate gene structure similar to that of the bluehead wrasse or broad-barred goby, which enables an actual sex-gender transition, it is demonstrably assured that humans cannot transition/transmute/transform into the opposite sex-gender.

Of the five examples outlined above, only the section discussing the 1970s superstar athlete Bruce Jenner features a self-identity that is in accord with the essential requirement of inter-quadrant congruence/harmony. Therefore, only this example represents a self-identity composition that can be accurately assessed as a truthful self-construction. The other four self-constructed and socially affirmed identities are ultimately revealed to be fallacious, i.e. deluded identity formations, as they are structurally characterized by quadrant confusion and, when actualized, noticeably present occurrences of quadrant discord.

The reader is invited to contemplate possible future manifestations in society of additional self-declared identities that are also characterized by quadrant confusion and, thus, dissociated in composition.

CHAPTER 4

A Woman's Right to Choose

A zygote [fertilized egg] is the beginning of a new human being. Human development begins at fertilization, the process during which a male gamete...unites with a female gamete or oocyte...to form a single cell called a zygote. The highly specialized, totipotent cell marks the beginning of each of us as a unique individual. (Moore, Keith L. and T.V.N. Persaud. The Developing Human: Clinically Oriented Embryology 7th Edition. Saunders: An Imprint of Elsevier, 2003)

You do not start as a cell. The egg cell is a cell. A particle of life, coming forth from the body of mother. When the egg cell is "fertilized," it transforms into something else: a zygote. A zygote is not a cell but an organism, a whole, therefore a body, a unicellular body. And this body is subdivided, sub organized in cells. In my view cells do not divide; cells multiply, that is their basic power, they reproduce, multiply. This means to me that the body is not the result or summation of a nearly infinite number of cell divisions but that you start as a body, and that you are body from the very beginning on. (van der Wall, Jaap. "NOT AS A CELL WE START! THE EMBRYO ABOUT GROWTH." embryo. nl, December 1, 2017)

> In the evolution of sexuality the critical event is that of the
> emergence of the cell with a nucleus, the eukaryotic cell.
> Hitherto, nature had worked through an asexual division
> ad infinitum of mother-daughter cells in which each gener-
> ation was exactly like the preceding one. The cell without a
> nucleus, the prokaryotic cell, was a stable, unchanging, and
> enduring system, but the cell with a nucleus introduces the
> radically destabilizing element of the individual. (Thomp-
> son, William Irwin. Imaginary Landscape: Making Worlds
> of Myth and Science. St. Martin's Press, 1989)

"It's a woman's right to choose." With an American history that, unfortunately, includes a very long period of time where women were
prohibited from exercising the complete array of individual liberties, one
can count on this acclamation, when taken at face value, to be quite persuasive. Related expressions include: "My body, my choice." "It could happen
to you, will you have a choice?" "You should not be punished for a birth
control mishap." "I'm pro-choice." "It's just a clump of cells."

A considered review of these vociferations will reveal that the underlying and indeed specific concern within this insistent demand for "choice"
is, most often, the use of abortion as a birth control method, i.e., an elective
abortive procedure employed to alter the course of a pregnancy. Therefore,
this present section is written solely focused on the utilization of abortion
as a birth control practice related to a pregnancy realized from consensual
sexual intercourse.

Just what is abortion? The word "abort" stems "from Latin *abortus*,
past participle of *aboriri*, 'to miscarry, be aborted, fail, disappear, pass
away',...The English word is attested from 1610s as 'to deliberately terminate' anything (intransitive), but especially a pregnancy in a human or
animal." Additional etymological research regarding the Latin compound
word "*aboriri*" reveals these details: "ab" conveys the meaning of "amiss"
and "oriri" signifies "appear, be born, arise...." Thus, when combined the
term "*aboriri*" would convey these meanings: "amiss to appear," "amiss to
be born" or "amiss to arise" (etymonline.com).

The word "abortion," in this present work, will represent the intentional
deviation from a developmental life process that, if left uninterrupted,

would result in the birth of an unconditionally novel member of the human species. Techniques of analysis intrinsic to the upper right quadrant of human experience, i.e., modern biological science, reveal with 100% accuracy that the life form developing within a pregnant woman is, in fact, a human being. Additionally, more extensive biological analysis of pertinent observables related to other compositional details of a human zygote, embryo or fetus will also reveal an unquestionably unique human, i.e., a human being, with a genetic composition differing from either parent. To reiterate, this knowledge is gleaned from the "see-touch" domain of human experience where precise classification of discrete domain intrinsic elements is a consummate practice and an exact level of accuracy is routinely achieved when comparing and contrasting observable entities. (Note: Psychologist Lawrence LeShan and physicist Henry Margenau, in their book *Einstein's Space and Van Gogh's Sky: Physical Reality and Beyond* [previously referenced], offer a complete explanation of the "see-touch" domain of human experience.) Since all mammals reproduce genetically distinct offspring, there is nothing idiosyncratic in this feature of a human mammal's process of reproduction. This quite basic scientific fact is made available to most every high school student in an introductory biology class.

Pregnancy has profound implications for a woman's psychological experience, emotional disposition, physical condition, economic situation, relationship dynamics and other lifestyle circumstances. And, when adding to these factors, the absolute scientific certainty that the developing young life form within the mother is, indeed, a genetically novel human being from conception, to the germinal phase of growth, proceeding to the embryonic stage, then to the fetal point of development and concluding in the actual birth of an infant, it is not unexpected that the social/psychological defense mechanisms of avoidance and rationalization would be employed in promoting abortion as a birth control method, e.g., "My body, my choice." This particular claim, while typically representing a legal claim or political position, is also immediately recognized as an expression of quadrant confusion, a social/psychological self-defense mechanism, as well as an overt attempt at obfuscation.

It is entirely obvious that the growing young human in the mother's body is not in any way comparable to her appendix, thyroid or spleen. It, therefore, follows that an abortion as a birth control method is not comparable to a healthcare procedure such as an appendectomy, the surgical removal of one's thyroid or a splenectomy. In fact, the individual human embryo demonstrably contains the genetic information, as well as corresponding rules of formation, to develop their own complex array of internal organ systems including an appendix, thyroid and spleen. In plain language, the human body developing inside the body of a pregnant woman is absolutely not her body. In a *National Geographic* article, author Rick Gore discusses the role of the human mammal's placenta, saying that "...it is invaluable. It not only nourishes the fetus in the womb, it also isolates the developing fetus from the mother's immune system. Otherwise, her immune cells would attack the fetus as a foreign object— after all, half its genes come from the father" ("The Rise of Mammals." nationalgeographic.com).

Hence, while a pregnant woman may exclaim "It's my body," the woman's very biological systems are nonetheless quite capable of correctly identifying that the developing human embryo inside her body is not her body. In the occurrence and progression of pregnancy among all mammals, the essential requirements for the sustenance of life have to do with two or more separate and unique bodies. Frankly, it seems unlikely that, for most educated and discerning persons, an incomprehension of basic biological science could reach a level of nescience that would allow for one to equate the body of a developing intrauterine human with that of the mother, even at the earliest stages of embryonic development. Yet, "In a 2019 CNN interview...former New York City Democratic politician Christine Quinn claimed that pro-life laws are wrong, arguing, 'When a woman is pregnant, that is not a human being inside of her. It's part of her body'" (Anderson, Ryan T., and Alexandra DeSanctis. *Tearing Us Apart: How Abortion Harms Everything and Solves Nothing*. Regnery Publishing, 2022). Again, when this particular argument is expressed, it typically represents either a legal posture or political proclamation. However, if offered in a literal sense, as noted above in the proclamation by Democratic politician Christine Quinn, this exclamation becomes employed as a simple ruse by biologically illiterate supporters of abortion as a birth control method.

The arguments and justifications for abortion as a birth control choice are most commonly focused on the following four issues: 1) The location in physical space, i.e., the temporary natural habitat occupied by a human being from conception to birth, e.g., "My body, my choice," 2) the total number of cells which comprise the physical size of the body of an intrauterine developing human, i.e., "It's just a clump of cells," 3) a young developing embryo or fetus cannot independently survive if separated from the mother and 4) an argument in favor of abortion as a birth control method that is based on emphasizing certain inherent latent abilities and capacities not presently demonstrated by a human embryo at a specific point of intrauterine development, such as the experience of physical pain or the possession of consciousness.

In addition to the explanation presented above, the first declaration forthrightly presents no consequence that is either scientifically or rationally persuasive, as every mammal requires a period of development within a mother. In truth, the female uterus has the singular purpose of protecting and nourishing a developing young human being and, without exception, every mother also developed within the uterus of her mother. (Note: Even the two egg-laying monotreme mammals, the platypus and echidna, keep the fertilized egg inside the mother for approximately one month.) The only physical location for the early developmental stage of all mammals is inside of their mother; there is absolutely no deviation from this biological fact. Regarding the identity of an in vitro embryo that is only 4 to 9 days post-fertilization (a blastocyst), prior to being deftly placed into a woman's uterus for the necessary nurturance and protection to support ongoing development, Dr. Leon Krauss, who holds a medical degree (as well as a Ph.D. in biochemistry) from Harvard and was the former chairman of the President's Council on Bioethics, offers the following scientific assessment: "One could go even further: the in vitro blastocyst is exactly what a human being is at that stage of human development. Only its extracorporeal location is different" ("Embryonic Issues." NR Staff. *National Review*, January 22, 2007, online).

Therefore, the fact that the offspring of a human mammal develops inside of a mother has no relevance whatsoever regarding the scientifically established truth of the easily detectable dissimilar body identities between the young developing individual human and the more developed individual mother. The error of reasoning manifested by this specific argument is akin to a non sequitur, i.e., it does not follow that, because the body of a human embryo develops inside of a human mother, the body of the embryo is therefore the mother. While a woman may justly claim legal jurisdiction over her body, she cannot, at the same time, assert that she has legal jurisdiction over someone else's body. It is therefore both inconsistent and patently incoherent for her to assert jurisdiction over the body of another human who is presently developing in her uterus, mindful that the sole function of a woman's uterus is to foster the life development and protection of another human's body. (Note: Certain tortuous variations of the "My body, my choice" argument, sometimes called the "argument from bodily rights," will be considered in the discussion to follow.)

In assessing the second frequently presented argument, i.e., "It's just a clump of cells," the social/psychological defense mechanisms of denial and rationalization are often seen in a combined arrangement leading to assigning moral value based on a curious "total cell count" derived-size comparison between the developing unborn human as contrasted with the "total cell count" magnitude of other older humans. This classification system is typically stated in terms of weeks of life development or in a "trimester" quantification system. To be more specific, this hierarchically ranked determination of human moral value is arrived at, in the most fundamental sense, through a loose quantitative accounting system which produces an estimate of the total number of cells that comprise each arbitrarily defined category of compared humans. This ambiguous system of "total cell count" size ranking, i.e., weeks of development or trimester phraseology, has been contrived to allow for the granting of a sanctioned societal license allowing for an individual woman, of greater cell quantity, to be the sole judge of whether another individual human, of lesser cell quantity, will continue to live or die. Remarkably, this "total cell count" size formula varies from State to State; yet, this entire proposition is manifestly based on a quintessential tautological assertion, to wit, all humans are "a clump of cells." The obvious truth and acceptance of this biological fact is universal.

Consequently, if one accepts this "clump of cells" rationale and moral value argument for justifying abortion as a birth control practice, then the following assertions must logically follow: a 35-day-old ("first trimester") human embryo is of less life importance than a 45-day-old ("first trimester") human embryo, who is then obviously of less life value than a 99-day-old ("second trimester") developing human, who is no doubt of less moral significance than a 144½-day-old ("second trimester") developing human fetus, who is plainly of less ethical value than a 234-day-old ("third trimester") developing human, who is clearly of less life value than a 281-day-old newborn human, who is of less moral value than a two-year-old toddler, who is of less ethical worth than an 4½-year-old child, etc.

"Your destiny, from day one" is the title of a feature written by Helen Pearson in the prestigious peer-reviewed scientific journal *Nature*, and begins with noting the following scientific findings:

> The mammalian body plan starts being laid down from the moment of conception, it has emerged....Your world was shaped in the first 24 hours after conception. Where your head and feet would sprout, and which side would form your back and which your belly, were being defined in the minutes and hours after sperm and egg united. Just five years ago, this statement would have been heresy. Mammalian embryos were thought to spend their first few days as a featureless orb of cells. Only later, at about the time of implantation into the wall of the uterus, were cells thought to acquire distinct "fates" determining their positions in the future body.

The implications of this scientific finding for biological researchers is noted in the conclusion of this article, which states that "What is clear is that developmental biologists will no longer dismiss early mammalian embryos as featureless bundles of cells—and that leaves them with some work to do" (nature.com, July 4, 2002).

Richard Stith, J.D., Ph.D., was a professor for over forty years at Valparaiso University. Over his many years as both a scholar and instructor, Dr. Stith has taught a wide variety of courses including "Philosophy of Law," "Rights of Juveniles and Mentally Handicapped," as well as "Law and Society." Stith wrote an article titled "Facing the Unborn" and offered a discerning quote by academic Jon Shields, which states that

> To say that "embryos are merely clumps of cells"...is to obscure scientific truth itself. This characterization suggests that an embryo is not biologically

different from what we might find under our fingernails if we were to gouge a bit of skin from our arms. It is to imply erroneously that they lack coherence, integrity, and self-direction as organisms.

Stith further explains that

Although we have considerable difficulty recognizing future continuity of being, we have little or no difficulty in seeing identity-despite-change when looking back into the past. We may doubt that a new sprout, or a barren vine, is really a tomato plant. We may doubt that embryos are persons, but as we look back upon ourselves or upon our neighbors, we realize that we and they were all once embryos. An embryo in a photograph may at first seem no more than a grain of sand, but if that embryo snapshot had been taken twenty years ago, just after our friend Mary was conceived *in vitro*, we may well exclaim, "Look Mary. That's you!" (firstthings.com, August 2015)

A lucid, impartial and rational judgment will affirm equal moral value of every human life based on the discrete reality of each unique individual human, not on a preposterous and distinctly grim "State-to-State" continuous variable formula of body dimension based on a hazy and enigmatic estimate of "total cell count." Certainly, the tautological, morally bankrupt and unscientific nature of this judgment device, directly related to the granting of a societal license to terminate the life of another human person, can be plainly seen. It is simply an indisputable fact that every discrete intrauterine developing human, as well as more developed postnatal humans, are both a "clump of cells" (upper right quadrant). Dr. Ryan T. Anderson and Alexandra DeSanctis in their new book (previously referenced) confirm this assessment and conclusion stating:

Some people try to deny this reality in order to justify abortion. They deny that the unborn child is really a human being. They try to dehumanize the child by using sterile terms outside the clinical context. (Has any expectant mother ever shared ultrasound pictures of her "fetus" with family and friends?) Some go further and refer to the child as a "clump of cells." (Organisms aren't clumps, but if we are going to speak this way, couldn't each of us be considered in some sense "a clump of cells," too?)

(Note: The later manifestation of physical features, organ structures, certain chemical processes, cognitive skills or the social abilities characteristic of a greater "clump of cells" person are not considerations in determining the accurate identity and moral worth of the intrauterine embryo; rather, they only underscore the kind of entity under consideration, i.e., a human person at an early stage of development.)

In all important respects, the third argument is not an argument at all; rather, it simply represents a confirming acknowledgment of a universal biological fact which applies to the primary developmental needs of all mammals. Without exception, each and every mammal is vitally dependent upon an immediate protective and nourishing relationship for early life sustaining needs, both internally within the mother as well as nursing at the mother's breast upon birth (or a substitute nurturer). In fact, the etymological meaning of nurse includes "…to nourish at the breast…bring up, nurture…" (etymoline.com). A human from conception to infancy, as well as through childhood, cannot survive without vital dependency on another human to provide nourishment, protection and shelter. The extent of both an unborn human, as well as a newly-born human, on another human for life-sustaining needs is comparable to an intubated critically-ill ICU patient, severely physically-disabled persons, profoundly mentally impaired people or even a comatose human whose residence in physical space is in a life-sustaining health care environment. Certainly, in some cases, having to do with treating a terminally-ill patient, family members and healthcare professionals will follow the dictates of a "living will" document created by the patient and conclude that ongoing extraordinary care will be futile in restoring vital health to the loved one. In such circumstances, vacating medical support may allow for certain death to be more immediately realized. Yet, the form of reasoning employed to permit abortion as a birth control method, when characterized by a forthright (and unrestrained) justification tied to human-to-human dependency, has led to social constructions (lower left quadrant) that justified the assertive life termination of several classifications of dependent humans.

For example, when governed by the National Socialist German Worker's Party, the nation of Germany socially constructed a reality that legitimized killing humans who were dependent on others due to physical and mental disabilities, as well as other categories of persons judged to have "useless lives." The quite basic observation and primordial understanding, in regard to the staged processes related to human life development, is well-depicted in the following variation of "The Riddle of the Sphinx," which states that "What reclines on no legs prior to arising, walks on four legs in the morning, walks on two legs in the afternoon, walks on three legs in the evening and rests without legs at night?" As the legend ultimately informs, the Sphinx became so extremely frustrated when confronted by a wise traveler with the true answer to this riddle that she committed suicide.

The fourth category of argument favoring abortion as a birth control practice has to do with a methodology whereby a supposed accurate determination of human identity and/or moral value is arrived at by placing exceptional and primary emphasis on the importance of a variety of latent physical skills, emotional competencies, social abilities or cognitive capacities. This category of argument has become the most expansive area of "pro-choice" debate and has no doubt become focused upon so as to avoid confronting the unassailable findings of biological research (upper right quadrant), which has factually established the unique individual identity of the intrauterine developing human person.

These arguments are typically revealed to be manifestations of social/psychological self-defense mechanisms, e.g., denial, avoidance, rationalization and intellectualization, as well as conspicuous tactics aimed at promoting obfuscation. An agnotological analysis of these arguments reveals cleverly fabricated intellectual proposals—as well as crafty rhetorical strategies—advanced by activists who support abortion as a birth control practice. These techniques are specifically designed to both diminish the cultural influence of objective analysis and facilitate the obfuscation of scientific evidence.

When critiquing the arguments of those who utilize the phenomena of latent human abilities and developed natural characteristics in their efforts to redefine what it means to be a human person (as well as reject the moral value of a human embryo), Dr. Patrick Lee, professor of philosophy at Franciscan University of Steubenville, offers the following comments:

> It is clear that one need not be actually conscious, reasoning, deliberating, making choices, etc., in order to be a human being who deserves full moral respect....Of course, human beings in the embryonic, fetal, and early infant

stages lack immediately exercisable capacities for mental functions characteristically carried out (though intermittently) by most human beings at later stages of maturity. Still, they possess in radical (= root) form these very capacities. Precisely by virtue of the kind of entity they are, they are from the beginning actively developing themselves to the stages at which these capacities will (if all goes well) be immediately exercisable....In this sense, even human beings in the embryonic, fetal, and infant stages have the basic natural capacity for characteristically human mental functions.

Lee continues his discerning comments on this matter, saying that

Some entities have intrinsic value and basic rights and others entities do not. Such a radical moral difference logically must be based on a radical ontological difference (that is, a radical difference among those entities themselves). And so the basis for that moral difference (a difference in the way they should be treated) must be the natures of those entities, not their accidental characteristics which involve merely quantitative differences. Or difference in degree. (By "accidental" qualities, we mean those attributes that do not help to define the nature of the entity. In humans, age, size, stage of development, state of health, and so forth are accidental qualities.) The immediately exercisable capacity to reason and make free choices is only the development of the underlying basic, natural capacity for reasoning and free choice, and there are various degrees of that development along a continuum. But one either is or is not a distinct subject with a rational nature (the traditional definition of a "person"). Thus, the radical difference in being that grounds the radical moral difference between a thing a mere thing and a subject of rights is the difference between a sub-rational thing and a being with rational nature. And a human embryo is a subject with a rational nature. ("Embryonic Human Beings." *Journal of Health Law & Policy,* Volume 22, Issue, 2006)

So, as to further reveal the specious nature of the notion that only immediately exercisable preferred—or arbitrarily chosen—abilities or capacities must be used to define the human person and determine when human moral value is realized, the following two examples are useful. A 25-year-old man may suffer from the biological medical condition called congenital analgesia where he does not feel pain and, remarkably, has never felt pain from conception, through full intrauterine development, during birth or up to his current age. And a 52-year-old woman may experience a particular type of coma due to an accident and is no longer in possession of consciousness. Yet, both living organisms in these two scenarios do not forfeit their identity as persons; rather, they continue to be valuable living human beings in spite of the absence of these particular human abilities, or any other human capacity for that matter. Succinctly stated, an intrauterine developing mammal is accurately identified as an individual human person based on a biological analysis of the DNA/ genetic composition of the body of the zygote, embryo or fetus. There is no known biological practice that identifies animal species based on the possession of specific abilities or the absence of those particular abilities. It is a truly odd, and noticeably discontinuous, intellectual conception to discount the value of a human life based on the absence of inherent latent abilities, which given known developmental timelines, will manifest at a later stage of life development. The fact of the staged unfolding of various skills and capacities from conception up until the age of about 25 is well understood by biological scientists and applies to a multitude of human features, e.g., organ development and maturation, biochemical processes, cognitive faculties, emotional skills, interactional social finesse as well as an array of physical capabilities. Most importantly, other than in the most heinous and debased of nation-states, there is no known "abilities test" commonly employed in the assessment of either the identity or moral worth of individual human persons.

To illustrate how abortion advocates use social/psychological defense mechanisms in defending certain abortion practices through employing arguments focused on emphasizing latent human characteristics and skills, as well as what Patrick Lee describes as "accidental qualities," an essay by Michael Standel published in the *New England Journal of Medicine* will be referenced. Standel contends that human embryos are actually different in kind as compared to humans at some later point of developmental, and to support his position, he puts forth the following analogy: "...although every oak tree was once an acorn, it does not follow that acorns are oak trees, or that I should treat the loss of an acorn eaten by a squirrel in my front yard as the same kind of loss as the death of an oak tree felled by a storm. Despite their developmental continuity, acorns and oak trees are different kinds of things" ("Embryo Ethics—The Moral Logic of Stem Cell Research." 351 New England Journal of Medicine, July 15, 2004).

Patrick Lee cogently critiques Standel's argument, stating that

Standel's purported analogy works only if he disregards the key proposition asserted by opponents to embryo-killing, namely, that all human beings, irrespective of age, size, stage of development, or condition of dependency, possess equal and intrinsic dignity by virtue of what (i.e., the kind) of entity they are, not in virtue of any accidental characteristics, which can come and go, and which are present in human beings in varying degrees. Oak trees and acorns are not equally valuable, because the basis for their value is not what they are (i.e., the kind of entity they are) but precisely those accidental characteristics by which mature oaks differ from acorns (in particular, the magnificence that comes only from maturity).

Lee continues his insightful response to Standel's proposition, arguing that,

However, unlike the magnificence of a mature oak, personhood is not an accidental characteristic, that is, a characteristic which one acquires at some point after he exists and may lose at another point. Being a person is being an individual who has the basic natural capacity to shape his or her life (by reason and free choice)—even though that natural capacity may not be immediately exercisable (as when someone is in a coma) or may take months or years to become immediately exercisable (as with a human infant, fetus or embryo). If not just sentience, but also being "capable of experience and consciousness" were required to be a person, then it would follow that infants and the comatose would not be persons either. Being a person, then, is not a result of acquired accidental attributes, but is being a certain type of individual, an individual with a rational nature. But human beings are individuals with a rational nature at every stage of their existence. We come into being as individuals with a rational nature, and we do not cease being such individuals until we cease to be (by dying). We did not acquire a rational nature by achieving sentience or the immediately exercisable capacity for rational inquiry or deliberation. We were individuals with a rational nature even during the early childhood, infant, fetal, and embryonic stages of our lives. If we are persons now, we were persons then. We were never "nonpersons."

Lee then extends his critique of Standel's analogy, saying that

...the differences between human embryos, infants, and adults, are in fact not differences in kind, but merely differences in stages of development and maturity for beings of the same kind. This is also true of the differences between acorns, saplings, and mature oaks...the reason for valuing oak trees, unlike the reason for valuing human beings, has to do, not with the kind of entity an oak is, but with the magnificence of (healthy) mature members of the oak species—an accidental quality in oaks (as in humans). ("Embryonic Human Beings." previously referenced)

Professor Richard Stith published an article titled "Construction vs. Development: Polarizing Models of Human Gestation" in the *Kennedy Institute of Ethics Journal* (Volume 24, Number 4, December 2014, pp. 345–384) which offers another challenging retort to Standel's acorn argument, which states the following:

Take a blue spruce. At what stage of its development would we say that a young plant becomes a blue spruce, that a blue spruce actually exists? At the very moment it germinates and begins to develop from the seed? (In analogy to human conception or fertilization.) When it sprouts and begins to carry water and nutrients inward from its environment? (In a strained analogy to a fetus with a heart just beginning to beat.) When it starts to look like a small tree? (In analogy to a fetus at around three months.) When it ceases to need constant care or is ready to be replanted? (Possible analogy to viability at birth.) Or perhaps when it finally achieves sufficient maturity to live up to the name "conifer" and bear cones? (Analogy to human puberty.)

Stith then succinctly answers these questions, saying that

The most appropriate response here is that these are all bad questions, ones that cover up rather than reveal our real perceptions and thoughts.

The growing plant never becomes a blue spruce because it always is a blue spruce....The plant develops, to be sure, from a sprout into a tree, but those are just stages of the same kind of plant—indeed, of the same individual living organism. It never was or could be any type of being other than a blue spruce. If we ask the nursery what those little sprouts are, the answer might well be "Those are blue spruces, but they've got a ways to go before they're ready to be replanted."

One can easily create a dynamic mental image of an adult person, who is a proponent of abortion as a birth control choice, taking a short break after reading Standel's article online on an unusually cold October day. Getting up from her white oak computer desk, the advocate walks across a recently installed red oak floor to an outdoor wood deck, kicking acorns off the surface as she moves with a discernible sense of purpose. The advocate is accompanied by a niece who quickly gathers up the acorns for use in target practice with her "always at hand" slingshot. A visiting young neighbor adds a musical interlude to the scene by grabbing an acorn and using the cupule (cup of scales) as a makeshift instrument to whistle "Yankee Doodle." After the brief "primitive woodwind concert," the adult reader grabs several well-seasoned oak logs and returns to the interior of the house to stoke the fire in a wood stove. As the advocate prints a copy of Standel's article on paper partly made of oak wood pulp, she gazes appreciably at both a young oak sapling and a magnificent mature oak tree visible through a large window overlooking an expansive backyard. At that very moment, the advocate recognizes that an acorn, an embryonically rooted acorn, a sapling, a small oak tree, a medium size oak or a large fully mature oak tree are all the same kind of entity, i.e., they are all oaks, just simply at different stages of life development. She then also realizes that the value of an oak is not based on the kind of entity it is (an oak), but rather on a variety of preferred features, particular characteristics or even certain accidental qualities, e.g., furniture material, flooring product, projectile, musical instrument, heating substance, printing paper or an object of visual beauty. The astute reader comes to understand that, while an embryo is not a mature adult human being (as an acorn is not a mature oak tree), the embryo is nonetheless a complete human person simply at an immature state of development, just as a newborn, a toddler, young child or teenager are human beings at different

stages of development. A human zygote, embryo or fetus are now seen by
the reader as having innate value and moral worth not based on accidental
characteristics or latent capacities which manifest at different stages of life
development, e.g., consciousness, cognitive reasoning ability, larger "total cell
count," advanced gross and fine motor skills or complex functions related
to social engagement; rather, they are morally valued precisely due to the
kind of entity they are, that is, a very young human person. And most
immediately, the advocate realizes that her niece is not valued for a variety
of developed skills, including being a superlative handler of a slingshot, nor
is the neighborhood child granted the recognition of being a human person
based on the developed and practiced characteristic of being an innovative
musician; to the contrary, all young persons (not yet fully mature human
beings) are rightly granted full recognition as members of the human family
precisely because of the kind of entity they are.

Those who support abortion as a birth control practice will often
agree with the unassailable scientific fact that an embryo is indeed a unique
"human being" with discernable bodily actions (upper right quadrant), but
then insist that the actual valuable "human person" is associated with and,
indeed, determined by the manifestation of latent characteristics such as
consciousness, choice making abilities, rational cognitive faculties or mental
capabilities allowing for complex social envisioning (upper left and lower
left quadrants), and therefore comes to be at some future point in time as
a developed phenomenon—a "dualist view" of the human being/person.
Yet, etymological research reveals that the meaning of the word "person"
is grounded in c1200 French: "...*persoun*, 'an individual, a human being,
from Old French persone 'human being, anyone, person'[12c., Modern
French personne] and directly from Latin *persona* 'human being, person,
personage'" (etymonline.com).

Pro-abortion advocates who maintain a dualist view (i.e., neo-Gnostic)
have clearly exerted efforts to use the terms "human being" and "human
person" in a manner that purportedly refers to different things, yet semanti-
cally, they are synonyms. In refuting this dualist view of the human person,
Lee offers the following explanation:

> ...a living thing that performs bodily actions is an organism, a bodily entity.
> But it is clear in the case of the human individual that it is the same subject

that perceives, walks and talks (which are bodily actions), and that understands and makes choices (what everyone, including anyone who denies he
is an organism refers to as "I"). It must be the same thing that perceives these
words on a page, for example, and understands them. Thus, what each of us
refers to as "I" is identically the physical organism which is the subject both
of bodily actions such as perceiving and walking, and of non-physical actions,
such as understanding and choosing. Therefore, you and I are essentially
physical organisms, rather than consciousness merely associated with physical
organisms. And so we came to be at conception, we once were embryos, then
foetuses, then infants, and so on.

Thus, a human being is a bodily entity that has, from the moment
of conception, the natural capacities (because of the kind of thing it is) to
demonstrate discerning mental functions, advanced motor skill operations
and complex social skills, given a nurturing and protective environment
allowing for ongoing development.

Lee continues to explain his position, saying that

Being a certain kind of thing, that is, having a specific type of substantial
nature, is an either/or matter—a thing either is or is not a human being. But
the accidental qualities that could be proposed as criteria for personhood
come in varying degrees: there is an infinite number of degrees of relevant
developed abilities or dispositions, such as for self-consciousness or intelligence. So, if persons were valuable as subjects of rights only because of
such accidental qualities, and not in virtue of the kind of things they are,
then, since such qualities come in varying degrees basic rights would be
possessed by human beings in varying degrees. ("THE PRO-LIFE ARGU-
MENT FROM SUBSTANTIAL IDENTITY: A DEFENCE." Bioethics ISSN
0269-9702 [print]; 1467-8519 [online], Volume 18, Number 3 2004)

Clearly, all human persons are of equal moral worth because of the
kind of entity or thing they are, each with latent skills and natural capacities
that develop in varying degrees of complexity and expression.

To substantiate the truth that a zygote, embryo or fetus is a complete
human person that possesses an array of latent abilities, natural capacities
and accidental qualities, in his book *Abortion and Unborn Human Life*,

Patrick Lee offers the following salient quote from the eminent French geneticist Jerome Lejeune, which responds to those who assert that the human embryo is not yet "humanized": "I must say very simply, as a geneticist, I have never heard any specialist in husbandry of animals thinking about the 'cattilisation' of cattle. They know that the embryo of a cow would be a calf....From all the genetic laws that we have tried to summarize, we are entirely convinced that every embryo is, by itself a human being" (The Catholic University of America Press, 1996).

Patrick Lee and his colleague, Robert P. George, offer the following conclusion regarding the certain identity of the human embryo:

> The human embryo, like the adult, is a self-integrating whole, a complete member of the species at a certain developmental stage....The human embryo, fetus, infant, child, adolescent, and adult differ not as to what they intrinsically are—they are human beings—but in respect of their age, size, stage of development, and condition of dependency....Our view, which we have defended in various writings, is that the dignity of human beings is inherent and that all of us, as members of the human family, are created equal. ("Embryonic Issues." *National Review*, January 22, 2007, online)

(Note: Robert P. George is the sixth McCormick Professor of Jurisprudence and Director of the James Madison Program in American Ideals and Institutions at Princeton University.)

Modern scientific research has determined with 100% certainty that the life of each human person begins at the point where a female oocyte/egg is fertilized by a male sperm. Whereas the individual egg and individual sperm are sex cells belonging to the mother and father, the fertilized egg, i.e., zygote (rapidly developing towards becoming an embryo, then a fetus and ultimately an infant) is a unique and integrated whole human body—that is to say, an individual human person (upper right quadrant). It therefore follows that this young human being who possesses in "radical (= root) form" a variety of natural capacities, "accidental characteristics" and latent capabilities is the exact tangible individual, with discernable "bodily actions," who is the very entity that allows for the assured and predictable manifestation of (quite secondary) non-tangible characteristics such as consciousness, problem solving skills, decision making functions, the cognitive faculties which allow for composing a variety of self-referential narratives (upper left quadrant), the mental capacity to envision a possible social world (lower left quadrant) as well as the social ability to engage others in complex interactional occurrences (lower right quadrant). Obviously, the individual person cannot itself be one of these "latent capabilities." Succinctly stated, a human person is a certain type of embodied individual entity that owns a wide variety of latent secondary characteristics and "accidental qualities," including a rational nature, from the point of conception forward.

Patrick Lee offers the following comment regarding this examination and conclusion:

> The pro-life position is not that unborn human beings are potential persons and therefore have a right to life. Rather, potentiality is important only because it is an indicator of what kind of thing is already present. From conception on, the unborn human being is a developing substantial entity with the basic, natural capacities to reason and make free choices. She right now is that type of thing or substantial entity. And it is the type of thing that matters, not the condition that thing is in, which may or may not allow her immediately to exercise all of her basic capacities. Only this position makes sense of the evident truth, that people who are asleep or in a (reversible) coma are equally subjects of rights as those who are awake and can immediately exercise all of their natural capacities. Only this position is consistent with the recognition that the actions of a thing (such as conceptual thought and free choice) flow from the kind of thing it is, its nature, rather than vice versa. And only this position is consistent with the principle that all human persons have equal basic rights.

Lee then concludes his analysis by saying that

> In sum, what is intrinsically valuable as a subject of rights is what you and I are. What you and I are, are human physical organisms. Human physical organisms come to be at conception (whether by a natural process or by lab technology). Therefore, what is intrinsically valuable as a subject of rights— and so can rightly be called a "person"—comes to be at conception. ("THE PRO-LIFE ARGUMENT FROM SUBSTANTIAL IDENTITY: A DEFENCE." previously referenced)

As proponents of abortion as a birth control method employ social/psychological defense mechanisms such as denial, rationalization and intellectualization to support their position, a variety of incongruous justifications and arguments ensue. For example, Dr. Joseph Fletcher was a theologian who transitioned his cosmological self-identity to that of an atheist. Fletcher was also a professor of medical ethics at the University of Virginia and is well known for advancing the concept of "situational ethics" or "social relativism." Given his professional identity as a medical ethicist, it is remarkably inconsonant that Dr. Fletcher would advance the following position, which not only denies the moral value of mentally disabled persons, but also rationalizes their extermination:

> Idiots are not, never were, and never will be in any degree responsible [because they cannot understand the consequences of action]. Idiots, that is to say, are not human. The problem they pose is not lack of sufficient mind, but of any mind at all. No matter how euphoric their behavior might be, they are outside the pale of human integrity.

Dr. Fletcher then inhumanely proclaims that "There is no such thing as a right to bring crippled children into the world" (Smith, Wesley J. "Joseph Fletcher's Dark Dreams Becoming our Reality." *Discovery Institute*, January 5, 2018, online).

Accompanying Fletcher in advocating for the life termination of disabled human beings is philosopher and Princeton University professor Peter Singer. Singer is known for his work in bioethics and is, ironically, credited as a key intellectual founder of the modern animal rights movement. Singer's views on this matter are discussed in an online February 8, 2020, article written by Naaman Zhou in *The Guardian* and titled "Peter Singer event canceled in New Zealand after outcry over disability stance." In this feature, the philosopher notes that certain conditions like hemophilia, Down syndrome and spina bifida make "the child's life prospects significantly less promising than those of a normal child." Zhou reports that Singer believes that parents of these children should be allowed to terminate their child's life. The bioethicist explains his viewpoint in the following manner, saying that "The position taken here does not imply that it would be better that no people born with severe disabilities should survive: it implies only that the parents of such infants should be able to make this decision." Singer makes sure to clarify that his proposal is not applicable to adults with disabilities; rather, it is specifically aimed at new-born infants who are without "rationality, autonomy and self-consciousness."

In a challenge to Singer's infanticide notions, Zhou quotes disability advocate Stella Young, who says that "He uses spina bifida as an example of a disability that might warrant infanticide....I have a number of friends who have spina bifida. One is Kurt Fearnley, who I expect we'll be hearing quite a lot about in the coming weeks as he competes in his third Paralympic Games in London." Singer's family history includes an account of his Jewish parents fleeing Nazi Germany while three of his grandparents were left behind and were murdered in the Holocaust. Given the inhumane horror that Singer's family members suffered, the following statement by the bioethicist is remarkably incongruous and distinctly lacks human empathy: "Human babies are not born self-aware, or capable of grasping that they exist over time. They are not persons [therefore] the life of a newborn is of less value than the life of a pig, dog, or a chimpanzee."

Judith Jarvis Thomson, Ph.D., a professor of philosophy at MIT, has supported abortion practices through insisting that only if the mother has voluntary agreed to the use of her uterus by the in-utero developing human, seemingly in a manner analogous to a "room and board landlord-tenant agreement" (lower right quadrant), does the embryo have a just right to the continued use of her body as a temporary nurturing and protective dwelling space. In arguing for this position, Thomson used this quite well-known comparison:

> But now let us imagine this. You wake up in the morning and find yourself back to back with an unconscious violinist. A famous unconscious violinist. He has been found to have a fatal kidney ailment, and the Society of Music Lovers has canvassed all the available medical records and found that you alone have the right blood type to help. They therefore kidnapped you, and last night the violinist's circulatory system was plugged into yours, so that your kidneys can be used to extract poisons from his blood as well as your own. The director of the hospital now tells you, "Look we're sorry the Society of Music Lovers did this to you—we would never have permitted it if we had known. But, still, they did it, and the violinist now is plugged

into you. To unplug you would be to kill him. But never mind, it's only for nine months. By then he will have recovered from his ailment, and can safely be unplugged from you." Is it morally incumbent on you to accede to this situation? (*Abortion and Unborn Human Life*, previously referenced)

This proposition is sometimes called the "argument from bodily rights" in favor of abortion. Thomson argues that pregnancy is analogous to one being innocently medically attached—through totally involuntary and unaware processes—to the important musician in order to provide vital support and concludes that one is not morally required to agree to this relationship with the violinist. Thomson's position regarding abortion is as follows:

> Thomson explicitly distinguishes between securing the death of a fetus, which she says is not morally permissible, and removing the fetus from the mother's body, an action she says is morally permissible if carrying the child involves great sacrifice for the mother. Thus, her argument can be accurately expressed as follows: There is a distinction between intentional killing (securing someone's death) and bringing about death as a side effect. (*Abortion and Unborn Human Life*, previously referenced)

However, if the fetus is not at a point of life development that she can survive without intrauterine life support, the argument proposed by Thomson is clearly a distinction without a difference, i.e., a logical fallacy.

A distinction without a difference is defined as follows: "The assertion that a position is different from another position based on the language when, in fact, both positions are the same—at least in practice or practical terms" (logicalfallacies.com). A more detailed definition is offered by University of Richmond's Elizabeth Southall in a 2012 publication, which states that

> "A distinction without a difference"—a colloquial expression employed by one wishing to recognize that while a linguistic or conceptual distinction exists between any number of options, any such distinction lacks substantive practical effect. To allege that a situation presents "a distinction without a difference" is to suggest that any difference between a given set of options is

a logical fallacy—purely a creature of erroneous perception. ("A Distinction Without a Difference? An Examination of the Legal and Ethical Difference Between Asset Protection and Fraudulent Transfers Under Virginia Law." https://scholarship.richmond.edu/law-student-publications/27/)

From the point of view of a 7-week-old embryo or a 14-week-old intra-uterine human—in very real "practical terms"—an abortion performed so as to remove the embryo or fetus from the mother's body or to intentionally kill the developing human is most certainly a "distinction without a difference." However, if a fetus at 29 weeks of development (or older) is carefully surgically removed from the mother's uterus there is a very good possibility that there can be a "distinction with a difference," as the survival rate for a fetus at that point of intrauterine life development is estimated to be 95% (https://www.bellybelly.com.au/baby/whats-the-earliest-a-baby-can-be-born-and-survive/). In a situation where an intrauterine human being cannot survive if removed from the mother's uterus, Thomson's argument is unquestionably a "distinction without a difference," as well as a blatant example of employing social/psychological self-defense mechanisms in an effort to support her argument, e.g., denial and rationalization. Lee and George offer the following assessment of Thomson's view on abortion: "According to this position, it is true that we once were embryos and fetuses, but in the embryonic and fetal stages of our lives we were not yet valuable in the special way that would qualify us as having a right to life" (Lee, Patrick and Robert P. George, "The Wrong of Abortion." contemporarythinkers.org).

Further review of Thomson's violinist comparison reveals a rather strangely structured composition, as it prominently features an innocence that is obviously misplaced. A closer comparison to the fully dependent life situation of an intrauterine innocent person to their mother can be more accurately represented by a hypothetical scenario where both a woman and a man, as members of the "Kidney Patient Benevolent Society," launch a unique clandestine investigation and determine that the woman has specific kidney characteristics and other biological features that can solely provide the support necessary to ensure both the health and full recovery of a favored kidney patient who is in critical condition. The couple, knowingly and willfully—not innocently—then collaborate in engaging in a social action where the terminally-ill kidney patient (who also happens to be a famous violinist) is surreptitiously rendered unconscious. While in this externally induced comatose state, the unaware and innocent violinist is kidnapped by the couple and becomes relationally entrapped through being attached to the woman with exclusive medical tubing and other specialized equipment in a hospital renal treatment ward. While the hospital administration was completely unaware of this covert operation, upon learning of this occurrence, they acquiesced to the arrangement based on their humanitarian policy of assuring healing and wellbeing to all persons regardless of their circumstances. The necessary procedure of using her kidneys to filter her blood, as well as that of the violinist, operationalizes a 9-month healthcare treatment plan, offering the one and only intervention that can both assure a sound recovery and realize ongoing life for the kidney patient. However, at a point significantly short of the requisite 9-month period of vital support, the woman decides that she no longer wishes to participate in this exclusive life support relationship and intends to detach her body from the ensnared kidney patient. Due to the fact that the woman willfully placed both herself and the unwitting violinist in this temporary 9-month human-to-human caretaker relationship, the innocent kidney patient has clearly been unconsciously entrapped into a vital dependent relationship with the woman with no ability to either initially approve of this social relationship or disagree with the woman's intention to later terminate the arrangement. The reader is invited to compare this altered scenario to Thomson's original scenario and reflect upon which comparison is closest to that of the vital dependency with which an innocent intrauterine human embryo has on their mother, as well as consider how evaluative conclusions may vary depending on which comparison is considered.

Moving the Thomson sketch from analogy to reality must necessarily require a discussion which involves an actual human embryo. Consider the situation of a single woman who wishes to become pregnant in order to realize her vision to be the mother of a child to which she has given birth. After several years of being unable to conceive, the woman undergoes a variety of medical tests which reveal damaged fallopian tubes. In order to realize her vision, she hires the services of a fertility clinic with the hope that their professional expertise may help her fulfill her desire. After reviewing details of her personal health history with clinic specialists, the woman decides to purchase a donated embryo and invite the embryo to be implanted in her uterus. While the procedure was remarkably successful, during the second trimester of pregnancy, the woman changes her mind, no longer wishing to be pregnant or become a mother and gains an abortion. Unquestionably, in this scenario, the scientifically-identified young human being (upper right quadrant) was both willingly invited and ensnared into a dependent relationship with the mother (lower right quadrant). In a similar manner, when a woman willingly has consensual intercourse with full knowledge that this action could result in an embryo becoming invited to be implanted into her uterus, she has likewise potentially created a situation where a young human person becomes entrapped into a temporary life-dependent relationship with her. In both cases, the intrauterine human person was innocently placed in a vital relationship with their mother, solely through her willful action.

As pro-choice advocates joined the postmodern credo asserting that there is no objective reality with theorizing guided by reductionism, the precise identification—and widely accepted moral recognition—of the objective "human being" (upper right quadrant) was discontinuously transformed into a socially-constructed entitled-to-rights "human person" (lower left quadrant), who is argued to be both mysteriously unsubstantial and unaccountably postnatal. As one would expect, the devaluing of human life quickly ensued, relegating the intrauterine human being to an arbitrary identification as a purchasable commodity or a mere "clump of cells." As described above, a woman can now actually purchase a human embryo and have the human being implanted in her uterus, but within a matter of weeks, choose to "return her purchase," through disposing of the intrauterine developing human person through an abortion procedure. Likewise, a woman can conceive either through consensual intercourse or by means of lab technology, and if she later chooses to no longer be pregnant, can also discard the intrauterine human being, now identified as a "clump of cells," by purchasing an abortion.

In further critiquing Thomson's argument, recall that the one and only purpose of the human female uterus is to nurture and protect a developing embryo, thus there exists no other "tenant" other than a human embryo that could possibly occupy this physical dwelling place. Furthermore, the female uterus is not an organ structure that is in place for the health and wellbeing of the woman, i.e., it is not a vital organ such as her kidney system, liver or heart; rather, it is a vital organ specifically positioned in her body for the life assurance of another human being—perhaps a developing violinist—and the female uterus is the only internal human organ that is so designated. As a matter of scientific fact, the zygote was invited and entrapped within the mother's uterus through the woman's conscious choice to willingly engage in sexual intercourse. Therefore, she (and the father) has willingly assumed full responsibility for the possibility of a male sex cell (sperm) entering her vagina and transforming her sex cell (egg/oocyte) into a separate and totally unique human being, i.e., a zygote (upper right quadrant). To reiterate, the mother, through consensually agreeing to sexual intercourse, has ensnared the transformed sex cell, now a fully embodied separate human being, into occupying her uterus as a place of dwelling, nurturance and protection.

To all appearances, the argument proffered by Thomson represents a de facto "landlord" arrangement between the consciously acting mother and the unaware, ensnared and innocent "tenant" embryo, as "eviction" in the form of an abortion is a possible occurrence. Of course, from Thomson's point of view, the social arrangement is a one-sided authoritarian structure. Yet, due to the fact that the very young human being was invited into a completely dependent "landlord-tenant" relationship, the mother has implicitly assumed responsibility for providing a "nine-month room-and-board contract." Research from the biological sciences (upper right quadrant) provides data that establishes, with a 100% level of certainty, that a sex cell cannot self-initiate a transition/transformation into a unique totipotent human zygote, i.e., her sex cell cannot autonomously transmute into a human zygote. Thus, if the woman had not chosen to engage in sexual intercourse, her sex cell would have remained her sex cell, and thus no separate human being as a temporary "tenant" could possibly occupy her uterus. Furthermore, because the human embryo was entrapped by the mother into occupying her uterus—the singular physical shelter on earth that can sustain its life development—the mother has, by default, acquired both a practical and moral responsibility to provide for the health and wellbeing of the invited young human person through providing ongoing nurture and protection until the point of birth. (Note: According to the online *Collins Dictionary*, "default" is defined as: "If something happens by default, it happens only because something else which might have prevented it…has not happened.")

Without question, the conscious choice of effectuating an embryo to be within the woman's uterus is the responsibility of the mother and the father; plainly, this cannot be a choice exercised by the ensnared, blameless and vulnerable intrauterine human person. The altered sex cell—now a zygote—was placed directly by the mother in a precarious life situation of total dependence within her uterus, as she alone possesses the one and only body that can offer the requisite protective and nurturing environment. Lee concurs with this assessment, saying that "In the vast majority of abortion cases, the man and woman freely perform an action, sexual intercourse, which they realize could result in the conception of a new human being. Thus, most pregnancy cases are different than simply finding that someone is dependent on one for his or her life. Rather, they are cases of having put someone in a position of being dependent on one for his or her life. Parents have a special duty to their children, partly because they have performed an action which they fully realized could result in the procreation of children" (*Abortion and Unborn Human Life,* previously referenced).

Therefore, in a surprising "turn of the tables," it is the entrapped and innocent embryo that arguably possesses the rightful and just "bodily rights" position, not the knowledgeable and completely accountable mother. Given that it is the mother that "plugged" the innocent—and totally dependent—embryo into her life-sustaining organ system, it is both baffling and incongruous that Thomson would make the following statement: "I am arguing only that having a right to life does not guarantee having either a right to be given the use of or a right to be allowed continued use of another person's body—even if one needs it for life itself" (*Abortion and Unborn Human Life*, previously referenced).

Lee and George provide this additional cogent comment related to Thomson's argument: "…the mother has a special responsibility to her child, in virtue of being her biological mother (as does the father in virtue of his paternal relationship). The parental relationship itself—not just the voluntary acceptance of that relationship—gives rise to a special responsibility to a child." Noting the totally exclusive nature of the human parental relationship, Lee and George add that

The physical unity or continuity of children to their parents is unique. The child is brought into being out of the bodily unity and bodies of the mother and the father. The mother and the father are in a certain sense prolonged or continued in their offspring. So, there is a natural unity of the mother with her child, and a natural unity of the father with his child. Since we have special responsibilities to those with whom we are closely united, it follows that we in fact do have a special responsibility to our children anterior to our having voluntarily assumed such responsibility or consented to the relationship. ("The Wrong of Abortion," previously referenced)

As previously discussed, some advocates who support the abortion of an embryo as a birth control choice will often justify their position by first acknowledging the biological truth that the embryo is indeed a human being (upper right quadrant), but then immediately insist that the actual valuable human person who is entitled to rights appears postnatally and is identified by the staged unfolding of certain favored accidental qualities or latent capacities, e.g., consciousness of products of perception and awareness of complex aspects of thought (upper left quadrant). Strangely, in this particular example, such a conceptualization represents an illusory, and rather ghostly, conceptualization of the human person. Assuredly, this is a notion formed through the employment of social/psychological self-defense mechanisms such as denial and rationalization, as well as a concept marked by quadrant confusion. Obviously, consciousness, rationality, as well as processes related to abstract problem-solving, are not embodied phenomena, but rather are impalpable faculties (upper left quadrant) possessed by palpable human beings (upper right quadrant). Furthermore, consciousness as a later developed and intangible capacity cannot own, use or somehow possess a tangible human body; rather, it is the embodied human person that owns consciousness as well as rationality, as predictably developed capacities located in the upper left quadrant of human experience. To insist that the identity of the valuable human person is determined by consciousness, or any other latent ability or accidental quality, represents a certain occurrence of quadrant confusion.

Lee and George critically examine this argument, saying that

Most will grant that human embryos or fetuses are human beings. However, they then distinguish "human being" from "person" and claim that embryonic human beings are not (yet) persons. They hold that while it is wrong to kill persons, it is not always wrong to kill human beings who are not persons.... Sometimes it is argued that human beings in the embryonic stage are not persons because embryonic human beings do not exercise higher mental capacities or functions. Certain defenders of abortion (and infanticide) have argued that in order to be a person, an entity must be self-aware (Singer, 1993; Tooley, 1983; Warren, 1984). They claim that, because human embryos and fetuses (and infants) have not yet developed self-awareness, they are not persons.

Lee and George continue their judicious analysis of this argument, saying that "These defenders of abortion raise the question: Where does one draw the line between those who are subjects of rights and those that are not? A long tradition says that the line should be drawn at persons. But what is a person, if not an entity that has self-awareness, rationality, etc.?"

Lee and George then extend their thoughtful critique of this position, saying that

This argument is based on a false premise. It implicitly identifies the human person with a consciousness which inhabits (or is somehow associated with) and uses a body; the truth however, is that we human persons are particular kinds of physical organisms. The argument here under review grants that the human organism comes to be at conception, but claims nevertheless that you or I, the human person, comes to be only much later, say, when self-awareness develops. But if this human organism came to be at one time, but I came to be at a later time, it follows that I am one thing and this human organism with which I am associated is another thing. But this is false. We are not consciousnesses that possess or inhabit bodies. Rather, we are living bodily entities. We can see this by examining the kinds of action that we perform. If a living thing performs bodily actions, then it is a physical organism. ("The Wrong of Abortion," previously referenced)

As earlier noted, the terms "human being" and "human person" are synonyms; yet, in order to bolster their pro-abortion argument, advocates have obscured the meaning of the term "human person" through an agnotological campaign. Thomas Sowell comments on this practice common among prepossessed intellectuals, saying that "One of the many signs of virtuosity among intellectuals is the repackaging of words to mean things that are not only different from, but sometimes the direct opposite of, their original meanings or the meaning that most other people attach to those words" (*Intellectuals and Society.* Basic Books, 2011). As tendentious abortion advocates employ cognitive processes guided by reductionism, they produce a preferred conception of the entitled to rights human person. This socially constructed notion (lower left quadrant) of a later-arriving immaterial human person is explicitly joined with postmodern philosophical conceptions that reject objectivity—leading to a fundamental separation from the objective intrauterine human being—and is further asserted to be the rightful possessor of vital moral value now denied to the tangible human being (upper right quadrant).

Seemingly, this conception is arrived at through a two-step process, with the first step comprised of employing obfuscating rhetorical techniques precisely aimed at advancing the claim that the actual meaning of the commonly-used and etymologically-grounded term "human person" actually refers to something other than the tangible and objective embryonic "human being." Once the term "human person" has been rendered vulnerable to a redefinition, the second step involves reducing the identity and meaning of the term "human person" to a variety of arbitrarily-selected latent qualities and developed capacities. (Note: Recall that LeShan and Margenau offer this pertinent comment with respect to the practice of reductionism: "...if one idea seemed...unacceptable, its meaning could be saved by reducing it to a more familiar or a more acceptable one" (*Einstein's Space and Van Gogh's Sky: Physical Reality and Beyond*, previously referenced). While some of these latent qualities, as well as developed capacities, may have to do with sophisticated abilities related to complex social engagement (lower right quadrant), others are amazingly attached to immaterial qualities of mind or consciousness, e.g., self-awareness or the self-reflective capacity to analyze the consequences of intentional action (upper left quadrant). Once this engineered intellectual composition and associated manipulative rhetorical operations are successful, in the sense of being sufficiently personally and socially persuasive, the pro-abortion advocate may now reduce the identification of the valuable and entitled-to-rights human person to the upper or lower left quadrants, having to do with intangible elements/processes of mind (Fletcher, Singer et al.), or the lower right quadrant, where complex inter-actional social phenomena characteristic of more mature human beings are expressed (Thomson).

However, these propositions and arguments are straightforwardly recognized as both products of quadrant confusion and techniques of obfuscation, as all objective individual entities (such as an embryo) are studied and given identity through the investigative methodologies of modern science (upper right quadrant), e.g., physics, astronomy, material science, geology, biology, inorganic and organic chemistry, as well as the taxonomies derived from the scientific disciplines of zoology, botany, entomology, etc. Precisely through employing the research techniques of modern biological science, an embryo existing within a woman's uterus is found to be a completely unique human being/person at an early stage of life development.

LeShan and Margenau have explained in their book *Einstein's Space and Van Gogh's Sky: Physical Reality and Beyond* (previously referenced) that an impartial researcher is first concerned with accurately identifying the specific domain of study, and then asking what observables exist within the identified realm. After achieving these first two determinations, the next concern is focused on what sort of measurements and analyses can be made with respect to the elements or observables encountered within the domain of inquiry. As discussed earlier, the powerful indexing capacity of post-postmodern Integral Theory has outlined four quadrants of human experience. When an investigative project has to do with tangible, i.e., "see-touch" individual entities, the upper right quadrant of human experience is the precise domain of study. A human zygote, embryo or fetus is quite obviously an embodied individual material entity existing in the "see touch" domain (upper right quadrant). Therefore, the methodologies appropriate to studying the intrauterine living entity are those related to modern biological science. When biologists analyze the genetic structure of a zygote, embryo or fetus, they are found to be a completely unique member of the human species at an early stage of life development.

Accidental qualities and latent features have no relevance whatsoever in reaching an accurate identification of the intrauterine human person, as all accidental qualities and latent features owe their very origin, as well as systematized manifestation, to the embodied developing embryo; they do not spontaneously appear "out of thin air" and somehow capture or "possess" the corporeal human person. Clearly, the human person does not owe its existence to an accidental quality or latent feature. Additionally, there is absolutely no mammalian species that is identified in terms of their accidental qualities or latent features. Certainly, the intrauterine cheetah is not required to first run at the adult speed of 65+ miles per hour (an accidental quality) before being fully identified as a cheetah, nor must an unborn wolf demonstrate the social assertiveness (a latent feature) associated with that of an adult alpha wolf pack leader prior to being recognized as truly a wolf. While the value of a particular mammal, other than a human, may be linked to a favored accidental quality or latent feature, their identity is never based on those characteristics.

As previously noted, French geneticist Jerome Lejeune has assertively concluded that "...I have never heard any specialist in husbandry of animals thinking about the 'cattilisation' of cattle. They know that the embryo of a cow would be a calf....From all the genetic laws that we have tried to summarize, we are entirely convinced that every embryo is, by itself, a human being" (*Abortion and Unborn Human Life*, previously referenced). Lee and George offer this decisive comment on the matter of human identity and value: "In sum, human beings are valuable (as subjects of rights) in virtue of what they are. But what they are are human physical organisms. Human physical organisms come to be at conception. Therefore, what is intrinsically valuable (as a subject of rights) comes to be at conception" ("The Wrong of Abortion," previously referenced).

Katy Lindemann wrote an article titled "Please, doctor, don't call my lost baby a 'product of conception,'" which concerns the death of her intrauterine baby (*The Guardian*, October 11, 2018, online). In describing the emotional pain that she and her husband experienced through the death of their baby, Lindemann writes:

> "There's your baby's heartbeat," said the sonographer, pointing to the screen as we listened to the thump-thump-thump that was the most magical sound I had ever heard. A week later, the next scan showed that this beautiful twinkling heartbeat had gone, and our baby had died. I couldn't face having to

wait to pass the pregnancy sac, so I opted for surgery: a procedure called an ERPC: "evacuation of retained products of conception." From the outset of your antenatal care, the NHS refers to "your baby," acknowledging that the stage of gestation doesn't determine the meaning of the pregnancy to the family. But as soon as the pregnancy is "non-viable," there's an immediate and stark switch in the language used. I remember thinking that "evacuation" sounded like something you'd have done to your bowels. "Products of conception" might be the correct clinical term, but to us, as a grieving couple, that was our dead baby: our much longed-for baby, who was already loved and anticipated as a unique human being, not simply an object to be discarded.

After reading Lindemann's article, writer Melanie McDonagh was moved to publish a feature in *The Spectator* (October 10, 2018, online) titled "The dishonestly of the abortion debate." McDonagh offered the following comments:

> I was moved by her account, of course, but it was baffling to read it without any reference to one obvious reason for this non-committal language, viz, the fact that you can in Britain kill the product of conception for virtually any reason up to 24 weeks' gestation, and up to birth in the case of foetal abnormality. So of course you don't talk lightly about babies, unless you're either a pro-lifer or a woman who actually wants to be pregnant. If you talk about the foetus in human terms you risk stigmatising the process whereby you can kill him or her quite legally. Abortion is what feminists mean when they talk about "reproductive rights."

McDonagh then effectively brings into focus the nature and function of social/psychological self-defense mechanisms arrived at through cognitive processes, which are guided by reductionism and then further supported by a linguistic sleight of hand—which then enables the social manifestation of quadrant discord through concrete human action, i.e., abortion as a birth control choice, in the following quote:

> So, how to produce language about the unborn human being that respects the sensitivities of parents who suffer a miscarriage without offending the

greater number of women who have had abortions. Answer: you can't. It's not possible for the same creature to be a baby in one reading, a product of conception in another. Yet it's the same human being. It's as if a foetus is human only if it's wanted; if it isn't, it ceases to be human, philosophically and linguistically, because otherwise abortion rights could be compromised. It's not what anyone could call a scientific approach.

In the interest of realizing consonance with scientific findings (upper right quadrant) and achieving sound intellectual integrity (upper left quadrant), the only truthful conclusion regarding the act of abortion as a birth control choice reveals that the practice of aborting (lower right quadrant) a young developing human being whose physical residence or temporary "natural habitat" is within a mother, is the killing of a distinct human person. The performance of human abortion as a birth control technique simply cannot be legitimately described in any other way, and attempts to retreat from this acknowledgement will necessarily require the employment of lies, trickery and obfuscation, as well as regression to a variety of social/psychological defense mechanisms.

As President John Adams expressed: "Facts are stubborn things; and whatever be our wishes, or inclinations, or the dictates of our passions, they cannot alter the state of facts and evidence." Thus, a woman's "choice" (upper left quadrant) can only be related to the developmental point of growth, from conception forward, where the act of killing (lower right quadrant) a separate and totally unique human life (upper right quadrant) will occur. Alfred Adler, the originator of the psychological model called Individual Psychology, stated that "A lie would have no sense unless the truth were felt dangerous" (alfredadler.edu).

In reality, societies throughout history have always sanctioned the killing of humans. An example of sanctioned killing includes government-directed capital punishment of a human judicially convicted of first degree murder. In addition, the execution of tens of thousands of suspected witches in Europe and America during the early modern period (1450–1750), the ceremonial sacrifice of young children among the Incas, democide of citizens who were judged to be blameworthy and/or undesirable among socialist and fascist regimes in the 20th century, as well as mass human killing as a result of war operations are conclusive examples of government sanctioned killing. Although in these occurrences, the moral worth of the individual human's life was denigrated or dismissed, typically there was no denying that a distinct human person was killed.

The list of rationalizations, denials, intellectualizations and other social/psychological defense mechanisms that persons who fully support abortion as a personal birth control choice employ, so as to avoid acknowledging that a distinct living human person with a totally unique genetic composition is being killed by means of an abortion, is sincerely astonishing. Through abortion, a totally helpless individual human being is undeniably sacrificed so as to ensure that the societal group identified as women is secured from the perceived and often expressed omnipresent threat of renewed or continuing oppression. Consequently, the protected societal class of women is judged to be of greater moral value than a defenseless individual human who lacks the autonomous ability to act in defense of their life and, presently, possesses no affiliation with a group owning codified societal security protections. Additionally, in what is truly a heartbreaking irony, in approximately 50% of all human pregnancies, the developing intrauterine human person is female and, through abortion, the yet-to-be-born female is forever denied membership among the protected societal class of women.

Undoubtedly, the most awe-inspiring and consequential powers possessed by humans are the following capabilities: 1) generating a new individual human life through the act of procreation, 2) saving a human life or 3) taking an individual life through an act of killing. In regard to the controversial issue of abortion as a birth control method, the grace afforded by human integrity, when grounded in both the utilization of sound reasoning and the full acknowledgement of unassailable scientific facts, will necessarily lead to the following two mutually exclusive ethical positions:

1. I believe, support and affirm that the killing of an individual human person whose physical residence is temporarily (ordinarily nine months) within their mother, solely based on a birth control choice by the mother, should be formally sanctioned by society.

2. I do not believe, support or affirm that the killing of an individual

human person whose physical residence is temporarily (ordinarily nine months) within their mother, solely based on a birth control choice by the mother, should be formally sanctioned by society.

Society surely will ethically benefit when domain/quadrant specific study of any legally-authorized social practice, of which there is considerable question and controversy, is pursued in an earnest validly-focused analysis. Only when the above outlined scientific truth regarding abortion as a birth control method can be fully acknowledged will society be freed from the lies, trickery and obfuscation surrounding this presently-sanctioned social practice.

In regard to the foregoing, a curious and plainly discrepant societal transaction must be referenced. Several well-known and long-established insurance companies will provide life insurance for an intrauterine young horse in the event of death. Remarkably, a life insurance policy is not available for an unborn human, as typically a young human person needs to be 15 days post-birth before life insurance can be acquired.

CHAPTER 5

Real Socialism Has Never Been Tried

What happened and existed in the Soviet Union was not socialism. It was authoritarian Communism....And Communism, whether in Cuba, whether in the Soviet Union or whether in other countries was marked by totalitarianism, was marked by throwing millions of people into the Gulag.
—Bernie Sanders, United States Senator and twice U.S. Presidential Candidate

Union of Soviet Socialist Republics (U.S.S.R.): The economic foundation of the U.S.S.R. was Socialist ownership of the means of production, distribution, and exchange. And the economy of the entire country was controlled by a series of five year plans that set targets for all forms of production. (Encyclopedia Britannica, online)

Constitutionally, Cuba is a socialist country ruled by the dictates of Marxism. The Communist Party of Cuba is the leading force both at the society level and in the state. (World Atlas, online)

Marx used many terms to refer to a post-capitalist society—positive humanism, socialism, Communism, realm of free individuality, free association of producers, etc. He used these terms completely interchangeably. The notion

*that "socialism" and "Communism" are distinct historical
stages is alien to his work and only entered the lexicon of
Marxism after his death. (Hudis, Peter. "Marx's Concept
of Socialism." Oxford Handbooks, June 2019, online)*

*No political experiment has been tried so widely, with so
many disparate people, in so many different countries and
failed so absolutely and catastrophically. Is it mere ignorance that allows today's Marxists to flaunt their continued
allegiance—to present it as compassion and care? Or is it
instead, envy of the successful, in near-infinite proportions?
Or something akin to hatred for mankind itself? How much
proof do we need?*

—Jordan Peterson, professor,
clinical psychologist and author

According to numerous and well-respected historical documentations,
as well as statements by the very founders and leaders of the Soviet
Union, the political and economic system of the nation has been unequivocally identified as socialist. And based on the history of Cuba since
the mid-twentieth century, as well as reviewing its current economic and
political structure, the country was and currently remains socialist. As noted
above, an examination of the very writings of Karl Marx published in an
Oxford Handbook reveals the terms socialism and communism were used
interchangeably, i.e., as synonyms, by the chief creator of this economic/
political system. With respect to the above introductory statement regarding the socialistic socioeconomic systems of both the USSR and Cuba by
Bernie Sanders, the senator plainly employed a communication strategy
characterized by lies, trickery and obfuscation. Yet, Bernie Sanders is not
alone in his employment of social/psychological defense mechanisms
when confronted with the 100% failure rate of socialism/communism.

For example, see the following quotes: "There hasn't been a shred of
socialism in the Soviet Union....It's got nothing to do with socialism" (Noam
Chomsky); "We can't concede the end of communism. Communism hasn't
been tried on a society-wide basis" (Professor Stephen Resnick, University
of Massachusetts); "Socialism has never been tried" (The Socialist Party of

Great Britain);"China and Cuba, like the former Soviet Union and Western bloc, have nothing to do with socialism" (The International Socialist
Organization) (Niemietz, Kristian. *Socialism: The Failed Idea That Never
Dies.* The Institute of Economic Affairs, 2019). These examples of social/
psychological defense mechanisms persist in spite of the dismal and, indeed,
tragic failure of socialism in numerous societies, from Poland and Hungary
to Laos and Cambodia, let alone the cataclysmic implementation of this
socioeconomic model in both the Soviet Union and China.

A succinct retort to the numerous deniers of the unassailable lethal
nature of socialist/communist systems of government is provided by Marion
Smith, the executive director of the Victims of Communism Memorial
Foundation, in the following statement:

> It is perhaps one of the biggest lies that exist in our culture today that the
> deadliest ideology in history is somehow not responsible for the regimes that
> it brought to life and the deaths that it caused....Ideas have consequences
> and there has never been a communist regime that did not end up killing
> its own people as a goal."

Smith provides further historical references to confirm his analysis,
saying that

> From Stalin's gulags to the Cambodian Killing Fields to Mao's famines, there
> is not a single communist government in history that was not both tyrannical
> and left horrifying death and destruction in its wake. According to the *Black
> Book of Communism,* regimes inspired by Marxist-Leninism are responsible
> for some 100 million deaths (and counting), making communism the 20th
> century's most fatal ideology.

And, to expose the deceitful nature of the social/psychological defense
mechanisms employed by socialist/communist apologists, Smith comments that "It would be indefensible to say...that fascism as an idea has
nothing to do with the sorts of regimes that fascism brought to life....But
it is the accepted opinion that Marxism is not responsible for the Soviet
Union or Mao's China" (Kirchick, James. "Communism's Victims Deserve
a Museum." *The Daily Beast,* April 14, 2017, online). The widely accepted

observation by the British historian Lord Acton is felicitous regarding Marx and Engels'socially constructed theory: "Power tends to corrupt and absolute power corrupts absolutely....Absolute power demoralizes" (Acton Institute, online).

Acclaimed economist Thomas Sowell adds to the critique of contemporary socialist/communist apologists, saying that "The Marxian vision took the overwhelming complexity of the real world and made the parts fall into place, in a way that was intellectually exhilarating and conferred such sense of moral superiority that opponents could be simply labeled and dismissed as moral lepers or blind reactionaries." Sowell then adroitly confronts the intellectual structure of Marxism with the observable facts of its real world applications, arguing that "...as it is applied in the real world, intellectual flaws and blemishes too slight to be noticed amid the heady rhetoric become manifest in terms as concrete as hunger, terror, and death." The socioeconomic folly that is Marxism can be accurately summed up by the following comment by Sowell:

> ...it represented the hubris of imagining that a whole society could be constructed from the ground up on the vision of one man, rather than evolving from the experience of millions, spread over the generations or the centuries. It was not simply that Marx happened to be unequal to the task, but that anyone was foredoomed to be unequal to such a task. (Sowell, Thomas. *Marxism: Philosophy and Economics*. Routledge Revivals, 2011)

Government is a compound word with the root "govern," conveying the following meanings: "be at the helm of...command, direct...to steer, to pilot...to guide." Additionally, the word govern is related to the Greek word *kyberman,* which means "to steer or guide a ship..." and is the root of the word "cybernetics" (etymonline.com). Professor of mathematics Norbert Weiner, in his book *Cybernetics: or Control and Communication in the Animal and the Machine* (The Technology Press, John Wiley & Sons, 1948), distinctly defined this term as "the science of control and communications in animal and machine." The suffix of the term government, i.e., "ment," is "added to verb stems to make nouns indicating the result or product, of the action of the verb" (etymonline.com). Just as the captain or pilot of a classic sailing craft would use written charts and a sextant to guide the direction of a vessel toward a predetermined destination by using information derived from tangible documents and the corrective information provided by detectible and measurable celestial coordinates, humans governing or piloting the direction of a nation-state use tangible documents and measurable "points of correction" to guide the dynamic movement of a country toward desired and predetermined goals. It is certainly no mere coincidence that, among the several appellations used to reference Mao Zedong by his followers, the phrase "Great Helmsman" was commonly expressed.

The ideas intrinsic to a composed concept of government are socially-constructed notions having to do with human social regulation, as well as the control of individuals, with an aim towards reaching a described and predetermined destination. Thus, notions and conceptions of government "exist" in the lower left quadrant of human experience. Internal concepts and abstract compositions of social organization and human management are brought into detectible form only through the production of tangible documents of order and procedure—and then enacted and performed by palpable, dutiful and cooperative human beings. These "agents of government ideas" coordinate their conduct in observable repetitious social arrangements according to actual documents of protocol and operation, and thus create predictable group behavioral patterns in society, thereby establishing peculiar social facts, i.e., "things." Additionally, these "agents of government ideas" typically operate within clearly identified tangible structures, e.g., buildings, vehicles and designated geographical areas. The animation of observable societal institutions (lower right quadrant), derived from intangible notions of government (lower left quadrant), is realized only by coordinated and repetitive human action (lower right quadrant). To reiterate, actual human players behave in accord with detectable documents containing the circumstances and prescriptions for social role performances derived from specific ideas of government; in this way, human "super-vision" and practical social management is actuated. (Note: Archaic tribal, contemporary gang, terrorist or warlord social arrangements, as well as management of a microsociety, are not a matter of specific focus in this present work.)

As an example, when a person receives a written notice of tax underpayment or an impending audit from the Internal Revenue Service (a societal institution operating within the detectible confines of the United States of America), the communicating IRS employee is coordinating their conduct in line with certain rules of operation related to an actual societal document crafted in order to provide human behavioral guidance in regard to matters of taxation; thus, giving form and function to this institution. If the individual tax payer challenges the IRS employee's interpretation of specific codified tax regulations based on written tax-payer procedures with respect to such matters, this protest will determine the next "behavioral move" by the IRS employee, who is again guided by specific rules of procedure found in conspicuous documents related to the functioning of IRS employees under such circumstances. Additionally, the citizen is enabled, based on written statute or policy, to employ defense tax attorneys (and/or accountants) with expertise in IRS tax matters to formally dispute particular interpretations and actions by the IRS employee. In this way, humans acting in accord with generally consonant interpretations of documented notions of government individually and jointly enact repeatable public performances, and thus create social facts, i.e., "things" (lower right quadrant).

As viewed within the framework of Integral Theory, government may be generally understood as a composite of an internal social construction, i.e., a set of ideas having to do with the supervision of human social ordering (lower left quadrant), that results in producing directly-related tangible documents that outline specific procedures for the guidance of human actors involved in the actual management of individual human conduct, as well as the control of social proceedings within a society (lower right quadrant).

In 1950, human actors in Romania dutifully followed the socialist/communist ideas of government (lower left quadrant), through putting into action a particular set of behavioral prescriptions for human conduct—having to do with social ordering—specified in the following decree (lower right quadrant). The following document is sourced from the online "Tour of Communism: A tour through the Communist history of Bucharest, Romania."

Decree 92 for the nationalization of real estate, issued on April 19, 1950, and published in the Official Bulletin, issue 36/April 20, 1950:

In order to support the strengthening and the development of the socialist economy of the people's Republic of Romania, In order to ensure the good management of the housing sector, which has been subjected to degradation through sabotage by rich landlords and exploiters who own a large number of houses, In order to confiscate from exploiters an important means of exploitation, The real estate mentioned in the addendum [...] will be nationalized. The following criteria were applied when compiling the list:

Real estate which belonged to former industrialists, former land owners, former bankers, former retailers, and other elements of the high-ranking bourgeoisie. Real estate owned by property speculators. Hotels, together with their entire inventory. Real estate still under construction, built for the purpose of exploitation, which have been abandoned by their owner, together with all construction materials, irrespective of where these materials are stored. Buildings damaged by earthquake or war, and built for the purpose of exploitation, whose owners have not invested into their repair or reconstruction.

Real estate belonging to workers, civil servants, independent craftsmen, professional intellectuals, and pensioners does not fall under the incidence of this decree. The nationalized buildings shall become property of the state, as goods of the entire people, without any compensation, and free of any property rights claims. "Real estate," as used in this decree, shall refer to both buildings and the land on which they are built, as well as all equipment or installations used for the maintenance of the buildings. "Real estate," belonging to the wife, husband or minor children of the same family is considered as belonging to a single owner. As a consequence of this decree, the State takes ownership of the real estate from the former owners. The former owners who currently live in these buildings shall become tenants of the State. [...] Destruction, damage or alienation of real estate in any form is punishable with 5–10 years of hard labor and confiscation of wealth. The same sanctions apply to anyone who tries to undermine the nationalization of real estate.

The Romanian socialist/communist notion and structure of government allowed for no codified recourse to allow challenges by professional accountancy firms or specific legal proceedings for citizens who had their property confiscated. Without question, the social regulation of the people of Romania in 1950 was based on the socialist/communist ideas of government as socially constructed by Karl Marx and Friedrich Engels.

The following two definitions are from the *Encyclopedia Britannica* (online):

> Socialism, social and economic doctrine that calls for public rather than private ownership or control of property and natural resources. According to the socialist view, individuals do not live or work in isolation but live in cooperation with one another. Furthermore, everything that people produce is in some sense a social product, and everyone who contributes to the production of a good is entitled to a share in it. Society as a whole, therefore, should own or at least control property for the benefit of all its members.
>
> Communism, political and economic doctrine that aims to replace private property and a profit-based economy with public ownership and communal control of at least the major means of production (e.g., mines, mills, and factories) and the natural resources of a society. Communism is thus a form of socialism—a higher and more advanced form, according to its advocates. Exactly how communism differs from socialism has long been a matter of debate, but the distinction rests largely on the communists' adherence to the revolutionary socialism of Karl Marx.

In conjunction with the clarification presented by Dr. Peter Hudis, the above definitions confirm that the terms socialism and communism both refer to the same Marx/Engels social construction having to do with a particular set of governmental ideas. Thus, this present work will use socialism and communism as equivalent notions of human socioeconomic regulation. The defining criteria that is to be used in determining whether appreciable societal institutions, as well as the conduct of humans working within these institutions, are derived from socialist/communist ideas and conceptions is based primarily on whether the society in question is characterized by: 1) government ownership, centralized control or autocratic confiscation, as well as transfer of private property and 2) fundamental societal/communal ownership or centralized authoritative control of the major means of economic production, e.g., mines, mills, factories, natural resources, farms, transportation structures, procurement and warehousing functions, sales and product distribution businesses, banks, etc. In a revealing, and quite succinct, expression of his authoritarian socioeconomic model and theory of government, Marx stated that "The theory of communism may be summed up in one sentence: Abolish all private property" (Cameron, Dan. "Understanding Marxist Socialism." medium. com, July 1, 2018). According to Marx and Engels, the abolition of private property is designed to occur "by means of despotic inroads" (see quote below) and includes individual financial gains, a significant progressive or graduated income tax on personal earnings, as well as the elimination of rights of inheritance:

> The Communist revolution is the most radical rupture with traditional property relations; no wonder that its development involved the most radical rupture with traditional ideas.
>
> But let us have done with the bourgeois objections to Communism.
>
> We have seen above, that the first step in the revolution by the working class is to raise the proletariat to the position of ruling class to win the battle of democracy.
>
> The proletariat will use its political supremacy to wrest, by degree, all capital from the bourgeoisie, to centralise all instruments of production in the hands of the State, i.e., of the proletariat organised as the ruling class; and to increase the total productive forces as rapidly as possible.
>
> Of course, in the beginning, this cannot be effected except by means of despotic inroads on the rights of property, and on the conditions of bourgeois production; by means of measures, therefore, which appear economically insufficient and untenable, but which, in the course of the movement, outstrip themselves, necessitate further inroads upon the old social order, and are unavoidable as a means of entirely revolutionising the mode of production.
>
> These measures will, of course, be different in different countries.
>
> Nevertheless, in most advanced countries, the following will be pretty generally applicable.
>
> 1. Abolition of property in land and application of all rents of land to public purposes.
> 2. A heavy progressive or graduated income tax.
> 3. Abolition of all rights of inheritance.
> 4. Confiscation of the property of all emigrants and rebels.
> 5. Centralisation of credit in the hands of the state, by means of a national bank with State capital and an exclusive monopoly.

6. Centralisation of the means of communication and transport in the hands of the State.

7. Extension of factories and instruments of production owned by the State; the bringing into cultivation of waste-lands, and the improvement of the soil generally in accordance with a common plan.

8. Equal liability of all to work. Establishment of industrial armies, especially for agriculture.

9. Combination of agriculture with manufacturing industries; gradual abolition of all the distinction between town and country by a more equitable distribution of the populace over the country.

10. Free education for all children in public schools. Abolition of children's factory labour in its present form. Combination of education with industrial production, &c, &c. (Marx, Karl, and Friedrich Engels. *Manifesto of the Communist Party.* Marxists.org, online)

Manifesto of the Communist Party (1848), as detailed above, visibly represents a tangible document (lower right quadrant) that reveals the social construction, i.e., an inter-subjective composition, of a set of ideas, conceptualizations and envisioned societal goals (lower left quadrant), which also includes an outline of specific behavioral prescriptions that will guide obedient and cooperating human actors in reaching the "destination" (as in the functioning of a "kyberman") of a socialist/communist nation-state (lower right quadrant).

Societal visions of a socialist state can be referenced as far back as Plato's *Republic*. Plato put forth a model of society structured upon three distinct groups: 1) a group of elite central planners, 2) police/military authorities and 3) a group of those that produce. The producers were to have much of their lives determined according to a specific master plan. The work of each person was assigned by the planning administrators of the state based on assessed ability. The nationalization of both property and material production by the central planners would allow for the distribution of produced goods based on individual needs, as determined by the master governing class. The award of social positions of prestige would, of course, also be determined by the ruling group.

The lower right quadrant of external human experience represents the observable domain of socioeconomic systems and political structures. The positive identification of advantageous governmental functioning affording broadly shared economic benefits (ascertained by means of quantitative analysis of pertinent data), as well as the existence of generally effective social systems, are the essential assessment criteria employed so as to determine the integrity, i.e., truth, of societal institutions. In other words, is the organizational system actually operating in the way that partisans, advocates and administrators contend based on objective data? Is the overall system a functional or dysfunctional social arrangement? And is there a wide availability of economic opportunity affording measurable "bread-and-butter" benefit for the largest portion of citizens? These discernable and measurable factors are among the key criteria that are used to determine the functional authenticity, i.e., truth of a social system. "Marx and Engels argued that an individual or an era must be judged not by what they intend or conceive, but by what they actually accomplish. Marxism itself cannot be exempt from this standard" (*Marxism: Economics and Philosophy*, previously referenced). The intentions of Marx and Engels, as well as their social construction of socialism/communism, are in in the left-hand quadrants of human experience, while the accomplishments realized through implementing the notions of socialism/communism are precisely located in the lower right quadrant.

More than one hundred and seventy years has passed since the publishing of the Marx and Engels socioeconomic model of socialism. Marx and Engels claimed that their socioeconomic model was a "scientific socialism" as compared to the "utopian socialist" society advocated by Robert Owen (New Harmony, Indiana), along with a number of other "utopian socialists." Therefore, the "accomplishments" (lower right quadrant) of applying the ideas and conceptions related to the system of human social ordering (lower left quadrant), as proffered by Marx and Engels, are most certainly subject to objective assessment via the methodologies of modern science. While the work of James Clerk Maxwell on electromagnetic radiation and field theory equations occurred during the lifetime of Marx and Engels, the impact on philosophy and modern science due to these findings was not fully appreciated during the life span of these two men. Thus, neither theorist could have intellectually entertained, or practically considered, a worldview remotely comparable to that offered by post-postmodern theory. The period during which Marx and Engels socially constructed their model of socialism/communism was most powerfully intellectually influenced by modernism, plus several critical challenges to certain tenets of the modern perspective, as well as the remaining philosophical and metaphysical considerations contained in the afterglow of a premodern worldview.

The perspective offered by contemporary Integral Theory affords an appraisal of the "accomplishments" of communism/socialism that is quadrant specific and, therefore, fittingly objective in methodology, ensuring fair and repeatedly testable results. Assuredly, the creators of socialism/ communism had heard the adage, "Be careful what you wish for, lest it come true!" (*Aesop's Fables*, 260 BC), because in arguing that an individual or era must be judged by "accomplishments," not simply intentions and abstract conceptions, their socially constructed ideas of government having to do with the political and socioeconomic organization of a nation-state, have realized nothing other than abject failure.

The theorists that socially constructed the socialist/communist socioeconomic conception of social order proposed that their theoretical model, aka "scientific materialism," would transform society into a "heaven on earth" via the realization of equity in both political power and material well-being. And, in the Soviet Union, the proponents of socialism also believed that these ideas of government would actually create "the new Soviet person." This new human creation would become selfless, learned and, of course, a faithful evangelist for the socialist revolution. Leon Trotsky remarked in detail about the "Communist man" or "man of the future," stating that

> Man will make it his purpose to master his own feelings, to raise his instincts to the heights of consciousness, to make them transparent, to extend the wires of his will into hidden recesses, and thereby to raise himself to a new plane, to create a higher social biologic type, or, if you please, a superman. (Trotsky, Leon. *Literature and Revolution*. Soviet Government, 1924)

Thomas DiLorenzo, a Mises Institute senior faculty member, notes a similar quote from Trotsky referencing the communist fanatic's near-magical belief in the transformative ability of socialism for every human being, saying that

> Socialist icon Leon Trotsky predicted that once socialism had destroyed the

division of labor: "[M]an will become incomparably stronger, wiser, finer. His body more harmonious, his movements more rhythmic, his voice more musical....The human average will rise to the level of an Aristotle, a Goethe, a Marx." Only a child (or infantile-minded adult) could believe such a thing. (DiLorenzo, Thomas J. *The Problem with Socialism*. Regnery Publishing, 2016)

The unmitigated grandiosity of Trotsky is plainly the equivalent of most any zealot of a fundamental religious ideology and was no doubt derived from, and surely encouraged by, the quite lofty beliefs set forth in the following quotes by two foundational theorists of socialism:

The Christian...imagines the better future of the human species...in the image of heavenly joy....We, on the other hand, will have this heaven on earth. (Hess, Moses. *A Communist Confession of Faith*. London, 1846)

In communist society, where nobody has one exclusive sphere of activity but each can become accomplished in any branch he wishes, society regulates the general production and thus makes it possible for me to do one thing today and another tomorrow, to hunt in the morning, fish in the afternoon, rear cattle in the evening, criticise after dinner, just as I have a mind, without ever becoming hunter, fisherman, herdsman or critic. (Marx, Karl. *The German Ideology*, 1845)

Marx's notion of socialism/communism is vehemently anti-religion, as shown in the following quote from Marx himself (Note: The subsequent quotes regarding socialism's atheistic character are sourced from slife.org/marxist-leninist-atheism/):

The abolition of religion, as the illusory happiness of the people, is the demand for their real happiness. To call on them to give up their illusions about their condition is to call on them to give up a condition that requires illusions. The criticism of religion is, therefore, in embryo, the criticism of that vale of tears of which religion is the halo. (Marx, Karl. *Critique of Hegel's Philosophy of Right*. Paris, 1844)

Marx further emphasizes his anti-religious position, stating that "Communism begins from the outset (Owen) with atheism; but atheism is, at first, far from being communism; indeed, that atheism is still mostly an abstraction..." (Marx, Karl. *Private Property and Communism*, 1844). Engels subsequently joins in the assault on religion in the following quote:

...when society, by taking possession of all means of production, and using them on a planned basis, has freed itself, and all its members, from the bondage in which they are now held, by these means of production, which they, themselves, have produced, but which confront them as an irresistible alien force, when, therefore, man no longer merely proposes, but also disposes—only then will the last alien force, which is still reflected in religion, vanish; and with it will also vanish the religious reflection itself, for the simple reason that then there will be nothing left to reflect....The real unity of the world consists in its materiality, and this is proved, not by a few juggled phrases, but by a long and wearisome development of philosophy and natural science. (Engels, Friedrich. *Anti-Dühring*. Leipzig, 1878)

The socialist/communist zealot Vladimir Lenin described scientific materialism as synonymous with Marxism, arguing that

Marxism is materialism. As such, it is as relentlessly hostile to religion as was the materialism of the eighteenth-century Encyclopaedists or the materialism of Feuerbach. This is beyond doubt. But the dialectical materialism of Marx and Engels goes further than the Encyclopaedists and Feuerbach, for it applies the materialist philosophy to the domain of history, to the domain of the social sciences. We must combat religion—that is the ABC of all materialism, and consequently of Marxism. But Marxism is not a materialism which has stopped at the ABC. Marxism goes further. It says: "We must know how to combat religion, and in order to do so we must explain the source of faith and religion among the masses in a materialist way. The combating of religion cannot be confined to abstract ideological preaching, and it must not be reduced to such preaching. It must be linked up with the concrete practice of the class movement, which aims at eliminating the social roots of religion." (Lenin, Vladimir. *Socialism and Religion*, 1905)

Professor Eric Voegelin, in his book *Science, Politics and Gnosticism* (Regnery Publishing, 1968), further establishes Marx's rejection of either a transcendent or immanent deity by referencing the following quote from Marx's doctoral dissertation of 1840–41:

> Philosophy makes no secret of it. The confession of Prometheus, "In a word, I hate all the gods," is its own confession, its own verdict against all gods heavenly and earthly who do not acknowledge human self-consciousness as the supreme deity. There shall be none beside it.

While originally from Marx's critique of Hegel, it was the dutiful student of Marx and Engels, Vladimir Lenin, who perhaps most assertively expressed the following phrase: "Religion is opium for the people."

There is no doubt Marx and Engels, as well as their socialist brethren, were intellectually smitten by the power of modern science to perform precise measurement of observables in the material world, and then to use this exact knowledge to accurately predict the status of related future material events, i.e., specific predictability. The intellectual seduction by modern science was arguably absolute as these theorists of "scientific materialism," aka socialism, conspicuously embraced a conceptual worldview now identified as "flatland." Corey deVos defines "flatland" as "1. When the interior quadrants (the Left-Hand path) are reduced to the exterior quadrants (the Right-Hand path). For example, scientific materialism....The 'bad news' of Modernity. See gross reductionism and subtle reductionism. 2. Using any one level as the only level in existence" (deVos, Corey. Flatland. integrallife.com, February 5, 2017). To add further clarity regarding the conceptual nature of "scientific materialism," the following definition is useful: "Materialism, also called physicalism, in philosophy, the view that all facts (including facts about the human mind and will and the course of human history) are causally dependent upon physical processes, or even *reducible* [emphasis added] to them" (*Britannica*, online).

While ostensibly rejecting religion and spirituality, Marx and Engels ironically evoked what is surely a "faith" in an intangible "spirit" plainly inherent within their peculiar worldview. They, along with other socialist theorists, endowed their worldview of a scientific materialism (lower left quadrant) with a superhuman and indeed near miraculous ability to create a manifest social world (lower right quadrant) where life for humans would be glorious beyond human precedent, fulfilling in every imaginable way and void of all material want. In this way, very material humans would create a "heaven on earth." Clearly, the Marx/Engels social construction of the notion of government known as socialism/communism is a system of belief as utopian as those proffered by either Robert Owen or Charles Fourier. And while the immaterial heaven, of which several religions maintain faith, is universally acknowledged as being unable to be analyzed by means of objective scientific methodologies, the tangible "heaven on earth" as prophesied by Moses Hess and other socialists is totally capable of being assessed by objective measures. In fact, the process by which truth is established in the lower right quadrant of human experience, where societal institutions are located, is precisely the modern scientific empirical method of investigation and study as derived from the Enlightenment.

In the year 2022, in all of Eastern and Western Europe, there is not a single nation that is socialist, including those in Scandinavia. Bernie Sanders, as well as other American politicians who are socialist/communist apologists and advocates, often state their desire for America to become a socialist nation like Sweden and Denmark. These statements are prime examples of lies, trickery and obfuscation. To wit, both Sweden and Denmark are free market capitalist nations where the private ownership of property is fully supported and private enterprise controls "the means of production." In an article published on October 31, 2015, the Danish Prime Minister Lars Lokke assertively states "I know that some people in the US associate the Nordic model with some sort of socialism.... Therefore, I would like to make one thing clear. Denmark is far from a socialist planned economy. Denmark is a market economy" (Yglesias, Matthew. "Danish prime minister says Bernie Sanders is wrong to call his country socialist." vox.com). Sweden is also clearly a free-market capitalist nation where private property rights are respected and the means of production is kept safely away from a central planning government institution.

In discussing the disaster that was Sweden's experiment with "democratic socialism," writer Rainer Zitelmann offers the following report:

The image of Sweden and other Scandinavian countries as strongholds of socialism harks back to the 1970s and 1980s. During the period of socialist welfare-state expansion from 1970 to 1991, Sweden dropped far behind many of its European competitors. Sweden's economic growth rate was lower than in a number of other countries, including Italy, France, Germany, the UK and the Netherlands. From fourth place in the Organisation for Economic Co-operation and Development's (OECD) per-capita GDP ranking in 1970, socialist-era Sweden had dropped to 16th place by 1995. In the decade from 1965 to 1975, the number of civil servants swelled from 700,000 to 1.2 million, a rise that was accompanied by increasing government intervention in economic affairs and the creation of a number of new regulatory authorities. Between 1970 and 1984, the public sector absorbed the entire growth of the Swedish workforce, with the largest number of new jobs created in the social services sector. In order to understand the full extent of Sweden's disastrous flirtation with socialism, it is well worth taking a closer look at the development of two key groups: In 1960, for every 100 "market-financed" Swedes (i.e., those who derived their income predominantly from private enterprise), there were 38 who were "tax-financed" (i.e., dependent on the public sector for their income, whether as civil servants or as welfare recipients). Thirty years later, that number had risen to 151.... These figures reflect Sweden's move away from a capitalist free-market economy to a socialist model during that period.

Zitelmann further comments that

From the 1990s, however, a counter-movement emerged in Sweden to push back against the clearly catastrophic effects of "democratic socialism." There was a major tax reform in Sweden in 1990/91: corporate taxes were slashed almost in half; the tax on share dividends was abolished; capital gains from shares were taxed at a greatly reduced rate, which was later eliminated completely; and the top marginal income tax rate was cut by a third. While income tax rates have come down considerably from their peak in the 1970s and 1980s, they are still higher than in many other countries. However, what many don't realize is that other taxes have been completely abolished in Sweden, including: wealth taxes; and inheritance and gift taxes. In stark contrast, socialists of Bernie Sanders and Elizabeth Warren's ilk want to drastically increase wealth and inheritance taxes in the United States. ("Bernie Sanders Dreams of 'Scandinavian Socialism.' The only problem? It has long since failed." forbes. com, Nov 11, 2019)

Most notably, Denmark ranks 8th in the "Free" category on the Heritage Foundation 2020 "Index of Economic Freedom" and Sweden is placed at 22nd in the "Mostly Free" class, only five places behind the USA. Every Scandinavian nation embraces free-market capitalism but maintains a high taxation level so as to fund expansive and expensive social programs, but their socioeconomic structure is categorically not socialism.

In order to make an accurate socioeconomic assessment of nations that have actually established state socialism, what was "intended" by political leaders and planners will be ignored; rather, the focus of objective analysis will be on that which was actually "accomplished," just as Marx and Engels insisted. As Marion Smith (previously referenced) states: "... Ideas have consequences...." Each country listed below reached a high level of governmental ownership, or centralized direction of the major "means of production," and also reached nearly-complete elimination of private property, substantial elimination of personal real estate, control of individual land ownership or the confiscation and transfer of private property— qualifying them as socialist/communist nations. (Note: All "observables," representing the "accomplishments" realized through the implementation of the socially constructed socioeconomic reality called socialism/communism [lower left quadrant] presented in the assessments of the nation-states to follow, are in the lower right quadrant of objective human experience.)

Romania: Along with significant confiscation of private property, as outlined above in "Decree 92…April 19, 1950," the socially constructed design and destination of this socialist central planning economic enterprise entailed destroying towns and communities across the entire country, as well as forcing residents to move to "agrotechnical centers" where they were required to work in government determined and forced work situations. One Romanian farmer, Constantin Surescu, reported on police conduct, saying that "They ordered us to destroy our own houses. Many people said, 'don't want to do this.' If you said 'No.' they came in the night and got you and beat you up." In the same newspaper article, another

Romanian citizen, Gheorghe Cristea, described roads lined with skele-
tons, stating that "Not even in war would it look like this" (Lederer, Edith.
"Villagers Lament Ceausescu's Razing of Homes: Romania..." *Los Angeles
Times*, March 4, 1990). That human beings resisted having their house
and property confiscated by government agents is not surprising. After
all, mammals are keenly interested in "territory," as home and property
are intimately related to the most basic of life-sustaining needs, as detailed
in Abraham Maslow's *Hierarchy of Needs*. Naturally, other mammals,
such as the bobcat and badger, also do not easily or willingly surrender
their "den" to predatory intruders! From 1947 to 1989, it is estimated that
over 400,000 people died of political/government actions, i.e., democide
directly related to implementing the socialist ideas of government. With
the socialist/communist government controlling the economy, Romania
recorded a significant economic decline at the end of the 1980s, resulting
in a massive reduction in living standards.

The citizens of Romania experienced dreadful circumstances in their
daily life where food shortages became common, requiring the socialist
government to introduce particular cards intended for a strict supervision
of food stocks. With socialist central planners in full control of the nation,
the attempt to solve the ongoing food shortages resulted in the following
government dictate: "In 1981, a restrictive decree stated that those who
purchased basic food products in quantities exceeding the needs of one
month of household consumption will be imprisoned for six months to
five years." Everyday citizens lived under constant fear of the socialist
government, as shown in the following quotation:

> Despite living in these harsh conditions, criticizing the Party was close
> to impossible, as whoever dared speak against the Communist regime
> was severely punished by the Department of State Security. The Securi-
> tate was the secret police agency of the Socialist Republic of Romania,
> and it closely monitored all Romanian citizens, especially the ones with
> foreign connections. Leaving the country was also a far-away dream
> for most of the citizens. Those who tried it risked many years of prison
> and torture. Going to church was also illegal, and the trust between
> friends or family was basically non-existent, as anyone could have been

a member of the secret police. (rolandia.eu/en/blog/history-of-romania/
romania-under-nicolae-ceausescu-s-communist-regime)

The socialist requirement of (1) a significant elimination of private
property and (2) government control or ownership of the major means
of economic production, resulted in widespread misery for Romanian
citizens, providing a clear demonstration of the inability of socialism/
communism to produce a functional human society.

Zimbabwe: On the continent of Africa, Robert Mugabe won election in
1980 as the first black prime minister in Zimbabwe. Prior to winning the
election, he spent ten years in prison for anti-government activities. While
incarcerated, Mugabe engaged in an intense study of the political and economic ideas of Marx and Lenin. After Mugabe reached power, he began to
implement the socialist/communist requirement of seizing private property.
"As a self-proclaimed communist and socialist, Mugabe installed a socialist experiment in Zimbabwe. His most notorious economic policy was
'land reform'....Government-backed ZANU militias were at the forefront
to enforce the 'land reform' with violence...." (Raleigh, Helen. "Dictator
Robert Mugabe Is What Happens When a Country Falls for a Charismatic
Leader." *The Federalist*, September 17, 2019, online). In forcibly confiscating
farmland, Mugabe was simply following the written directions of Marx and
Engels, as outlined in their social construction of a socialist/communist
model of government, which clearly insists on the appropriation of private
property by means of despotic inroads (*Manifesto of the Communist Party*,
previously referenced). Before the establishment of the socialist/communist
government of Mugabe, Zimbabwe was known as the "breadbasket" of
Africa and exported 40% of its agricultural production. With the occurrence
of farms confiscated by the government, new and inexperienced farmers
produced not food, but rather a catastrophe. Zimbabwe soon ended up
with a need to import more than 60% of its food needs.

As Mugabe concentrated the nation's economic activities under centralized socialist control, the results were as follows:

> The rest of the economy fell along with the agriculture industry: Banks closed,
> factories shut down, and the unemployment rate skyrocketed. Zimbabwe's

gross domestic product per capita dropped from $1,105 in 1980 (the begin-
ning of Mugabe's reign) to $397 in 2007. Average life expectancy dropped
from 60 years in 1980 to 46 in 2007, the lowest in the world. (*The Federalist*,
previously referenced)

In order to keep firm control of the nation, Mugabe used torture,
imprisonment and murder, resulting in up to 50,000 deaths (Kudenga, Kel-
vin. "Mugabe should be jailed for his murderous crimes." *The Zimbabwean*,
July 21, 2017, online). To clearly illustrate the economic fiasco that is realized
when a socialist/communist government manages a nation, Zimbabwe
ranks second in history as reaching the highest level of inflation: "Imagine
prices doubling every twenty-four hours. That's exactly what happened in
Zimbabwe's run-in with hyperinflation in November 2008 when inflation
reached unheard-of levels of 79 billion percent." Furthermore, "…attempts
to redistribute land from white Zimbabweans for political capital sent the
economy into a free fall, prompted capital flight, and sent people running
for the hills" (Henderson, Andrew. "The Five Worst Cases Of Hyperinflation
In World History." *Nomad Capitalist*, December 29, 2019, online). As a
result of this hyperinflation, Zimbabwe had to abandon its currency and
begin to use the US dollar and the South African Rand.

Cambodia: A seven year-long civil war in Cambodia ended in 1975 with
the victory of the Khmer Rouge, i.e., "Red Khmers." This political group
was composed of ferociously zealous Marxist socialist/communists. With
socialists firmly in charge of supervising, and practically managing, Cambodian society, farms and factories were commandeered by communist
forces. Citizens were not only prevented from engaging in religious practices, but family ties were also severed. In 1977, children were taken from
their parents and placed into labor camps and taught to see the "State" as
their family. All cities and towns were emptied by the military.

The Khmer Rouge claimed that they were creating Year Zero through their
extreme reconstruction methods. They believed that Cambodia (which was
called Kampuchea from 1975–79) should be returned to an alleged "golden
age" when the land was cultivated by peasants and the country ought to be
ruled for and by the poorest amongst society. They wanted all members of

society to be rural agricultural workers rather than educated city dwellers, who the Khmer Rouge believed had been corrupted by western capitalist ideas....Khmer Rouge ideology stated that the only acceptable lifestyle was that of poor agricultural workers. Factories, hospitals, schools and universities were shut down. Lawyers, doctors, teachers, engineers and qualified professionals in all fields were thought to be a threat to the new regime. ("Khmer Rouge Ideology." Holocaust Memorial Day Trust, online)

With the socialist/communist party having complete control of both property and all economic matters, citizens were forced into slavery work situations. Any resistance to the human actors carrying out the ideas of socialism/communism was met with brutal force.

Victims of the Khmer Rouge could be shot for knowing a foreign language, wearing glasses, laughing, crying or expressing love for another person. Minority ethnic groups were also victims of the Khmer Rouge. Ethnic Chinese, Vietnamese and Thai people became targets of the racism encouraged by Pol Pot. Religious believers were sought out and half the Cham Muslim population was murdered alongside 8,000 Christians. By 1977 there were barely any functioning Buddhist monasteries left in Cambodia. (Holocaust Memorial Day Trust, previously referenced)

It has been estimated that between one and three million citizens were murdered by dutiful human agents following the socialist/communist notions of the Khmer Rouge governing structure. Yet, according to researcher Kristian Niemetz, "...Khmer Rouge socialism was once seen as romantic, agrarian, back-to-the-roots by some mainstream intellectuals." And after objectively assessing the actuality, not the intent (per Marx and Engels), of the socialist/communist Cambodian government's management of this nation (lower right quadrant), Niemetz comments that "It is virtually impossible to find a Western supporter of the Khmer Rouge today" (Niemetz, Kristian. *Socialism: The Failed Idea That Never Dies.* The Institute of Economic Affairs, 2019). The nation of Cambodia under socialist governance quickly became an economic disaster of horrendous proportions, and for everyday citizens, most certainly not a Hessian "heaven on earth," but rather a very real hell on earth!

Cuba: In 1959, after a three-year battle against the Fulgencio Batista-led government of Cuba, the revolutionary leader and socialist Fidel Castro emerged victorious. The Castro-led central planning government and socialist economic system was characterized by extreme authoritative directives supposedly aimed at achieving the universal socialist goals of economic equity and political egalitarianism.

> During his nearly five decades of rule in Cuba, Fidel Castro built a repressive system that punished virtually all forms of dissent, a dark legacy that lives on even after his death....The repression was codified in law and enforced by security forces, groups of civilian sympathizers tied to the state, and a judiciary that lacked independence. Such abusive practices generated a pervasive climate of fear in Cuba, which hindered the exercise of fundamental rights, and pressured Cubans to show their allegiance to the state while discouraging criticism....Many of the abusive tactics developed during his time in power—including surveillance, beatings, arbitrary detention, and public acts of repudiation—are still used by the Cuban government. (Human Rights Watch, November 26, 2016, online)

Over 140,000 citizens have been killed by agents of Cuba's socialist government (Rummell, R. J. "How Many Did Communist Regimes Murder?" hawaii.edu/powerkills/COM.ART.HTM).

With total control of economic central planning, an iron fist management of the citizenry, and guidance from enlightened socialist economists, as well as other sapient stewards of government, Castro certainly should have been able to shepherd Cuba into the desired and expected socialist/communist "heaven on earth" (per the socialist theorist Moses Hess). In a 2016 article, economist Tim Worstall outlined details regarding the results of Castro's application of socialist ideas, stating that "...in 1959, when Castro took power, GDP per capita for Cuba was some $2,067 a year. About two thirds of Latin America in general and about the same as Ecuador (1,975), Jamaica (2,541), Panama (2,322) and two thirds of Puerto Rico (3,239)...by the standards of the time, doing reasonably well." Worstall adds the following data: "...By 1999, 40 years later, Cuba had advanced hardly at all, to $2,307, while Ecuador had, relatively, jumped to 3,809, Jamaica to 3,670, Panama to 5,618 and Puerto Rico to 13,738." Worstall further offers this concise assessment of the economic accomplishments of socialism/communism:

> That scientific socialism of the Soviet type makes one great claim—or at least it did when it could still be said without people bursting into great gales of laughter. That by planning the economy, by doing away with the exploitation of capitalism and the chaos of markets, socialism would make the people rich. We then ran the world's largest economic controlled experiment, something we call the 20th century, and found that socialism does not achieve this. ("Fidel Castro's Economic Disaster in Cuba." *Forbes,* November 26, 2016, online)

North Korea: The online *Encyclopedia Britannica* provides the following facts concerning North Korea: "The first constitution of the Democratic People's Republic of Korea was promulgated in 1948 and was replaced with a new constitution in 1972…Revisions were made in 1992, 1998, 2009, and 2016…." The constitution is characterized as "The DPRK Socialist Constitution…." The socioeconomic model of the nation is described as follows: "North Korea has a command (centralized) economy. The state controls all means of production, and the government sets priorities and emphases in economic development. Since 1954, economic policy has been promulgated through a series of national economic plans….North Korea's economic goals have always been linked to the general government policy of self-reliance (juche, or chuch'e)." The general arrangement of land ownership and farming in North Korea is described by Yoo Gwan Hee in an article at *Daily NK* (March 5, 2010, online.), which states that

> The collective farming system, implemented over the course of 1954–1958, resulted in farmers becoming employees on collective farms. The pretext for the collective farming system was communal ownership under the socialist system, but in reality it was a way to realize state control. Article 5 of the Land Reform Law was abolished and the farmers' dreams of personal and equitable land ownership were swept away in the name of socialist modernization.

Human Rights Watch (hrw.org/world-report/2019/country-chapters/north-korea) reports that personal employment, as well as individual occupational pursuits in socialist/communist North Korea, are anything but "free," with government officials both appointing people to specific jobs and managing forced labor camps, which includes child labor. A large majority of citizens perform labor with no compensation at some point in their lifetime. And, if a worker fails to appear at their workplace, this "crime" can result in three to six months of forced work in a hard labor camp. With the above details in mind, the North Korean socioeconomic system and land ownership structure undeniably fit the socialist model of government.

The "accomplishments" of the socialist structure of North Korea are extremely dismal. The GDP (per capita) of North Korea reflects the poor economic performance of the nation: 2013 = $1,800, 2014 = $1,800 and 2015 = $1,700. Comparing these figures to South Korea reveals the following figures: 2015 = $37,600, 2016 = $38,500 and 2017 = $39,500 (all in 2017 US dollar valuation). And assessing the GDP "purchasing power parity" of North Korea reveals these figures: 40 billion 2013, 40 billion 2014 and 40 billion 2015 (in 2015 US dollar valuation). The comparable South Korean numbers are: 2015 = $1.918 trillion, 2016 = 1.972 trillion and 2017 = 2.035 trillion (in 2017 US dollar valuation) (Indexmundi.com/factbook/compare/south-korea.north-korea/economy). According to online *Trading Economics*, the North Korean 2019 GDP value represents 0.01 percent of the world economy.

The socialist/communist central planning structure of North Korea has also contributed to tragic famine. Erin Blakemore wrote an article titled "North Korea's Devastating Famine" and revealed that, during the 1990s, "...a huge famine...affected the 25 million-person country due to poor planning, isolation and a misguided policy of self-sufficiency. But though the famine may have killed many millions, its true extent has never been understood in the West, and it appears never to have been publicly acknowledged by North Korean officials." Blakemore also indicates that, as of 2018, United Nations officials suggest that 40% of North Koreas are malnourished, experience insufficient health care and cope with poor sanitation conditions (history.com/news/north-koreas-devastating-famine). The most horrendous "accomplishments" of North Korea's socialist/communist governmental system are related to imprisonment and murder. Katie Dangerfield, writing in *Global News*, indicates that, with a long historical practice of imprisoning citizens for political reasons, North Korea is still estimated to have 200,000 adults and children in concentration camp/prison environments ("North Korean prisons: UN reports torture, starvations and executions." August 9, 2017, online). The total number of murders committed by the agents of the socialist/communist North Korean system of government, between the years 1948 to 1987, is reported to stand at 1.66 million (https://healthresearchfunding. org/19-shocking-statistics-democide/).

In summarizing the horrific human rights violations of North Korea's socialism/communism system of government, the *NZ Herald* published an article titled "Hell on earth: The Horrors of North Korean torture camps" (June 20, 2017, online), noting that

> In a 2014 report, the United Nations Human Rights Commission called North Korea "a state that does not have any parallel in the contemporary world" due to the country's "systematic, widespread and gross human rights violations." Beatings are widespread in the camps, in which guards are given near-absolute authority to abuse and kill prisoners, according to survivors who have survived to speak out.

Venezuela:

> Despite having the world's largest oil deposits at about 1.3 trillion barrels, Venezuela has taken socialism's path downward from the 4th to the 82nd wealthiest nation on Earth. Venezuela in 1950 had the fourth largest domestic GDP per capita at $7,424 per capita versus $9,573 for the United States as the world's leader. The United States is still the world's leader in 2019 at $65,061, but Venezuela has collapsed to just $3,100. (Street, Chris. "Venezuela's path from 4th to 82nd wealthiest nation." *American Thinker*, 2019, online)

Venezuela, in 1950, maintained a democratic style of government and was easily the richest nation in South America. When oil prices fell to extremely low levels, the nation found itself deeply in debt. To deal with this crisis, economic decisions were made by officials that included making cuts to social programs, eliminating certain price controls and overvaluing the nation's currency. "The big mistake was not diversifying the economy and being so dependent and so reliant on the petroleum sector. That's virtually the only thing that Venezuela produces, said Michael Shifter, president of the Inter-American Dialogue, a think tank in Washington." (Margolis, Jason. "Venezuela was once the richest, most stable, democracy in Latin America. What Happened?" pri.org, February 7, 2019.)

While Venezuela has the largest oil reserves in the world, corruption contributed to siphoning off huge profits made by the nation's oil production activities, leading to widespread resentment within the general population. Into this climate of social exasperation, and the clamoring for change demanded by the poor and disillusioned citizenry, entered Hugo Chavez. Chavez won the presidency in 1998, and according to an August 17, 2007 report in *The Telegraph*, Chavez intended to make himself "president for life" through certain dramatic changes to the Venezuelan constitution; however, this particular effort failed (McDermott, Jeremy. "Hugo Chavez to make himself president for life." telegraph.co.uk, online). Chavez was initially a member of the "Movement of the Fifth Republic" (formerly the Bolivarian Revolutionary Movement 200), which rejected democracy and sometimes advocated for violent overthrow of existing governmental structures. In 2007, Chavez brought this party into his new political organization called the "United Socialist Party of Venezuela." With the notion of a socialist/communist government as a guide, Chavez embarked on predictable socialist strategies in an attempt to achieve social fairness, political empowerment and economic equity for the citizens of Venezuela.

> There are three main policies implemented by Chavez since 1999 that produced the current crisis: Widespread nationalization of private industry, currency and price controls, and the fiscally irresponsible expansion of welfare programs.... One of Chavez's first actions was to start nationalizing the agriculture sector, supposedly reducing poverty and inequality by taking from rich landowners to give to poor workers. From 1999 to 2016, his regime robbed more than 6 million hectares of land from its rightful owners....After agriculture, the regime nationalized electricity, water, oil, banks, supermarkets, construction, and other crucial sectors." (Di Martino, Daniel. "How Socialism Destroyed Venezuela. (economics21.org, March 21, 2019)

And what have been the "accomplishments" of socialism/communism in Venezuela? The nation's food production fell by 75% over a period of 20 years as the population increased by 33%. And, as noted in an article by Nathan J. Robinson, as of 2018, the poverty rate in Venezuela reached 82% and inflation was almost 1300% ("What Venezuela Tells Us About Socialism." *Current Affairs*, May 29, 2018, online). With 90% of the population living in poverty, an average of 24 pounds of weight has been lost by each citizen (Sequra, Vivian. "Venezuelans report big weight losses in 2017 as hunger hits." *Reuters*, February 21, 2018, online). In 2017, there have been 2,800 cases of child malnutrition and 400 deaths. Adding to poverty and widespread hunger, agents of the socialist government have detained, killed or injured a multitude of civilians, leading to more than 4 million citizens fleeing Venezuela (Beck, Glenn. *Arguing With Socialists*. Threshold Editions, 2020).

Union of Soviet Socialist Republics (Soviet Union): Friedrich Engels, the co-author of the *Manifesto of the Communist Party*, died on August 5, 1895. Engels was preceded in death by his co-writer, Karl Marx, by almost 12 years. Engels' wish for his burial was to be cremated and his ashes cast into the sea. Among the small group in the boat carting Engels' ashes to a watery grave was Eduard Bernstein, the recognized protégé of Engels. Surprisingly, it was Bernstein who first noticed and wrote that Marx and Engels' prediction, regarding the inevitable collapse of capitalism due to ever increasing impoverishment of the working class, was seemingly not occurring, even a half-century after the major communist treatise was published. In support of his observations, Bernstein published a series of articles entitled "Problems of Socialism." For example, "He pointed out that trade unions and democracy had vitiated the raw power of capitalists and had ameliorated capitalism. It no longer made sense, he said, to draw a 'heavy line…between capitalist society on the one side and socialist society on the other,' nor to assume 'an abrupt leap' from one to the other. Moreover, to believe that socialism would somehow accord a solution to all problems was to assume…'miracles.'" Bernstein summarized his developing sense of a re-envisioned socialism in his book *Evolutionary Socialism* (Stuttgart, 1899).

In regard to the published evolutionary socialist ideas of Bernstein, a young Vladimir Lenin commented to his brother in Moscow: "There is only one answer to revisionism: smash its face in!" (Muravchik, Joshua. *Heaven*

On Earth: The Rise and Fall of Socialism. Encounter Books, 2002). Lenin concluded that, while the gap between the capitalists and the proletariat may be shrinking, effective revolution does not necessarily require their uprising. Lenin concluded that with a suitable and effective political organization it could be done for them. In 1917, Lenin led a militant political coalition called the Bolsheviks in a violent takeover of the Russian post monarchy Provisional Government. The Bolsheviks, who changed their name to the Russian Communist Party, immediately established a ruling structure called the Russian Soviet Republic, directed by a Central Committee called the Politburo. For a few years, violent encounters continued with oppositional forces, but with Lenin's group eventually winning out, the Soviet Union was established in 1922. Following Marxist ideology, the Soviets were, of course, interested in changing both the economic system as well as cultural practices. Lenin advocated for, and practiced, his belief in the power of socialism/communism to create a new type of human being: "the new soviet person," i.e., a "superman." Thus, the Soviets focused on altering various aspects of culture, especially religion and education. Challenges to socialist ideology were dealt with by closing opposing newspapers and using censorship to curtail objecting voices in community journals and other publications. A censorship institution was set up in 1922 called the Glavlit. This bureaucratic structure had ultimate censorship power over the arts and all printed materials.

"Public," rather than private, ownership of private property is notably a key ingredient of socialism as outlined by Marx and Engels. Thus,

> In 1929, with only 4% of farms in collectives, Stalin ordered the confiscation of peasants' land, tools, and animals; the kolkhoz [Rus., = collective farm] replaced the family farm. The state would decide how much of what crops were to be produced, how much would be paid to the peasants for their work, and how much would go to the state at what price. Farmers who resisted were persecuted, exiled, even killed....By 1931, more than half of all farms had been collectivized. Low productivity and inordinate government diversion of farm production contributed to a devastating rural famine in 1932–33. ("Collective farm: In the Soviet Union." infoplease.com)

In order to reach the Marxist ideal of controlling the major means of economic production, the private ownership of businesses, manufacturing, financial functions and natural resources was essentially eliminated and came under the supervision and management of agents of the socialist/ communist governmental system. It was illegal for individuals to own a significant property share or engage in private enterprise. In this way, socialist Soviet control of businesses and manufacturing operations reached a total number approaching 45,000.

A series of five-year socioeconomic plans were created by the elite central planners within the Politburo, working dutifully within the socialist/communist governing structure. In order to realize control over the populace and maintain iron-fist management of the citizenry, aggressive and violent measures were implemented by political operatives of the Soviet Union. As perhaps could be expected, a multitude of persons did not readily cooperate with their property being confiscated and being forced into work situations not of their choosing. Estimates of the number of killings, imprisonments, starvation deaths and exiling of private citizens by government agents implementing the notions of a socialist system of human management in the USSR are likely to be over 50 million. Just in the two year period called the "Great Terror" (1937–38), approximately 1 million people were killed (*Arguing With Socialists*, previously referenced).

Establishing a network of forced prison camps was a brutal and infamous socialist/communist technique of human domination and control.

> The Gulag was a system of forced labor camps established during Joseph Stalin's long reign as dictator of the Soviet Union. The word 'Gulag' is an acronym for Glavnoe Upravlenie Lagerei, or Main Camp Administration. The notorious prisons, which incarcerated about 18 million people throughout their history, operated from the 1920s until shortly after Stalin's death in 1953. At its height, the Gulag network included hundreds of labor camps that held anywhere from 2,000 to 10,000 people each. Conditions at the Gulag were brutal: Prisoners could be required to work up to 14 hours a day, often in extreme weather. Many died of starvation, disease or exhaustion—others were simply executed. The atrocities of the Gulag system have had a long-lasting impact that still permeates Russian society today. ("Gulag." history.com, August 21, 2018)

With the population subdued, and socioeconomic central planning firmly in the hands of the wise leaders of the Communist Party, just what were the economic "accomplishments" of this socialist nation? In regard to agricultural management, Georgy Manaev reports the following:

> The USSR got the money for its industrial revolution by exporting crops and grain, which drained food from the whole country. In 1928, all grain stocks that were seized from the peasants, farm products, and other goods were sent abroad. In 1928, the export amounted to 7.4 million rubles. In 1929, it was 3 times more—23 million rubles. A ninefold jump in 1930— 207 million rubles....By the end of the 1920s, in cities, food began to be rationed via food stamps. Not everyone got the necessary rations. State security reported to Stalin what workers were saying: "This fish is rotten like the whole five-year plan is. If it gets worse and worse every day now, then nothing good can be expected in the future. The workers are now so humiliated that they are fed worse than cattle. Delayed earnings, there is no money." ("The human cost of Soviet five-year plans." *Russia Beyond*, October 15, 2020, online)

The dramatic limitations of an economic central planning system to cope with fluctuating consumer needs, realize an adequate supply of demanded goods, maintain an efficient distribution of products, as well as setting effective pricing structures, resulted in chronic shortages of basic consumer items including food, with bread lines an all-too-common feature of life in the USSR.

> By 1970, the Soviet economy reached its high point, with a GDP estimated at about 60% that of the United States…in 1989, its $2,500 billion GDP had dropped to just over 50% of the United States' $4,862 billion. Even more telling, the per capita income in the USSR (pop. 286.7 million) was $8,700, compared to $19,800 in the United States (pop. 246.8 million). Despite Brezhnev's reforms, the Politburo refused to increase the production of consumer goods. Throughout the 1970s and 1980s, average Soviets stood in breadlines as Communist Party leaders amassed ever greater wealth. Witnessing the economic hypocrisy, many young Soviets refused to buy into the old-line communist ideology. As poverty weakened the argument

behind the Soviet system, the people demanded reforms. (Longley, Robert. "Why Did the Soviet Union Collapse?" *ThoughtCo*, March 30, 2019, online)

If the Soviet Union had not had vast reserves of oil and gas enabling export to the west, the economic situation of the nation would have been much worse. For example, during the late 1970s and into the 1980s, oil production increased from 31 million tons to 312 million tons and natural gas generation grew from 9.5 billion cubic meters to 156 billion cubic meters. With chronic economic malaise, enduring social strain experienced by the populace, as well as the general dysfunction of the governmental systems produced by socialist/communist management of the nation, a point of economic collapse was reached in 1991 when the USSR abandoned socialism.

China: The Chinese socialist/communist political phrase and rallying cry "The Great Leap Forward" assuredly ranks among the most grandiose and oxymoronic political utterances on record. *The Black Book of Communism: Crime, Terror, Repression* (Courtois, Stephane et al. Harvard University Press, 1999) records the number of human deaths, due to implementing the notions of socialism/communism in China under the leadership of Mao Zedong, to have reached as many as 65 million. This estimate of human death in China tied to socialism/communism is corroborated by other academics including Dr. Lee Edwards of the Heritage Foundation and Dr. Rudolph Rummel of the University of Hawaii. In following the dictates of socialism, which require that the major means of production must be owned or controlled by governmental structures, and that the private ownership of land must be transferred to a centralized governmental arrangement, severely curtailed or handed over to others persons selected by elite socialist planners, when the Chinese Communist Party was established in 1949, deputies of the socialist government immediately implemented what was called "land reform."

Work teams of Communist Party members were sent to villages to assign each villager to one of the five classes: landlord, rich peasant, middle peasant, poor peasant, or laborer. Most landlords and rich farmers were rounded up and either executed or sent to labor camps. Local governments confiscated their belongings, such as cattle and land, and redistributed them to landless and impoverished farmers. (Raleigh, Helen. "When Communists Redistributed Private Property, My Grandfather Lost Everything." *The Federalist*, June 18, 2017, online)

Recall that Marx and Engels emphatically state, in their *Manifesto of the Communist Party*, that "despotic inroads" are to be justly used to confiscate private property; and subsequently, as many as 10 million farmers had their land confiscated and redistributed to other persons. However, to trust a system of government which has no qualm about using intimidation and deadly force to confiscate private land and property, is to be a fool of the highest order. For example,

> In 1953, the Chinese government announced agricultural collectivization that gradually clawed into state ownership the land it had handed out to poor farmers. By 1958, there was no private land ownership. Private farming was prohibited, and anyone who engaged in it was labeled a counterrevolutionary and persecuted. Farmers were required to sell their produce to the government, and no private sales were allowed. Farmers had a rude awakening when they realized that what the government gives, the government can take it away. (*The Federalist*, previously referenced)

It is not an unexplainable or bewildering coincidence that, one year later in 1959, a horrendous famine developed, which lasted until 1961 and is estimated to have claimed the lives of well over 30 million human beings. In continuing to adhere to the theory and practice of socialism within the nation of China, Mao and his "enlightened" planners developed "The Great Leap Forward," which entailed a second 5-year plan. The intent of this plan was to transform China from a primarily agrarian society to an industrial powerhouse. Beginning in 1958 and continuing through 1960,

> Mao hoped to increase China's agricultural output while also pulling workers from agriculture into the manufacturing sector. He relied, however, on nonsensical Soviet farming ideas, such as planting crops very close together so that the stems could support one another and plowing up to six feet deep to encourage root growth. These farming strategies damaged countless acres

of farmland and dropped crop yields, rather than producing more food with fewer farmers. (Szcepanski, Kallie. "The Great Leap Forward." *ThoughtCo*, September 3, 2019, online)

In an ill-conceived effort to accelerate industrialization and reduce the need to import manufacturing machinery and raw steel, the socialist government transferred millions of people into not just farming communes, but also industrial cooperatives. The workers in the industrial communes were directed to create small iron-making furnaces. Out of desperation to meet strict production quotas, scrap metal from kitchen items and farming tools were often melted so as to achieve production goals. The quantity realized from these primitive metal making operations was, of course, meager, and the metal produced was typically very poor in quality, being virtually useless in practical application (*ThoughtCo*, previously referenced).

In regard to ongoing food production, the accomplishments of socialist central planning remained pathetic, as

...the government in 1953 closed the grain market and monopolized grain trade by fiat, making it illegal for anyone other than the government to engage in large-scale grain trade. In 1954 it expanded the control to include oil seeds, cotton, pork, and other key agricultural commodities. Extracting agricultural surplus was further hampered by the lower level of agricultural productivity in China as compared to more developed countries. With nearly 90 per cent of the population living in the countryside China was producing barely enough food and wearable fibers to meet basic domestic needs. Estimates suggest that the daily average food energy intake in China in the 1950s was around 2000 calories per capita, below the 2350 calories recommended by the United Nations. (Li, Wei. "Maoist Economics." *The New Palgrave Dictionary of Economics*, December 13, 2016, online)

Socialist China has a disastrous record of farm production, an extremely feeble economic performance history, a grim past of utilizing brutal labor prisons, an infamous tradition of employing forced re-education camps and an aggressive practice of banning religion—including outright persecution of Christians, Muslims, Buddhists and Falun Gong. Chinese deputies, charged with indoctrinating the citizenry with the ideology of socialism, demanded rejection of historically anchored sacred practices with a compulsory adoption of faith in Communist Maoism and atheism. The ghastly human rights history, and astonishingly dysfunctional socioeconomic record of socialist/communist China, leads to the accurate assessment of a failed nation-state.

China adopted certain economic reforms in 1979 leading to the nation opening up to foreign investment and trade, as well as moving toward a for-profit market economy, which came to be called by the Chinese Communist Party, "socialism with Chinese characteristics." Predictably, China has since become a much-wealthier nation. Objective data that substantiates the superior functionality (i.e., truth in the lower right quadrant) of a capitalist economy as compared to the dysfunction (i.e., falsity in the lower right quadrant) intrinsic to a socialist/communist economic system is documented, in the case of China, by historian and sociologist Dr. Rainer Zitelmann:

> Today, China is the world's leading export nation, ahead of the United States and Germany. Above all, never before in history have so many people escaped poverty in such a short time as in the past decades in China. According to official World Bank figures, the percentage of extremely poor people in China in 1981 stood at 88.3%. By 2015 only 0.7% of the Chinese population was living in extreme poverty. In this period, the number of poor people in China fell from 878 million to less than ten million. ("China's Economic Success Proves the Power of Capitalism." *Forbes*, July 8, 2019, online)

Unfortunately, social freedom and individual liberty have not expanded in the same manner, as a relic of the socialist/communist authoritarian governmental structure still controls the nation, as evidenced by the maintenance of "re-education camps" as well as the active oppression of both political opposition and free religious practice.

When expanded, the list of failed socialist/communist nation states will include: Yugoslavia, Poland, Mongolia, East Germany, Czechoslovakia, Bulgaria, Albania and Afghanistan. If numerous, third-world countries were added to the list of nations that adopted the deeply flawed, and demonstrably worthless, socioeconomic model of socialism, the number would increase significantly (*Heaven on Earth: The Rise and Fall of*

Socialism, previously referenced). A much easier task is to list all of the world's nations who have achieved a functional governmental system of human social management judged by ensuring trustworthy "bread and butter" basic human needs, engendering broad based economic benefits, enhancing individual and social freedoms, sustaining growth of the country's GDP and supporting widely available social as well as educational advancement through implementing the defining principles of socialism/communism: 1) "Zero."

Thus, there exists an absence of scholars and researchers documenting and lauding the success of socialism/communism when adopted as the guiding governmental system for nation-states; rather, there is a plethora of economic research reports, academic papers and books detailing the disastrous failure of socialism/communism as a theoretical model for the supervision and practical management of a country. Because assessment of political and socioeconomic systems occurs in the lower right quadrant of human experience, objective analysis of relevant data has been replicated producing accordant findings, as evidenced by the consistent judgment of applied socialism/communism as a failed economic theory, as well as a dangerous political model for use by human beings.

The socialism of Mao's China, Lenin-Stalin's USSR, Cambodia, North Korea, Yugoslavia, Ethiopia, Indonesia, Afghanistan, Rwanda, as well as other 20th century socialist/communist-ruled nations, caused as many as 100 million government-connected deaths of private citizens (*The Black Book of Communism: Crimes, Terror, Repression*, previously referenced). In point of fact, as many as seven or eight times more private citizens were killed by socialists/communists in the 20th century than by the German Nazis. While the National Socialism (Nazism) of 20th century Germany is universally (and correctly) perceived as an unacceptable and invalid, i.e., "untrue," social construction of reality, it is completely inconsistent that the far more deadly socialist political conception created by Marx and Engels maintains ardent proponents among certain intellectuals, journalists and politicians in the 21st century. Without resorting to lies, trickery, obfuscation and the employment of social/psychological self-defense mechanisms, support for this preposterous, and extremely lethal, model of human social supervision and system of practical economic management simply cannot be maintained in the face of the compelling amount of objective data (lower right quadrant) invariably revealing the lack of legitimacy, rectitude and functionality of the socialist/communist theory of government.

As an analogy, imagine if the civil engineering firm of "Max and Angels" had socially constructed a "Manifesto of the Superlative Master City" and boldly claimed that their system of municipal design was based on "scientific social theory" and possessed the ability to create a "heavenly city on earth." Several key factors of their design model were emphasized as absolutely essential in order to bring about a city where ordinary men and women would transition to become "supermen" and "superwomen" and this transformation would not be the exception; rather, they would represent the typical inhabitant of these wondrous cities. However, in following the detailed construction specifications and closely implementing the overall model of design for gas mains, water pipes, buildings, rail lines, bridges, sewer systems and road designs—the consequences when completed by city engineers—resulted in dysfunctional sewer systems spreading disease, broken water lines leading to water shortages and life-threatening dehydration, failing building structures causing multiple human casualties, exploding gas mains creating massive numbers of injuries and deaths, roads fracturing under everyday use contributing to a multitude of vehicle accidents and collapsing bridges preventing the shipment of goods and food to the city resulting in shortages of essential human needs. One would expect that it would only take a single city experiencing the catastrophic design failures described above to cause other municipalities to reject and completely abandon the "Max and Angels" model of city design. (Note: no "supermen" or "superwomen" were found among the survivors of the devastation in this "Max and Angels" designed city—or for that matter, among the survivors of the socialist/communist nation of the USSR.)

As noted above, there remain a number of contemporary intellectuals who serve as apologists, as well as advocates, for socialism and there continues to exist organizations that unabashedly claim that they are led by trained Marxists, Cultural Marxists, Neo-Marxists or Race Marxists/Critical Race Theorists (See: Lindsay, James. *Race Marxism: The Truth about Critical Race Theory and Praxis*. New Discourses, LLC, 2022). Amazingly, these social phenomena linger in spite of the plainly observable fact that there is not a single nation on the planet that is presently thriving under the socioeconomic model of socialism/communism and, to reiterate, no nation has ever succeeded (lower right quadrant) following this socially constructed reality crafted by Marx and Engels (lower left quadrant).

Author and journalist Tom Bethell wrote a feature titled "The Mystery of Eric Hoffer" in *The American Spectator* (April 3, 2020, online), and quotes the following discerning assessment offered by Hoffer regarding intellectuals who express support for social theories that promise a classless society:

> The intellectual knows with every fiber of his being that all men are not equal, and there are few things that he cares for less than a classless society. No matter how genuine the intellectual's altruism, he regards the common man as a means. A free society is as much a threat to the intellectual's sense of worth as an automated economy is a threat to the worker's sense of worth. Any social order…which can function well with a minimum of leadership will be an anathema to the intellectual.

Again, objective research is widely available that describes in stark detail the inability of the social conceptions (lower left quadrant) intrinsic to socialism/communism to realize a continuously viable, and truly functional, human society (lower right quadrant). Excepting those persons who are thoroughly ignorant of political and economic history, it is completely obvious that only through the employment of social/psychological self-defense mechanisms such as denial, rationalization and intellectualization, as well as the projection of blame, can one express belief that socialism can successfully be used as a set of social conceptions (lower left quadrant) that will guide humans to produce a functionally valid socioeconomic management system for a nation-state (lower right quadrant). Author Kristian Niemietz, in his book *Socialism: The Failed Idea That Never Dies* (previously referenced), suggests that social psychologist Johnathan Haidt's "social intuitionist model" may offer some measure of understanding of how support for socialism can be maintained in the 21st century, saying that "Haidt showed that a lot of our moral and political reasoning is post-hoc rationalisation. Its primary purpose is not to arrive at a conclusion, but to justify a conclusion after we have reached it.…Intuitions come first, strategic reason comes second." From Haidt's research on "motivated reasoning," Niemietz notes that "Psychologists now have file cabinets full of findings on 'motivated reasoning,' showing the many tricks people use to reach the conclusion they want to reach." Niemietz adds to Haidt's work, Bryan Caplan's theory of "rational irrationality" by offering the following observation: "Caplan shows that there are a lot of economic policy ideas that are demonstrably wrong and rejected by economists of virtually all political persuasions and methodological schools—but nonetheless remain widely popular." Niemietz then summarizes Caplan's research as follows:

> Thus, holding on to a demonstrably wrong belief can be entirely rational, if that belief is a source of pleasure, pride, emotional comfort and perhaps even a sense of identity. It only seems irrational if we erroneously assume that the person holding that belief is motivated solely by a desire to know the truth. Beliefs that are emotionally appealing confer a benefit on the person holding them, irrespective of whether or not they are true.

Yet, ironically as well as distressfully, there may be two additional explanations for how a person in the 21st century can maintain allegiance to the failed socially constructed notion of socialism/communism. The first is faith. Faith is defined as a "firm belief in something for which there is no proof" (*Merriam-Webster*, online). Similarly, faith is also defined as "strong or unshakable belief in something, esp. without proof or evidence" (*The Free Dictionary*, online). A reference to faith as an aid in developing an explanation for why there are persons who continue to maintain a dedication to a socioeconomic system and theory of government that has a tragic failure rate of 100% in dozens of nations is not simply hyperbole. Political Science Professor Paul Kengor, writing at *Crisis Magazine*, offers the following research findings and comments:

> Marx and Engels viewed the initial draft of their manifesto as a revolutionary "catechism" for an awaiting world. More than that, they saw it and referred to it, certainly in the initial draft stage, as a literal Communist Confession of Faith, before opting for the title that stuck. "Think over the Confession of Faith a bit," Engels wrote to Marx in November 1847. "I believe we had better drop the catechism form and call the thing: Communist Manifesto."

Even then, the document was, for these proud atheists, very much a cat-echetical confession of faith for communists. Their communism became their religion, even as they scoffed at religion as something for superstitious idiots. Truly, their manifesto was and became their catechism—their bible.

Kengor also adds the following insightful comment:

...Marion Smith, director of the Victims of Communism Memorial Foun-dation, likes to say that Christians go to heaven, whereas socialists go to communism. That is indeed the transitionary process, and Smith's language is apt, given that the communist views full communism as a sort of New Jerusalem. The atheistic communist, whether realizing it or not, subscribes or aspires to a messianic vision. ("The Communist's Catechism." *Crisis Magazine*, September 2, 2020, online)

The Italian Neo-Marxist Antonio Gramsci, noted as the progenitor of "Cultural Marxism," maintained and emphasized the messianic religious essence of socialism, saying that "Socialism is precisely the religion that must overwhelm Christianity....In the new order, Socialism will tri-umph by first capturing the culture via infiltration of schools, universities, churches, and the media by transforming the consciousness of society" (Kiska, Roger. "Antonio Gramsci's long march through history." www. action.org/religion-liberty/volume-29-number -3, December 12, 2019).

The second additional explanation, that may clarify how one could possibly sustain continued devotion to the thoroughly discredited socio-economic model of socialism/communism, is the grim universal human experience of "Thanatos." Thanatos is a psychological phenomenon first detailed by physician and psychologist Wilhelm Stekel, a professional associate of Sigmund Freud. In Freudian psychology, "Eros" represents the human drive towards life, i.e., propagation, survival and sex. Than-atos is the opposing drive to Eros and represents a movement towards dissolution, destruction and death. The human phenomenon of Thana-tos is understood to be closely associated with the human behaviors of aggression, violence, self-destructiveness and repetitive compulsion. The death drive, i.e., Thanatos, is plainly inherent in the writings of Marx. Within the *Manifesto of the Communist Party*, Marx openly insists that despotism, i.e., tyranny with its naked brutality, must be used to confiscate private property.

> The Communists disdain to conceal their views and aims. They openly declare that their ends can be attained only by the forcible overthrow of all existing social conditions. Let the ruling classes tremble at a Communistic revolution. The proletarians have nothing to lose but their chains. They have a world to win. Working Men of All Countries, Unite! (marxists.org, previously referenced)

It is certainly no mere coincidence that Marx would frequently recite the following line from the character Mephistopheles in *Faust*, which was his favorite play by Goethe: "...for all that comes to be deserves to perish wretchedly..." (Kengor, Paul. *The Devil and Karl Marx: Communism's Long March of Death, Deception and Infiltration*. TAN books, 2020). That Marx agreed with this sentiment of Mephistopheles is demonstrated by his unwavering plan to destroy the ownership of private property, religion, as well as the social and economic situation of successful farmers and business operators. A reading of some of the poetry written by Marx prior to developing the *Manifesto of the Communist Party* is most pertinent, as it reveals what is clearly an ominous and grim character structure. Professor Kengor in his recently published book (2020) quotes the following poem by Marx:

> Look now, my blood-dark sword shall stab
> Unerringly within thy soul.
> God neither knows nor honors art.
> The hellish vapors rise and fill the brain.
> Till I go mad and my heart is utterly changed.
> See the sword—the prince of darkness sold it to me.
> For he beats the time and gives the signs.
> Ever more boldly I play the dance of death.
> I must play darkly, I must play lightly,
> Until my heart and my violin burst.
> The Player strikes up on the violin,
> His blond hair falling down.

> He wears a sword at his side,
> And a wide wrinkled gown."

Economist Murray Rothbard emphasizes the same distinctly morose character of Marx in the following quote:

Marx expressed both his megalomania and his enormous thirst for destruction:

> Heaven I would comprehend
> I would draw the world to me;
> Living, hating, I intend
> That my star shines brilliantly …

and

> Worlds I would destroy forever,
> Since I can create no world;
> Since my call they notice never …

In another poem, Marx writes of his triumph after he shall have destroyed God's created world:

> Then I will be able to walk triumphantly,
> Like a god, through the ruins of their kingdom.
> Every word of mine is fire and action.
> My breast is equal to that of the Creator.

And in his poem "Invocation of One in Despair" Marx writes,

> I shall build my throne high overhead
> Cold, tremendous shall its summit be.
> For its bulwark—superstitious dread
> For its marshal—blackest agony.

(Rothbard, Murray. "Marx's Path to Communism." Mises Institute, September 6, 2012, online)

Economist and social philosopher Thomas Sowell, through most of his academic years as a student, considered himself a Marxist. However, he states that it took one experience as an intern with the U.S. Department of Labor to begin swiftly distancing himself from socialist theory. Sowell offers the following comments after his many years of studying the empirical results in nations that actually implemented the ideas of Marx:

> Socialism is a wonderful idea. It is only as a reality that it has been disastrous. Among people of every race, color, and creed, all around the world, socialism has led to hunger in countries that used to have surplus food to export….Nevertheless, for many of those who deal primarily in ideas, socialism remains an attractive idea—in fact, seductive. Its every failure is explained away as due to the inadequacies of particular leaders. ("Socialist Dream Crashes in Venezuela." higherrevolution.com, December 7, 2015)

In regard to the socioeconomic notion of socialism, entomologist and two-time Pulitzer Prize winner E. O. Wilson adds this concise comment: "Karl Marx was right, socialism works; it is just that he had the wrong species" (Daw, Sonya. "Carpenter Ant." Nps.gov, November, 2019).

Unquestionably, without an intellectual retreat to social/psychological self-defense mechanisms, a desperate emotional appeal to blind faith and/or the dominating presence of a desire to destroy, i.e., Thanatos, an objective analysis of the "accomplishments" (per Marx) of socialism/communism (lower right quadrant) simply cannot support an intellectually coherent justification for a serious discussion—let alone a practical consideration—of the thoroughly discredited model of socioeconomic dynamics, and human social governance, socially constructed and propounded by Marx and Engels. As a sharp rejoinder to the lies, trickery and obfuscation used by devotees and apologists for socialism, "real socialism" has been tried, numerous times, and just as there has never existed an actual Shangri-La, Atlantis or a paradisiacal Arcadia, the fantasy of a socialist/communist "Heaven on Earth" has never existed and, indisputably, will never be realized.

The envious and abiding preoccupation among socialists/communists with owning the major means of production, as well as property within a society, coupled with the recommended tactic of using tyranny, i.e., despotism, to confiscate these assets, has never been a successful economic enterprise. Through the use of this ill-formed—and distinctly destructive—strategy, the "proletariat" have always remained the "proletariat," or put in much worse life circumstances!

Ironically, the very capitalist system that socialists/communists despise and blame for creating and maintaining the poor economic situation of "workers," has created a way for these very same wage earners to reach a greatly improved economic position in society. Through the system of free-market economics, the financial structures of both tax-delayed and taxable investment accounts have been developed. Members of society are thus free to choose actual shared ownership in a variety of "stock market index funds," which can represent as much as 95% of the stock market. This figure clearly represents a huge portion of the "major means of production." Additionally, if one so chooses, investments can also be made in a "Real Estate Investment Trust" (REIT) which includes a broad range of real estate property within its structure. In this way, workers can truly own a wide portion of property in society.

As a practical example, if a worker were to avoid purchasing retail coffee, soda or food items and invest the dollar value of those products, equaling just $3.00 per day for a 5-day work week to total $15.00 per week (or $15.00 divided by 7 days = $2.14 per day) in an Individual Retirement Account using a "S&P 500 stock market index fund" from age 18 to the full social security retirement age of 67 and given an average return of roughly 8% (from 1957 through 2018 the S&P 500 average is about 8% per investopedia.com), the financial situation of the worker would include a private retirement account worth over $430,000.00 (Simple Savings Calculator, bankrate.com). Moving the private investment at age 67 to a more conservative account that earns 4.5% will allow for confidently withdrawing 6% ($25,800.00) of the retirement account per year. This financial strategy will result in a monthly income of $2,150.00, plus Social Security payments. At this altered rate of return within the self-owned retirement account, coupled with the specified rate of withdrawal, the "worker" can maintain this income level for about 29 years and 11 months ("How Long Will Your Savings Last," dollortimes.com).

The website businessinsider.com indicates that the average retirement account for people age 65 and up is $192,887.00. Remarkably, the thought-provoking situation for the financially independent and wise "worker" in the scenario outlined above is that they have slowly, but assuredly, transformed themselves from a member of the "proletariat" to a member of the once-despised "bourgeois," and nobody got killed or had their property stolen by agents of the government dutifully following written procedures of sanctioned social conduct! Many workers have, of course, done something similar to the retirement investment strategy outlined above. However, far too many persons have not been financially prudent and, thus, have left themselves monetarily unprepared and, therefore, both psychologically assailable and emotionally vulnerable to the rhetoric of predatory, authoritarian, as well as economically incompetent politicians.

With respect to the manipulative social techniques of lies, trickery and obfuscation, regarding those persons who maintain an ongoing advocacy for the failed socioeconomic theory of socialism/communism, the following observation by Eric Hoffer is most discerning: "Hatred is the most accessible and comprehensive of all unifying agents....Mass movements can rise and spread without belief in a God, but never without belief in a devil" (Hoffer, Eric. *The True Believer: Thoughts on the Nature of Mass Movements.* Harper & Row, Publishers, Inc., 1951). Regarding this particular point, the philosopher and writer Roger Scruton comments on the political and socioeconomic views held by the Hungarian Cultural Marxist Gyorgy Lukacs, saying that

> With Lukacs we have to do not with the anti-bourgeois snobbery of Foucault....We have to do with hatred. And while this hatred embraces all the "appearances" of the "bourgeois " world, it is directed beyond and behind them, to the hidden devil that they conceal. The devil is "capitalism, " and hatred of capitalism is total and unconditional, justifying every moral breach.

Scruton then notes the following telling quote by Lukacs: "At the time we all felt a bitter hatred for capitalism and all its forms. We wanted to destroy it at all costs and as quickly as possible. You cannot just sample Marxism…you must be converted to it" (Scruton, Roger. *Fools, Frauds, and Firebrands: Thinkers of the New Left.* Bloomsbury Continuum, 2019).

CHAPTER 6

Conclusions from A
Post-Postmodern Philosophy

There are two ways to be fooled. One is to believe what isn't
true; the other is to refuse to believe what is true.
—Søren Kierkegaard

A point of view can be a dangerous luxury when substituted
for insight and understanding.
—Marshall McLuhan

The practice of lying, tricking others into believing something that is incorrect, and obscuring truth is a primordial human practice. In a feature titled "Why We Lie: The Science Behind our Deceptive Ways," author Yudhijit Bhattacharjee offers this quote by Sissela Bok, an ethicist at Harvard University: "Lying is so easy compared to other ways of getting power." Bok also makes the following (rather dramatic) point: "It's much easier to lie in order to get somebody's money or wealth than to hit them over the head or rob a bank." In the same article, the author reports research by Kang Lee, a psychologist at the University of Toronto, revealing that children get better at lying as they get older. In a carefully structured psychological experiment, just before the researcher briefly exited the interviewing room, children were told to not look at a secret toy placed under a solid cover. A summary of the results of this experiment demonstrate that typically three-and-four-year-olds quickly disclosed their transgression when asked whether they looked or not, five-and-six-year-old children were more capable of using deceptive language and seven-and-eight-year-olds were quite adept at lying about their conduct (nationalgeographic.com, June 2017).

Illustrating that neither advanced academic achievement nor higher intelligence provides for a proscription against lying, Thomas Sowell, in his book *Intellectuals and Society* (previously referenced), notes that

> The preservation of the vision of the anointed has led many among the intelligentsia to vigorous and even desperate expedients, including the filtering out of facts, the redefinition of words and—for some intellectuals—challenging the very idea of truth itself. Many among the intelligentsia create their own reality—whether deliberately or not—by filtering out information contrary to their conception of how the world is or ought to be. Some have gone further. J. A. Schumpeter said that the first thing a man will do for his ideals is lie. It is not necessary to lie, however, in order to deceive, when filtering will accomplish the same purpose. This can take the form of reporting selective and atypical samples, suppressing some facts altogether, or filtering out the inconvenient meanings or connotations of words.

Dr. Richard Paul and Dr. Linda Elder, Fellows of the Foundation for Critical Thinking, in their book titled *Fallacies: The Art of Mental Trickery and Manipulation* (Foundation for Critical Thinking Press, 2008), state that "The human mind has no natural guide to the truth, nor does it naturally love the truth. What the human mind loves is itself, what serves it, what flatters it, what gives it what it wants, and what strikes down and destroys whatever 'threatens' it." With respect to the matter of a valued belief, Paul and Elder offer the following observation: "…most people are resistant to recognizing poor reasoning when it supports what they intensely believe in." In further substantiation of this observation, Paul and Elder note that "Any argument, any consideration, any mental maneuver or construction that validates emotionally-charged beliefs seems to the believer to be justified. The more intense the belief, the less likely that reason and evidence can dislodge it." The authors explain that most people are unaware of the following internally held premises: "1) It's true if I believe it. 2) It's true if we believe it. 3) It's true if I want to believe it. 4) It's true if it serves my vested interest to believe it." When personal preference and premeditated intent are operative in relation to advancing a favored social perspective,

Paul and Elder explain: "Manipulators do not use their intelligence for the public good. Rather they use it to get what they want in alliance with those who share their vested interests."

Robert Proctor is a Stanford University professor whose field of study is the history of science. Proctor, along with his colleague Londa Schiebinger, published a book through Stanford University Press in 2008 titled *Agnotology: The Making and Unmaking of Ignorance*. Proctor generated the word "agnotology" and, in the title of the preface, provides this rather succinct definition: "A Missing Term Used to Describe the Cultural Production of Ignorance (and its Study)." In their book, Proctor and Schiebinger offer the following beneficial suggestion: "We need to think about the conscious, unconscious, and structural production of ignorance ..." The authors further designate one specific category of cultural ignorance which is most relevant to this present work: "...ignorance as a deliberately engineered and strategic ploy (active construct)." Thus, the concept of agnotology certainly has to do with the practice of obfuscation, i.e., "...to make obscure or unclear...darken..." (*Merriam-Webster*, online). Proctor is perhaps best known for studying the practice of obfuscation as employed by the cigarette industry, revealing that giant tobacco corporations spent billions of dollars obscuring the scientific facts related to the health hazards of smoking. In emphasizing the ability of scientific knowledge to free humans from ignorance, Proctor offers the following quote from Johannes Kepler: "... ignorance was 'the mother who must die for science to be born.'"

The academic study of lies, trickery and obfuscation, i.e., agnotology, underscores that both individuals and large segments of society are subject to being deceived by well-engineered techniques of linguistic deception employed by cunning representatives and advocates of various misleading and erroneous socially constructed realities.

Greek astronomer and mathematician Aristarchus of Samos (310–c. 230 BCE) developed the first known heliocentric theory of the solar system. Yet, it is Nicolaus Copernicus who is widely credited as the originator of the heliocentric model of the solar system. Most historians agree that while Copernicus was aware that Samos had developed an astronomical model having to do with a moving Earth, he seemingly didn't understand that his theory was also fundamentally heliocentric. The model developed by Copernicus maintained the archaic idea that the movements of celestial bodies must be perfect circles. This restraining notion required him to create the concept of epicycles. i.e., each planetary body moved in a small circular pattern while also orbiting the Sun. Thus, the Copernican theory was quite complex and rather dissatisfying. Particular religious objections as well as the complexity of this theory hindered the model from being broadly accepted.

Johannes Kepler improved upon the Copernican theory through the use of methodologies related to the practice of modern science, including precise observation, rigorous measurement and detailed calculation. Thus, Kepler was able to convincingly demonstrate that the Earth orbits the Sun without the need to employ the cumbersome and manifestly erroneous idea of planetary epicycles, leading to a much wider acceptance of his model. In his book *The New Astronomy* (1609), Kepler effectively demonstrated that the geocentric worldview worked out by Greek theoreticians, and further developed by the Alexandrian astronomer and mathematician Ptolemy (about 150 CE), was untrue. Kepler was working in the "see-touch" domain of human experience (upper right quadrant) and thus his theoretical correspondences having to do with observable objects in the solar system could be precisely tested and re-tested. And, indeed, they have been re-tested with the results that, even in the 21st century, Kepler's concepts, laws and formulae are still used for crucial astronomical calculations. With the investigative methodologies of modern science continuing to dispel the ignorance intrinsic to many premodern perspectives and socially constructed realities, Kepler was a central figure in the transition from a premodern cosmology to a modern worldview.

Contemporary post-postmodern Integral Theory represents a potent intellectual indexing guide able to direct the investigative and truth-finding methodologies of modern science to the two external quadrants of objective human life, while at the same time, guiding specific practices associated with postmodern perspectives, as well as certain long-established premodern spiritual systems of inquiry, to the internal quadrants of human experience. In discerning that humans have genuine experience in four distinct quadrants/domains (with sub-domains), Integral Philosophy is able to avoid much of the quadrant confusion and reductionist thinking (as outlined by LeShan and Margenau) intrinsic to premodern worldviews, modern theorizing and Postmodern Philosophy.

Additionally, the absolutism and radical relativism characteristic of contemporary postmodern thinking and writing is averted, reducing the occurrence of quadrant discord as socially constructed conceptions are practically exercised in society.

The "socially constructed realities" selected for analysis in this present work were chosen based on their enduring controversial nature, the significance of their actual consequences in society, as well as the ability of modern scientific analysis to achieve, as stated by Proctor, the "Unmaking of Ignorance," thus establishing truth. Just as Johannes Kepler used modern philosophy's practice of science to expose the ignorance inherent in the geocentric worldview proffered by premodern theorists, the powerful indexing capacity of post-postmodern Integral Philosophy and Domain Theory was employed in this present work to "unmake" the lies, trickery and obfuscation used to compose and promote the spurious socially constructed realities herein critiqued.

The belief that a human being can, by means of psychological processes, volition, hormonal manipulation and applied surgical technique, transition/transform into the opposite sex-gender is absolutely false. Once again, there is no real "Teiresias" and humans do not possess the duplicate gene structure of either the bluehead wrasse or the broad-barred goby which allows for an actual, i.e., true sex-gender transition. A human mammal's binary sex-gender is a genetically determined dimorphic reproductive biological organization unconditionally based on a peculiar chromosome arrangement, as well as two types of gametes: 1) small mobile male sperm or 2) large stationary female oocytes/eggs (upper right quadrant). The social phenomena involving a man assertively insisting that he has fully "transitioned" into an actual woman and yet lacks the foundational genetic structural arrangement of a human female mammal and is functionally incapable of being an egg/oocyte donor or be impregnated—coupled with the human occurrence featuring a woman adamantly asserting that she has "transitioned" and has become in fact a man, but is demonstrably unable to generate sperm so as to sell to a sperm bank or impregnate a female human, offers explicit and incontrovertible examples of sex-gender self-identity structures that are dissociated in composition as well as delusional. Thus, such trans-sex-gender identity structures are confused in composition (i.e., quadrant confusion), due to failing to satisfy the veracity requirement of inter-quadrant congruence. Most importantly, a human's inherent binary gamete structure, as well as other directly-related procreative physical organ systems, are entirely arranged for, and concerned with, the reproduction of the human species—not with a person's psychological predilection and emotional disposition in relation to these binary biological reproductive characteristics and systems.

The uniquely human and intangible psychological processes related to the construction of one's sex-gender identity (upper left quadrant) are precisely associated with an unquestionably later-occurring event in the development of a person's life experience. Furthermore, this particular immaterial inner self-identity structure (upper left quadrant) features a delimited psychological organization that may be: 1) congruent with one's genetically determined binary sex-gender, i.e., identical, 2) incongruent with (and, indeed, psychologically dissociated from) one's genetically determined sex-gender, i.e., not identical—and preferentially self-formulated so as to conform with pertinent characteristics acquired/adopted from the opposite sex-gender or 3) vacillating between, or revolving around, the two (and only two) sex-gender human mammalian male or female reproductive biological/physical realities. To reiterate, agender, non-gender, etc. are categorically not sex-gender identity compositions. (Note: In her book *The End of Gender* [previously referenced], Dr. Debra Soh succinctly presents the following scientific facts regarding gender: "There are only two genders....There is zero scientific evidence to suggest that other genders exist....Gender is not a continuum or a rainbow or a diverse spectrum. It exists as two discrete categories, female and male....")

Proffering the belief that an intrauterine young human embryo is not an equally valued individual human person based on: 1) an incomprehensible dismissing of an absolutely requisite intrauterine temporary domain of residence for the primary stage of every mammal's early life development, 2) an arbitrary determination of moral worth based on a vague calculation of body size, i.e., "total cell count" estimates (e.g., weeks of embryo development or trimester phraseology), 3) disregarding the essential dependency on a mother for the initial nutritional (and protective) developmental needs required by all mammals and 4) placing extraordinary, primary and, indeed, vital emphasis on accidental characteristics and latent abilities, i.e., multifarious capacities and features, that predictably unfold within a human's staged life development up to the age of about 25—represents a perspective characterized by lies, trickery and obfuscation that is remarkably obvious at even the most rudimentary level of reasoned analysis. First and foremost, when employing a scientifically-based bio-logical investigation of the body composition of a young intrauterine human being (upper right quadrant), a conclusion is reached positively identifying the zygote, embryo or fetus as a separate and distinct human person with a completely novel genetic configuration. This is indeed a factual finding of 100% accuracy. To wit, "A zygote [fertilized egg] is the beginning of a new human being.…This highly specialized totipotent cell marks the beginning of us as a unique individual" (*The Developing Human: Clinically Oriented Embryology*, previously referenced). Engaging in unlimited replications of this specific scientific investigation will result in no exception from this absolute truth.

Dozens of nation-states have organized their socioeconomic and human social management structures based on the socially constructed conceptions (lower left quadrant) contained in the *Manifesto of the Communist Party* written by Karl Marx and Frederick Engels and published in 1848. Yet, no socialist nation has been a successful governing enterprise as objectively assessed by its "accomplishments" (per Marx) with regard to delivering broad and sustained economic growth (GDP), providing assured "bread and butter" benefit to its citizens, protecting individual liberty, fostering social freedoms, creating systems offering social, educational and economic advancement, as well as realizing ongoing societal stability—clearly demonstrating that, when actually implemented—soci-oeconomic structures derived from the ideas of socialism/communism do not meet the essential test of truth peculiar to external social systems, i.e., functional integrity (lower right quadrant). Thus, there are "zero" books available with a detailed study of the success of a socialist nation that can be used as a "how-to" guide in initiating and building a vibrant and successful socialist country. Among the many nations that have adopted socialism, all of them have proudly stated that they were "socialist." So, when intellectuals, academics, journalists, politicians or other naïve apologists for socialism say that "real socialism has never been tried," they are blatantly lying. Furthermore, based on the 100% failure rate of socialism, it is both reasonable and absolutely consistent with relevant objective data (lower right quadrant) to conclude that the socially constructed socioeconomic "reality" of Marx and Engels is not a "reality" at all; rather, it is one more fashionable utopian fiction concocted amidst this particular craze in the 1800s, along with that of Robert Owen, Henri de Saint-Simon, Etienne Cabet and Charles Fourier.

While Marx possessed exceptional scholarly abilities and read the works of economists such as Adam Smith and David Ricardo, he was not educated as an economist nor was he trained as a scientist. In 1841, after studying mythology, art and law, he was granted a Ph.D. from the University of Jena after writing a thesis focused on certain philosophical ideas. Engels demonstrated a keen intellect and unofficially attended some unknown number of university lectures; however, he dropped out of high school one year before graduation. More than one hundred years before the *Manifesto of the Communist Party* was published, Francis Hutchison (1694–1746) taught the economic concept of scarcity to the young student Adam Smith between 1737 and 1740 at the University of Glasgow.

In regard to this specific economic principle, economist Thomas Sowell notes that "The first lesson of economics is scarcity: there is never enough of anything to fully satisfy all those who want it. The first lesson of politics is to disregard the first lesson of economics" (Sanchez, Dan. "Free Everything and Thomas Sowell's First Law of Politics." realclearmarkets. com, August 5, 2019). The fanciful socialist economic conceptions, and the preposterous ideological political notions, of Marx and Engels demonstrate that it is not just politicians that "disregard the first lesson of economics." Lord Bolingbroke (1678–1758) was a prominent English politician and political philosopher. While Bolingbroke certainly could not have had an understanding of post-postmodern philosophy, he nonetheless expressed a keen understanding that, as an internal social vision (lower left quadrant) is actualized, the functionality of the derived social system (lower right quadrant) reveals matters of truth intrinsic to both domains: "History is philosophy teaching by example, and also by warning."

Socialism: Utopian and Scientific was the title of a pamphlet Engels published in 1880. This document plainly represents a rhetorical ploy in the continuous effort to distance the socialist ideas proffered by Marx and Engels from the "fantasy" of other contemporary utopian socialists.

Yet, as noted by Joshua Muravchik in his book *Heaven on Earth: The Rise and Fall of Socialism* (previously referenced),

> Before Marx, Robert Owen always characterized his activities as scientific (as did Saint Simon, Fourier and the other utopian socialists), and the claim was valid. Owen hit upon the idea of socialism and then set about to test it by creating experimental communities. Such experimentation is the very essence of the scientific method. Owen strayed from science only at the point that he chose to ignore his results rather than reconsider his hypothesis. Engels and Marx replaced experimental socialism with prophetic socialism, and claimed thereby to have progressed from utopia to science.

Thelma Lavine received a Ph.D. in philosophy and psychology from Harvard University just 40 years after Eduard Bernstein wrote, in his book *Evolutionary Socialism* (Stuttgart, 1899), a critical evaluation of Marx and Engel's prognostication that the proletariat would produce an inevitable revolution against the bourgeois capitalists. Lavine subsequently became an accomplished professor of philosophy and distinguished author. In her book *From Socrates to Sartre: The Philosophic Quest* (Bantam Books, 1984), which also formed the foundation for a 30-part television series with the same title, Lavine provided the following summary of her professional assessment of Marx and Engel's *Manifesto of the Communist Party*:

> Is the *Manifesto* science? Or is it philosophy? Clearly it is not science—the use in the *Manifesto* of the metaphysical, Hegelian laws of dialectic and the call for revolutionary action both disqualify the *Manifesto* from being considered a scientific statement. Nor is it philosophy as philosophy is usually understood, since if we compare the *Manifesto* with Hegel's *Lectures on the Philosophy of History*, for example, we see a profound difference: The *Manifesto* does not merely interpret or explain history, it inspires, incites to action, it is a revolutionary guide to action for the future, addressed not to mankind but to a particle group in society, the industrial proletariat.

Professor Lavine concludes that Marx's writing in the *Manifesto* reveals a work of overt ideology, stating

> But then has not Marx fallen into the trap of ideology which he himself set—and which he used to entrap and condemn all past theories? Is not his own theory an ideology, a system of ideas conditioned by class conflict at a particular historical stage, a distorting type of consciousness reflecting the interest of the proletariat against the bourgeoisie? And is he not, like all ideologists, seeking to promote the interests of a specific social group?

Lavine continues her astute analysis of Marx's writings by noting that

> It was Marx himself that taught us to be ideologically suspicious of theory. As for Marx's own position on this matter, he held that all thought is ideological, being conditioned by social class and historical period, and therefore offering only a distorting, falsifying picture of human reality; but he also claimed that his own views, although conditioned by social class and history, escape the ideological trap and are objectively true. But Marx does not explain how this is possible.

Professor, clinical psychologist and author Jordan Peterson offers the following insightful appraisal of ideologies:

> Ideologies are powerful and dangerous. Their power stems from their incomplete but effective appropriation of mythological ideas. Their danger stems from their attractiveness, in combination with their incompleteness. Ideologies tell only part of the story, but tell that part as if it were complete. This means that they do not take into account vast domains of the world. It is incautious to act in the world as if only a set of its constituent elements exist. The ignored elements conspire, so to speak, as a consequence of their repression, and make their existence known, inevitably, in some undesirable manner....Ideology confines human potential to a narrow and defined realm. Adaption undertaken within that realm necessarily remains insufficient, destined to produce misery....(Peterson, Jordan B. *Maps of Meaning: The Architecture of Belief.* Routledge, 1999)

The "sleight of hand" trickery inherent in Engels' 1880 pamphlet, in an effort to present the socioeconomic conceptions of an ideal social world (lower left quadrant) as outlined in the *Manifesto of the Communist Party* (lower right quadrant) as "scientific materialism" or "scientific socialism," did nothing to change the essence of the ideological utopian fiction that is socialism/communism. As the renowned Indiana poet and author James Whitcomb Riley famously expressed, "When I see a bird that walks like a duck and swims like a duck and quacks like a duck, I call that bird a duck." This wise adage has become known as the "Duck Test" and is viewed as a pithy representation of abductive reasoning, where a cluster of distinctive characteristics of that which is observed provides sufficient data to suggest a most probable identification. For example, if the leaders of a nation-state mistakenly identified a fictional utopian political/economic conception as an authentic "real world" socioeconomic model, and then actually implemented both the economic notions and prescriptions for political/social management derived from this fanciful conception, the results would surely be the sort of widespread dysfunction in organizational social systems and the enormous collection of authenticated human tragedies, as well as deaths, which have occurred in the many countries that have actually adopted the ideas intrinsic to socialism. Recall the disasters seen in the fantastical "heavenly city on earth" designed by the imaginary civil engineering firm of "Max and Angels"; now juxtapose the tragic outcomes in this fictional case with the real world catastrophes produced by the implementation of the utopian fiction called socialism in dozens of nations as documented by Kristian Niemietz, Joshua Muravchik, Rudolph Rummel and the authors of *The Black Book of Communism*. From the vantage point of the 21st century, informed intellectual discussion should not be concerned with whether "real socialism" has been tried or not; of course it has, but rather, with the accurate identification of socialism (including a "Duck Test") as the stuff of illusory dreams starring fantastical "supermen" and featuring "heaven on earth" utopian social arrangements characterized by idyllic political, social and economic equity.

The following childlike expressions of the utopian socialist theorist and philosopher Karl Marx regarding the assured wonders of a socialist society are worth repeating, as they well disclose the evident fantasy of his socioeconomic worldview:

> In communist society, where nobody has one exclusive sphere of activity
> but each can become accomplished in any branch he wishes, society reg-
> ulates the general production and thus makes it possible for me do to do
> one thing today and another tomorrow, to hunt in the morning, fish in the
> afternoon, rear cattle in the evening, criticise after dinner, just as I have a
> mind, without ever becoming hunter, fisherman, herdsman or critic. (Marx,
> Karl. *German Ideology*, 1846)

Yet, an objective analysis of "society" reveals that it is not comprised of
"brownies" or "elves" doing the daily work of productive farming, exercising
technical mining operations, accomplishing very detailed manufacturing
processes, carrying out skilled construction tasks, engaging in the efficient
distribution of goods, performing extremely complex scientific research
projects, professionally educating the populace, delivering exceedingly
technical medical treatments and adeptly managing complicated finance
functions—while socialists "...hunt...fish...rear cattle...criticize...." In
reality, "society" consists of adaptive and determined human beings, many
with actively acquired specialized training often requiring numerous years
of focused study, possessing differing intellectual capacities, experiencing
unique vocational aptitudes as well as owning varying degrees of individual
conscientiousness—who then concretely engage in specific and dedi-
cated economic performances in order to realize "the general production,"
achieve effective social functioning and assure the ongoing economic
well-being of society.

Bluntly stated, no coherent and capable socioeconomic theory would
claim the ability to create a socioeconomic "heaven on earth" or the power to
transform ordinary human beings into "supermen." To reiterate, an objective
assessment of socialism completely based on "accomplishments" reveals a
100% rate of failure in numerous nations. Without exception, socialism/
communism has been demonstrated to be simply another utopian social
fiction presented in an involved faith-related ideological structure with a
philosophical lineage stemming from the works of Jean-Jacques Rousseau,
Immanuel Kant, Johann Fichte, G. W. F. Hegel, as well as the influence
of Marx's contemporaries such as Ludwig Feurerbach and the group of
German Intellectuals known as the "Young Hegelians."

The term "utopia" is derived "from Modern Latin Utopia, literally 'nowhere,' coined by Thomas More (and used as title [sic] of his book, 1516, about an imaginary island enjoying the utmost perfection in legal, social, and political systems)..." (etymonline.com). Obviously, a social fiction (lower left quadrant) of any level of complexity cannot be successfully implemented in a non-fiction human society (lower right quadrant). The socioeconomic model socially constructed by the philosopher Karl Marx, in conjunction with his businessman and would-be revolutionary companion Friedrich Engels, should presumptively be removed from the class of genuine economic and political theories and placed adjacent to the following utopian fictions: Bacon's *New Atlantis*, More's *Utopia*, Plato's *Republic*, Al-Madina al-Fadilaby Al-Farabi's perfect religious state and the utopian dreams outlined by Adolf Hitler in *Mein Kampf*. In an article titled "Hitler and Stalin's utopian dreams," historian Laurence Rees states that "...despite their many differences, the leaders of Nazi Germany and the Soviet Union were united by a common passion: to create their own warped version of a paradise on Earth." The feature concludes by noting that "...Hitler and Stalin believed that they had uncovered the secret to existence" (historyextra.com, January 13, 2021). The comments of French Nobel Laureate Andre Gide, regarding his impressions of life in the socialist nation of the Soviet Union, offer the following compelling assessment: "In my opinion, no country today not even in Hitler's Germany is the spirit more suppressed, more timid, more servile than in the Soviet Union" (art-bin.com).

When utilizing the effective indexing capability of both Domain Theory and Integral Theory, quadrant confusion and intellectual reductionism can be much avoided, supporting a more accurate analysis as well as persuasive critique of questionable and contentious matters within contemporary society. In this way, the lies, trickery and obfuscation intrinsic to certain spurious social constructions within culture and society can be straight-forwardly identified as engineered techniques used to foster falsehoods and effectively dismissed as menacing agnotological strategies of social manipulation. Additionally, through the metatheoretical perspectives of Integral Philosophy and Domain Theory, the desultory—and often contradictory—nature of the radical relativism intrinsic to contemporary postmodernism, as well as the unrestrained absolutism frequently expressed by postmodern theorists, becomes effectively revealed, convincingly identifying this philosophical perspective as inherently regressive and dangerously authoritarian.

Just as the young niece was able to free herself from a position of subservience in a world of obfuscation and falsehood socially constructed by the trickster uncle and his offspring team of liars, it is assured that the discerning and effective analytical capability of post-postmodern Integral Philosophy/Theory can be used by the reader to achieve freedom from an array of socially constructed falsehoods commonly encountered in contemporary society.

Recommended Reading List

Anderson, Ryan T., *When Harry Became Sally*. Encounter Books, 2019.

Anderson, Ryan T., and Alexandra DeSanctis. *Tearing Us Apart: How Abortion Harms Everything and Solves Nothing*. Regnery Publishing, 2022.

Bateson, Gregory. *Mind and Nature: A Necessary Unity*. E. P. Dutton, 1979.

———. *Steps to an Ecology of Mind*. Jason Aronson Inc., 1972.

Bateson, Gregory, and Mary Catherine Bateson. *Angels Fear: Towards an Epistemology of the Sacred*. Macmillan Publishing Company, 1987.

Beck, Glenn. *Arguing with Socialists*. Thresholds Editions/Mercury Radio Arts, 2020.

Berger, Peter L., and Thomas Luckmann. *The Social Construction of Reality: A Treatise in the Sociology of Knowledge*. Anchor Books, 1967.

Courtois, Stephane, et al. *The Black Book of Communism: Crimes, Terror, Repression*. Harvard University Press, 1999.

Dansky, Kara. *The Abolition of Sex: How the "Transgender" Agenda Harms Women and Girls*. Bombardier Books, 2021.

DiLorenzo, Thomas J. *The Problem with Socialism*. Regnery Publishing, 2016.

Heying, Heather, and Bret Weinstein. *A Hunter-Gatherer's Guide to the 21st Century: Evolution and the Challenges of Modern Life*. Portfolio/Penguin, 2021.

Hicks, Stephen R. C. *Explaining Postmodernism: Skepticism and Socialism from Rousseau to Foucault*. Ockham's Razor Publishing, 2011.

Hicks, Stephen R. C., and David Kelly. *The Art of Reasoning*. W. W. Norton & Company, 1994.

Hoffer, Eric. *The True Believer: Thoughts on the Nature of Mass Movements*. Harper & Row, Publishers, Inc., 1951.

———. *The Passionate State of Mind*. Harper & Row Publishers, 1954.

Kengor, Paul. *The Devil and Karl Marx: Communism's Long March of Death, Deception and Infiltration*. TAN Books, 2020.

Kuhn, Thomas S. *The Structure of Scientific Revolutions*. The University of Chicago Press, 1970.

Lavine, T. Z. *From Socrates to Sartre: The Philosophic Quest*. Bantam Books, 1984.

Lee, Patrick. *Abortion and Unborn Human Life*. The Catholic University of America Press, 1996.

Lee, Patrick, and Robert P. George. *Body-Self Dualism in Contemporary Ethics and Politics*. Cambridge University Press, 2012.

LeShan, Lawrence, and Henry Margenau. *Einstein's Space and Van Gogh's Sky: Physical Reality and Beyond*. Macmillan Publishing Company, 1982.

Lindsay, James. *Race Marxism: The Truth about Critical Race Theory and Praxis*. New Discourses, LLC, 2022.

Mayer, Lawrence S., and Paul R. McHugh. "Sexuality and Gender: Findings from the Biological, Psychological, and Social Sciences." *The New Atlantis: A Journal of Technology & Society*, Number 50, Fall 2016.

Maturana, Humberto R., and Francisco J. Varela. *The Tree of Knowledge: The Biological Roots of Human Understanding*. Shambhala Publications, Inc., 1987.

Muravchik, Joshua. *Heaven on Earth: The Rise and Fall of Socialism*. Encounter Books, 2002.

Murray, Douglas. *The Madness of Crowds: Gender, Race and Identity*. Bloomsbury Continuum, 2019.

Moore, Keith L., and T. V. N. Persaud. *The Developing Human: Clinically Oriented Embryology*. Saunders: An Imprint of Elsevier, 2003.

Niemietz, Kristian. *Socialism: The Failed Idea That Never Dies*. The Institute of Economic Affairs, 2019.

Peterson, Jordan B. *Maps of Meaning: The Architecture of Belief*. Routledge, 1999.

Pluckrose, Helen, and James Lindsay. *Cynical Theories: How Activist Scholarship Made Everything about Race, Gender and Identity – and Why This Harms Everybody*. Pitchstone Publishing, 2020.

Popper, Karl R. *Objective Knowledge: An Evolutionary Approach*. Oxford University Press, 1979.

Saad, Gad. *The Parasitic Mind: How Infectious Ideas Are Killing Common Sense*. Regnery Publishing, 2020.

Scruton, Roger. *Fools, Frauds and Firebrands: Thinkers of the New Left*. Bloomsbury Continuum, New edition, 2019.

Shrier, Abigail. *Irreversible Damage: The Transgender Craze Seducing Our Daughters*. Regnery Publishing, 2020.

Soh, Debra. *The End of Gender: Debunking the Myths about Sex and Identity in Our Society*. Threshold Editions, 2020.

Solzhenitsyn, Aleksandr. *The Gulag Archipelago* (with a foreword by Jordan B. Peterson). Vintage Classics, 2018.

Sowell, Thomas. *Intellectuals and Society*. Basic Books, 2011.

———. *Marxism: Philosophy and Economics*. Routledge Revivals, 2011.

Wilber, Ken. *A Brief History of Everything*. Shambhala Publications Inc., 1996.

———. *Integral Psychology: Consciousness, Spirit, Psychology, Therapy*. Shambhala Publications Inc., 2000.

———. *Sex, Ecology, Spirituality: The Spirit of Evolution*. Shambhala Publications, Inc., 1995.

Thompson, William Irwin. *Imaginary Landscape: Making Worlds of Myth and Science*. St. Martin's Press Inc., 1989.

Voegelin, Eric. *Science, Politics and Gnosticism*. Regnery Publishing, 1968.

von Mises, Ludwig. *Socialism: An Economic and Sociological Analysis*. Liberty Fund Inc., 1981.

About the Author

John Ross Brown received an undergraduate degree in Sociology and History from Indiana State University. He also earned a Master of Arts in Education, as well as a graduate degree in Clinical Mental Health Counseling from Roosevelt University. Prior to retiring, he was a clinical member of the American Association for Marriage and Family Therapy and held professional licenses in Clinical Social Work, Marriage and Family Therapy and Mental Health Counseling. He worked for several years in the steel industry, including supervision of iron-making blast furnace operations, served for five years as a Social Caseworker in the housing projects of Gary, Indiana, provided well over 50,000 hours of direct psychotherapeutic care, recorded numerous hours of clinical supervision as well as professional instruction in both theories of psychopathology and techniques of psychotherapeutic intervention. His clinical experiences include: Director of a residential center for male adolescent offenders diagnosed with a variety of psychiatric disorders, Clinical Supervisor of a therapeutic day treatment program, Outpatient Therapist for several Community Mental Health Centers (including addiction services), Behavior Consultant and Therapist for emotionally troubled children within therapeutic school environments as well as maintaining a private psychotherapy practice for more than twenty years. Additionally, he was a founding member of the Gregory Bateson Society of Chicago, has served as a member of the Board of Directors for Gestalt Integrated Family Therapy Institute, Boys and Girls Clubs, People Helping People (an organization focused on serving persons living with Multiple Sclerosis), is currently serving on the Board of Directors for Family Concern Counseling and is a member of the Heterodox Academy.

Printed in the USA
CPSIA information can be obtained
at www.ICGtesting.com
JSHW011909121123
51825JS00014B/94